The Geography of
Peace and War

The Geography of
Peace and War

Edited by
DAVID PEPPER and ALAN JENKINS

BASIL BLACKWELL

© Basil Blackwell Ltd 1985

First published 1985

Basil Blackwell Ltd
108 Cowley Road, Oxford OX4 1JF, UK

Basil Blackwell Inc.
432 Park Avenue South, Suite 1505,
New York, NY 10016, USA

British Library Cataloguing in Publication Data
The Geography of peace and war.
　1. War　2. Peace　3. Geography, Political
　I. Pepper, David　II. Jenkins, Alan, *1940–*
　327.1　　　JX1952
　ISBN 0-631-13559-6
　ISBN 0-631-14069-7 Pbk

Library of Congress Cataloging in Publication Data
Main entry under title:
The Geography of peace and war.
　Includes index.
　1. Military geography—Addresses, essays, lectures.
2. World politics—1945–　—Addresses, essays,
lectures. 3. Peace—Addresses, essays, lectures.
I. Pepper, D.M. (David M.)　II. Jenkins, Alan.
UA990.G36　1985　　　355'.033'004　　　85–6228
ISBN 0-631-13559-6
ISBN 0-631-14069-7 (pbk.)

Typeset by Katerprint Co. Ltd, Oxford
Printed in Great Britain by Billing and Sons Ltd, Worcester

Contents

INTRODUCTION

Geographers in Search of Peace

David Pepper

This book is a contribution, largely by geographers, to that growing body of knowledge which is frequently called 'peace studies'.

'What's peace studies? Why, obviously it's *war* studies, you dummy!' This was how an American participant at a recent conference on peace studies in higher education described his subject. We think he was at least half correct, which is why this book is called *A Geography of Peace and War*. For it rests substantially on the proposition that if geographers want to make a contribution to peace they must certainly *know* about war, if not preparing for it. The first two parts of this book therefore examine conflict and cold war, arms manufacture and trading, and the awful prospect and consequences of a nuclear exchange – all from geographical perspectives: emphasising, that is, their spatial, locational and environmental aspects and their cartographic representation. Part 3, however, deals directly with the topic of 'peace'; first by examining geographical attempts to limit nuclear arms escalation and the geographical extent of the peace movement, and then by raising directly the issue of the (geographical) academic's role in peace education and in working for peace.

But why should there be a *geography* of peace and war, and what have geographers got to say in this well-worn debate which people at large need to know? This kind of question has been asked of all other subjects which contribute to peace studies. Particularly, it has been asked by people who believe philosophy, theology, history and politics to be the central disciplines which are crucial to an understanding of the issues of peace and war. If they are correct, then geography is probably peripheral and unimportant – a view that might, indeed, be supported by the extraordinary dearth of geographical studies up to now concerning the problems of peace and the threat of war.

We think that this view is incorrect, and that geography belongs squarely with the central disciplines. This is because so much of the war–peace problematique is inherently highly geographical, all the time requiring us to think about territories, spatial perceptions, geopolitics, potential place annihilation, the developed–underdeveloped world dichotomy, the locational ramifications of military doctrines and the potential spatial effects of nuclear weapons. We contend not only that there is this inherent geographical content (one has only to read military journals and 'peace' publications to see that), but also that this content is at present insufficiently recognised and studied.

Thus, one area which is of clear geographical interest concerns the superpowers' perceptions of each other's territorial ambitions, and of their own locational positions and contexts. Is the Soviet Union beleaguered, and encircled by hostile territories, or is it on the other hand an expanding empire, threatening from its heartland all the countries on its periphery? Whatever the answer, the very fact that these two highly different perceptions currently inform superpower military strategies leads to potentially dangerous mismatches in nuclear doctrines between the two protagonists.

Similarly, we get an enhanced sense of incongruity and danger if we bring a spatial perspective to bear on the vexed question of long-range theatre nuclear forces in Europe. Geography helps us to appreciate, perhaps more readily than is possible for non-geographers in the West, why the USSR objects vehemently to the cruise and Pershing deployments, and why there is a qualitative difference between these missiles and the SS-20s which they are supposed to 'balance'. While all three weapons are classed as 'intermediate' in terms of range, the really vital difference is that the SS-20s cannot reach the American heartland, while cruise and Pershing, stationed in Europe, *can* reach the Soviet heartland; to the Russians they are not at all 'intermediate', they are strategic, and their use would evoke a strategic response. NATO apologists for this controversial deployment appear not to see, or to want to see, this very basic geographical point.

Again, if we were to think more consciously and systematically about the *spatial* dimensions of the Rogers Plan to enhance 'conventional defence' in Europe, we might conclude that this plan, far from promising greater stability and raising the nuclear threshold, is a dangerous one. It commits NATO to a switch from forward defence – fighting along a well-defined front – to deep strike, that is, making forays by air and land deep into Warsaw Pact territory from the commencement of battle. A kind of territorial anarchy could well result, in which relatively isolated and independent conflicts could break out all over the European theatre, up to including the westernmost Soviet military districts. The potential danger here is obvious: the first use of nuclear weapons (which NATO reserves the right to make) could break out anywhere on the very extensive battlefield – particularly since deep strike brings with it heavy pressures to devolve (spatially) to field commanders the authorisation to use nuclear weapons as and where 'appropriate'.

Thus, there is a particular value in the geographical perspective, which we hope the following chapters will demonstrate in their specific subject matters. That perspective adds another dimension to our thinking about international political, strategic and military matters, and by increasing awareness may contribute to peace.

There are many other areas in which the geography of peace and war can help to advance our thinking. The spatial analysis of weapons effects and attack scenarios can give us a more realistic picture of what to expect in time of war. Terrain analysis can help us to evaluate the potential effectiveness of certain military doctrines such as purely defensive conventional defence, which is substantially based on 'fortified' front lines, and harassment in depth against an invading force. Applied climatology can build up a picture of the nature and extent of the nuclear winter and the global spread of the ultimate pollutant, radiation; already, this area of geography is persuading many politicians to stop thinking of war as being in any way winnable. The presentation of all this research will, and does, rely heavily on cartographic techniques, and it is greatly to be desired that the general public should understand and appreciate how cartography can 'bend' and selectively use information to fit an ideology.

However, all this is only part of the potential scope of the kind of geography which this book is developing; for it should not be forgotten that many proposals for peace and disarmament are themselves *geographical* responses to the problems. One thinks here of arms control treaties verified by remote sensing satellites, or of nuclear weapon free zones; of unilateral (nuclear) disarmament, or of nuclear weapons sanctuaries in space or in the sea; and of course some would wish to add here measures for strengthening 'deterrence', such as the dispersal of missiles (MX and cruise) in mobile formations, the improvement of weapons accuracy or the development of technologies and doctrines for fighting geographically limited wars (on the grounds that, if war can be limited, then the threat of going to war in retaliation for aggression becomes a more credible one).

Given this immense potential range and scope of peace and war geography, readers will inevitably discern some gaps in the coverage of this book; they may wish, too, to ask questions about its approach. The emphasis, as we have said, is on war rather than direct 'peace' studies. Furthermore, on balance the approach is at least overtly empirical and rational, sometimes fairly descriptive, and often positive rather than normative. It accords, in other words, considerably with the image of the truth-seeking, detached and 'scientific' academic which most geographers still have (and growingly cultivate), notwithstanding radical and humanistic influences on their discipline during the 1970s.

There might be reservations about both of these emphases. First, it might be argued that, in focusing so much on war studies, and especially on their spatial and environmental aspects, we are simply describing and analysing the superficial manifestations of deep structural problems, and are thereby missing the point. We are failing to consider the root causes of war and how to remedy them. These causes may partly be inherent in the economic and social structures of world societies, as George Orwell and Noam Chomsky argue, and they may partly be recognised at the level of the individual and be concerned with the psychological and 'structural' violence done to and by people, as John Galtung argues.

A second set of reservations, amounting substantially to an extension of the first, may come much more from within geography – indeed, from those who are termed 'radical' geographers. On the one hand, they might concede that in this book we are studying subjects which are relevant to the everyday lives and problems of the mass of people – and this is a positive step forward from the kind of geography which existed before the 1970s. But the problem might come in the *way* we study them. Our radical critics might argue, with Richard Peet, that there is no such thing as an objective, value-free and politically neutral science; that the function of established science is to enable the established economic and social order to survive by throwing up 'partial' solutions (such as nuclear weapon free zones?); and that scientists 'play a leading role in laying down the ideological strata which disguise the causal processes behind societal problems'. On the other hand, radical science, with which this book is *not* concerned, 'traces the relationships between "social problems" at the surface and deep societal causes', and proposes, in an explicitly value-laden way, a radical political programme for restructuring society. In other words, geography should be the agent of revolutionary political change, whereas the contributors to this volume hardly mention revolutionary political change.

If such charges are brought against this book, then we plead partly guilty on most counts. In mitigation, we would submit that Alan Burnett explicitly uses his technical expertise to suggest a range of propaganda maps that peace campaigners could construct; that Tony Ives writes as a member of the Campaign Against the Arms Trade; that Alan Jenkins argues vigorously for structural change in the classroom in order to show people how to be peaceful and to create a social order in which they can be so; that Frank Barnaby is an inveterate peace campaigner whose ideas have contributed towards a potentially radical shift in NATO perceptions of what is 'defence'; and that Academician Gerasimov calls on geographers from East and West to join in working openly 'against the arms race and the nuclear war threat'.

To this extent, we are contributing to a political position of the sort that Bill Bunge spelled out when in 1973 he called for geographers to labour 'to make sure that the earth's surface truly becomes the home of man, that mankind comes to some peace, some rest, some harmony, and ultimate unity with nature'. We are now addressing these issues in a 'professional' capacity (though Bunge does not like the word), recognising that it is the geographer's *job* to do so. In making this kind of start (or almost a start, for we do not forget Bunge's *Nuclear War Atlas* or Daniel Deudney's excellent 'Worldwatch' paper on *A Geopolitics of Peace*, both published in 1983), we hope that geographers will go on to work in future at both structural and non-structural levels, producing both relatively objective and subjective work.

We hope also that the approaches in this book will be continued and strengthened, since there is much to recommend them. Each contributor has built up, over the years, a formidable depth of scientific expertise in the topic on which he writes. Now this expertise is being brought to bear on an area of human activity that has previously been substantially closed off to open, serious, scientific and academic debate. Questions of conflict, military doctrine, propaganda, arms manufacture and dispersal, nuclear attack scenarios, civil defence and nuclear weapons effects – traditionally, most of these have been largely the province of scientific 'experts' from within a closed military–industrial–bureaucratic establishment. But the rise of the peace movement in the 1960s and again in the 1980s has made it impossible for the issues to remain closed and secret; they have become matters for open discussion in both the East and the West. Much of the debate has been emotional (and why not?), simplistic and uninformed. But, particularly in the 1980s, it has developed also at another level. 'Professionals' of all kinds – scientists, physicians, lawyers, electronics specialists, architects – have developed their own expert critiques of where we are at in the nuclear arms race, why we are here and where we are going.

This volume should be seen within the context of this development. And a highly significant development it is; for with it the war-making industry has been shown no longer to have a monopoly on rationality and 'common sense', on cool scientific appraisal and logical argument. Indeed, in many cases the established official view has been exposed as highly deficient on its own terms. Its experts do not necessarily know best. Thus, the intellectual foundations of the deterrent strategy have been under-mined; nuclear weapons have been shown to be incredible and unusable; 'flexible response' has been revealed as inflexible; and so on – all this because the scientists of the war-making establishment have at last been subjected to the kind of peer review which is the norm in academic life.

Some of our contributors have already figured in this process. Open-shaw and Steadman, in a running battle with the British Home Office, have forced the British government to admit that its civil defence pro-gramme is founded on a partial appraisal of inadequate data. As a spokes-man for Scientists Against Nuclear Arms put it in the magazine *Computing* (July 5, 1984), 'There is evidence that the Home Office has changed its plans because of information from us [particularly Openshaw, Steadman and their colleagues]. And even if people disagree with us, they can respect the quality and objectivity of our research; it raises the level of discussion.' Similarly, Zeigler and his colleagues have brought to light how inadequate are the evacuation assumptions of the American civil defence planners; while a host of American, European and Soviet climatologists, reviewed here by Elsom and Gerasimov, have spelled out what a nuclear exchange would really mean. The spectre of the nuclear winter has been one of the factors leading to pressure on NATO to renounce nuclear first use and opt for conventional doctrines. Barnaby has produced, with his colleagues, positive and logical arguments for making those doctrines truly defensive and for limiting the contagion of nuclear weapons. As Per Berg and Gunilla Herolf say in SIPRI's 1984 Yearbook, if conventional capabilities can be enhanced in credibility, the public may be willing to foot the bill. 'The consensus on NATO [nuclear] policy has suffered considerably because of this lack of credibility; the dilemmas and untenability of an "early first use" policy have dawned on the public much as a result of the peace education process that has taken place in the shadow of the Euro-missiles.' And the kind of knowledge which Ives and Anderton and Isard produce has helped to focus the glare of publicity on those, in the arms manufacturing business and in governments, to whom the arms race is good news.

Most of this may not be pitched at 'revolutionary' or 'structural' levels, but none the less we regard it as a very positive contribution to a change in the climate of informed opinion, and therefore, we hope, to a more peaceful and stable world – though we would agree that true and lasting peace is inseparable from social and economic justice.

However, just as formidable forces are ranged against the peace movement, so are there formidable pressures on geographers *not* to work for peace. Jenkins describes how these pressures impinge on the geography teacher, and many people know of the troubles which have beset geographers like Bunge and the Medvedkovas, who have attempted to campaign overtly and politically. In addition, we have to consider the geographer as a researcher, and therefore the sources of his or her funding. Like so many scientists in the developed world, some geographers in universities have 'lined up in the service of the war technique', as Chomsky, in *For Reasons of State*, has reminded us. Climatologists, remote sensing specialists, geomorphologists, political and economic geographers – their work is usable, and has been used, in the enhancement of warfighting capability.

Indeed, some of the work in this volume could be useful to, and justifiably funded by, the military. Chomsky feels that military funding of scientific research is all part of the militarisation of American society. We would echo his view that geographers, like all other academics, should resist such militarisation, but the $64,000 question, literally, remains: Where is the funding for peace research going to come from? While in the UK there is a profusion of government funds for war and defence-related departments, professorships and readerships, and for Institutes of Strategic Studies, of 'International' (military) Affairs and of the Royal United Services, there is but a protracted series of financial difficulties for the Bradford University School of Peace Studies, and for the peace studies units at Lancaster and Sussex. In 1982 the UN Secretary-General, Perez de Cuellar, called on scholars to create the preconditions for peace and disarmament. 'Being removed from the passions and prejudices which so often sway human decisions', he said, 'it is the scholars and scientists, the leaders of thought, who can open fresh horizons and suggest new perspectives for the pursuit of humanity's common good.' So they can, but they are not so far removed from 'passions and prejudices' that they can exist on nothing. Scholars, including geographical scholars, need money for their pursuit of peace. To this end the UN should make the funds from its own university more accessible and plentiful to academics. And it should try to bring unremitting pressure to bear on governments – on the hostile and aggressive governments of the USA and UK to divert funds from war to peace research, and on the tunnel-visioned USSR government to permit and encourage its academics to be critical of *both* sides in the arms race, not merely the West.

This collection of papers does display a healthy and fair degree of criticism of both sides. It is structured logically, we hope, into three parts. The first reviews events and processes which have led to the present state of international tension, conflict and cold war; the second examines the possible forms and consequences of a nuclear exchange; the third is, as we have said, about some of the ways in which geographers can contribute to the advancement of peace. We have encouraged our authors to concentrate on those matters which currently preoccupy popular opinion, especially in the peace movement. This has been done not in ignorance of the breadth and complexity of the issues of war and peace, but in response to such breadth and complexity. The focus has been placed on *nuclear* issues out of pragmatism – meeting the need to limit our scope in a short volume – and also because of the extraordinary nature of the nuclear threat, which somehow transcends and eludes human comprehension.

In part 1, Herman van der Wusten reviews data on postwar conflict, classifying it into three sorts: that involving the process of Third World decolonisation; that following such decolonisation and involving superpower attempts to establish spheres of influence; and that involved in the building of Third World states. Most wars and casualties have been from the last kind of conflict. It seems that, while the appearance of nuclear weapons may have limited warfare frequency, it is not the case that fewer people have died in warfare since the 'nuclear deterrent' – though the focus of conflict has emphatically shifted from the developed to the Third World. Patrick O'Sullivan examines the emergence of nuclear deterrence, and its subsequent partial eclipse by flexible response doctrines and possibly by nuclear war-fighting/first strike philosophies under Presidents Carter and Reagan in the USA. Drawing on some of Mackinder's concepts, he describes the US policy of containment of the USSR, and the latter's sense of encirclement by hostile forces in the rim countries surrounding the Soviet heartland. He also draws attention to Europe's uncomfortable position. O'Sullivan concludes that the idea of the Soviet Union being intent upon world domination is a myth; that since the 1950s the arms race has gained a momentum independent of geopolitical circumstances; and, most controversially, that a distance-decay function still holds, whereby the political, economic and military influences of the superpowers diminish steadily the further they go from their heartlands. We consider this notion to be important because it runs counter to the idea that Soviet and US influence is becoming more ubiquitous and uniform within their agreed spheres of influence – and even world-wide, given the advent of space-based surveillance and ICBMs. Here is a useful area for further political geographical research.

Part of the motor that drives the Cold War and the nuclear arms race is the NATO and Warsaw Pact perception of each other as aggressively expansionist. Governments play upon and strengthen this perception by using particular cartographic devices in their official literature, as Alan Burnett illustrates for us. He calls such maps 'maps for armament'; however, the peace movement also uses propaganda cartography to produce 'maps for disarmament' which emphasise the danger of being a nuclear target. His chapter makes us look more carefully and discriminatingly at the maps and posters of both camps, and it prompts the peace movement to develop more and different ways of imprinting on the consciousness of ordinary people the horrific scale of death and destruction which would follow a nuclear war.

Another cold war motor is arms manufacture and trading. Tony Ives considers patterns of arms dispersal, whereby the USA, USSR, Western European countries and Japan are getting rich by supplying increasing volumes of sophisticated weapons technology to the Third World, particularly the Mid-East, South-East Asia and sub-Saharan Africa. He feels that geographers should study the relationships between arms dispersal and (a) the incidence of conflict and (b) the prospects for economic development and welfare in less developed countries. He wants us to see arms dispersal as just part of a general cycle of repression of such countries by the developed world, which also fights proxy wars in these countries.

But the economic benefits of arms manufacture are, in fact, very partial, as Anderton and Isard show. Developed countries with the lowest proportion of defence spending, such as Japan and Germany, are doing best economically, while there is evidence that military spending is not the way to create most jobs. Having said this, it is not easy to trace what jobs are created via this spending, or where. While the Pacific, West South Central and South Atlantic regions of the USA are the chief beneficiaries of prime defence contracts, for example, this pattern soon begins to change and diffuse via the process of subcontracting.

Spatial analysis of a different kind commences part 2. Openshaw and Steadman continue their pioneering work on possible nuclear attack scenarios and the resultant death and casualty patterns for the UK. They refine figures given in their book *Doomsday* (Blackwell: 1983) from county to district level, and build into their model allowances for more of the uncertainties inherent in making casualty computations. They conclude that their *Doomsday* estimates were conservative, and that a 219 megaton attack on the UK would annihilate most of the country's population – partly because of its crowded geography, and partly because wind directions will probably be variable rather than constant. Geographical factors are thus likely to mean that for the UK the distinction between an attack on people and one on military targets is purely academic: nuclear war of virtually any sort would be national suicide.

Of course, this would anyway be the case if the 'nuclear winter' hypothesis were correct. While Derek Elsom presents us with the views of those who believe that the hypothesis is not proven, his valuable review of the complex and prolific literature shows that there is a balance of research and opinion for the notion that cold and darkness will envelop the Northern Hemisphere for some months after a nuclear exchange, followed by overheating and exposure to harmful radiation from space. A spillover of effects into the Southern Hemisphere seems likely, following radical changes in the zonal circulation pattern.

In the light of such evidence, civil defence by sheltering is futile; but some hold that, as a geographical response to nuclear attack, evacuation might, in huge countries like the USA, be a more successful policy. However, Don Zeigler shows us that current US evacuation planning is unrealistic in the light of the Three Mile Island experience and other evidence. More people will want to evacuate, and to travel much further from, the urban centres than the authorities envisage. But to try to get them all away before an attack might, perversely, *provoke* an attack, since an evacuation during international tension might signal to the Soviets that the USA was preparing a pre-emptive strike on them.

One of the major geographical contributions to peace could be the nuclear weapon free zone, in which such weapons are not produced, tested, stored or deployed. In part 3 Frank Barnaby reminds us that these zones exist already, by agreement, in the earth's commons – the Antarctic, the seabed and outer space. But it is clearly vital to extend the concept into the most likely 'theatre', that of Europe, especially through something like the neglected Rapacki Plan, or a nuclear-free 'strip' running down the East–West German border. However, Barnaby points out that, while we are saddled with nuclear deterrence, it is actually important to stability to preserve some areas as nuclear weapon *sanctuaries*; specifically, the North Polar Basin could be declared a haven from anti-submarine warfare, making some strategic weapons invulnerable on both sides and thereby decreasing the likelihood of one side believing a pre-emptive strike could succeed.

The nuclear freeze is another major idea which the peace movement promotes. Stanley Brunn tells us of the widespread pattern of voting for a freeze which has taken place in the USA. He also shows us the extent and diversity of purpose and activities of the US peace movement. Unsurprisingly, it is centred on Boston, New York, Philadelphia and Washington DC, but there is a perhaps unexpected secondary centre in southern California. One geographical imbalance which looks sorely in need of redress is that there is a profusion of US peace and disarmament research centres, while such provision in Europe is scant by comparison.

Our book finishes by considering the question of the role of the academic, particularly the geographer in working for peace – the theme of much of this introduction. It is encouraging to read Academician Gerasimov, who represents the mainstream of Soviet geographical thinking, when he says that all other global problems are subordinate to that of creating peace and preventing nuclear conflict, and that geographers must play a key role in the task. Gerasimov here echoes the words of the Presidents of the Institute of British Geographers and the Association of American Geographers, delivered in presidential addresses in 1983 and 1984. While it would be naive to believe that this unity of accord will lead directly to an accord between the political leaders of East and West, it would equally be unduly cynical and destructively negative not to read it as a sign of hope.

And a sense of hope and optimism – let us say that much-maligned word *idealism* – is what geographers as teachers must seek to inspire in their students. The enormity of the challenge is spelled out by Alan Jenkins, who calls uncompromisingly for us to do no less than eliminate hierarchical, authoritarian and patriarchical relationships in the classroom. We must tackle the problem of 'structural violence' at its root, by focusing on method as well as content in teaching, and by examining and challenging squarely the hidden curriculum that teaches our young mistrust and a sense of hopelessness and helplessness. As has been indicated above, this is ultimately the most important and difficult of our tasks. We hope that this volume will encourage geographers of all specialisms to stop thinking about it and to get on with it! As we know our only 'non-geographer', Frank Barnaby, would say, time is desperately short. It is not on our side.

PART I

The Geography of the Cold War and the Arms Race

CHAPTER 1

The Geography of Conflict since 1945

Herman van der Wusten

Introduction

The end of the Second World War marked a turning point in the history of the international system. As a result of this global conflict, the ranking of states according to their power position and the relations between states were to a considerable extent transformed. The old cores of the international system declined and their colonial empires were dismantled. The USA and the USSR went to the top of the international hierarchy, and they in their turn made efforts at empire-building. The state-makers of the political units which were established as a result of decolonisation tried to make their countries viable.

In the second section of this chapter I will describe the serious conflicts which have arisen as part of postwar trends – conflicts which have accompanied the granting of independence to former colonies, the rise to pre-eminence of the superpowers and the struggle for survival of Third World states. In the third section I will indicate the impact of the new nuclear armaments which have been perfected since the war, with their immense explosive loads, increasingly accurate long-range transportability and sophisticated informational devices. These assets have provided some political units, and the superpowers in particular, with an unprecedented resource base of coercive power.

The concept of conflict, generally, refers to social units having incompatible goals and to the mutual behaviour resulting from these incompatibilities. The seriousness of a conflict may be assessed in several, not necessarily corresponding, ways: by the distances between the values and goals of the contenders, by the quantity and quality of the means mobilised and by the consequences of their application. In what follows I use the harm inflicted by a large amount of violence, or the threat thereof, as an indication of serious conflict. In these cases incompatible values and goals are assumed. The assessment of seriousness is based on the consequences of the use of violence. War – that is, large-scale organised violence with at least one state as a party – and the threat of war, particularly nuclear war, are the central concerns of this chapter.

Most data are from Small and Singer (1982); their data refer to war. For the superpowers in particular I will also describe other forms of conflict behaviour based on different data sets (Blechman and Kaplan, 1978; Kaplan, 1981). Small and Singer have used numbers of battle-connected fatalities (e.g. 1000 per year) as the most important basis for regarding a violent conflict as war. In addition, the number of 'victims' indicates the severity of a war; this number was calculated only from those directly involved in fighting, not from the innocent bystanders, owing to the fact that no reasonably reliable casualty figures for innocent bystanders were to be had. By their rigorous definitions and counting rules, Small and Singer have considerably improved on earlier efforts in this direction such as Richardson's (1960). But there is a problem of validity when these figures are used to suggest the sum total of war consequences.

However, information on victims, together with the periods of involvement of the various parties in war, allows fairly precise, comparable and explanatory statements on war to be made. Such statements appear to lack the horror, fear, cruelty and suffering that warfare implies. This, however, is so only to the extent that one allows oneself to forget the significance of the victim numbers because they are compressed into a statistical category. Reader and writer should beware of letting this happen. We *are* dealing with extreme events, on account of the human suffering inflicted and the disruption of social life implied.

Geographers can use these data for two kinds of approach. First, they can contribute to general explanations of war characteristics (e.g. time of outbreak, contenders, duration, severity, victory/defeat) by using the explanatory power of factors such as distance and accessibility, which are their central concern. This is potentially fruitful because results so far indicate that such geographical factors are important in reaching explanations (Weede, 1975; Singer, 1981).

Second, geographers can use these data as a baseline for describing and characterising particular wars. These descriptions can form the starting point of a geographical investigation of the intricate combinations of local circumstances that bear on each individual event.

So far, geographers' efforts to exploit conflict data have been negligible. In this chapter I use such data to explore the frequencies and patterns of warfare that accompanied the major processes of political change. These processes involved three kinds of conflict: decolonisation conflict, superpower empire-building conflict and Third World state-making conflict. My major concern is with the parties that are directly involved, that is to say those taking part in the fighting with their own military manpower.

The demise of colonial empires and the construction of superpower empires and Third World states have occurred simultaneously on a global scale. However, in particular locations decolonisation and Third World state-making were, by definition, sequential, so the serious conflicts which accompanied these processes can be separately classified. Where colonial empires dwindled, superpowers did sometimes interfere directly or indirectly in the ensuing conflicts. The USA was anxious not to let Western influence slip away, and it generally supported particular parties in a conflict with a view to promoting an early transfer of power to a moderate new government. But direct military interference did not occur. The USSR was anxious to acquire as much influence as possible among newly independent countries, and on the whole it supported liberation movements with that aim in view. However, in no way did the USSR engage its own military force directly. Therefore there is no confusion between imperial superpower wars and decolonisation wars in our data.

However, the building of superpower empires and the efforts of Third World state-makers could, and sometimes did, interact directly. While superpowers tried to establish new dominance relations, state-makers were caught between the two rivals, or wanted to steer their own course. As a result, the serious conflicts which accompanied these processes could not necessarily be exclusively placed in either one of the two categories of superpower involvement or Third World state-making.

The fall and rise of empires and the making of states

Decolonisation conflicts

While the growth of colonial empires sometimes took centuries, they all broke down very rapidly. Decolonisation to some extent reshuffled the political map of the world; but although political authority was transferred from foreign governments and their local delegates to indigenous elites, initially the colonial borders hardly changed.

Colonies had been administered internally through rules approved by mother countries, which were also responsible for their external defences, and the mother country–colony relationship had been internationally recognised. The colonial empires were primarily extensions of European states, of which only the British, French, Dutch, Belgian and Portuguese empires were still relevant by 1945.

After the Second World War more and more colonies became independent. Very often mother countries were pressed hard to cut the links with their colonial dependencies, even though some dependencies were reluctant to break them. There were various reasons for the acceleration of decolonisation: waves of nationalism propagated by elite groups prompted an acute demand for constitutional changes, while in the mother countries support for the continuation of colonial relations began to waver on ideological and economic grounds. The fact that colonial powers were reduced in status as a consequence of the Second World War was not lost on the indigenous elites; it made the former less self-confident than they otherwise would have been. Furthermore, the new world leaders were critical of colonialism.

To some extent, colonial empires fell apart through strife and exhaustion and a lack of political will on the part of the leadership of the mother countries. To some extent also, the transfer of sovereignty was a managed process of running down an institution that had outlived its usefulness. Relations between mother country and former colony were then consciously reorganised and evolved on a new basis.

The process of decolonisation involved a complicated series of moves and countermoves, with the process sometimes stopping for a time, more or less successfully, and sometimes speeding up. Reciprocal moves could be made by small groups of officials in negotiations or by huge crowds in impressive demonstrations. While a large part of the process was nonviolent, there were ugly flares of violence during riots and repressive actions, and violent struggles during long-drawn-out guerrilla wars and counter-insurgency operations.

Decolonisation was a massive process. The five mother countries of the UK, France, the Netherlands, Belgium and Portugal granted independence to 82 countries during the period 1945–82, and there are now very few dependent territories left in the world. The number of colonies acquiring independence per year was rather irregular. This was to be expected, as independence movements in the different regions of the Third World gained momentum at different times and the general policies of mother countries differed as well.

While most acts of independence resulted from peaceful (though not necessarily unstrained) political change, about 14 out of the 82 newly independent states gained their status in the wake of at least sporadic acts of organised violence by at least two warring parties. But in only a handful of these cases did severe organised violence occur, notably in the French colonial wars in Indochina (1946–54) and Algeria (1954–62).

Table 1.1 lists these 14 cases. It is, in fact, a list of cases on which two sources agree. Cases mentioned by only one source are left out. There is also some disagreement between the sources on dates; as conflicts did not begin with a formal declaration of war and did not necessarily die down precisely on independence day. The two most serious of these decolonisation conflicts, which appear in bold type in the table, are the only ones included in Small and Singer's collection, because in these wars the number of battle-connected fatalities exceeded 1000 military personnel belonging to the coloniser per year, and this was the figure Small and Singer used as a threshold for this type of war. In fact, in Indochina 95,000 French soldiers died during over eight years of struggle, and in Algeria

Table 1.1 Organised violence in decolonisation struggles, by empire*

British	French
Malaysia (1948–59)	**Indochina (1946–54)**
Kenya (1952–6)	Tunisia (1952–4)
Cyprus (1955–9)	Morocco (1952–6)
South Yemen (1963–7)	**Algeria (1954–62)**
South Rhodesia (1967–79)	Cameroon (1955–63)
Dutch	*Portugal*
Indonesia (1945–9)	Angola (1961–74)
	Guinee-Bissau (1963–74)
Belgium	Mozambique (1964–74)
–	

*The worst cases appear in bold type.

Source: Kende, 1978; Chaliand and Rageau, 1983.

18,000 died in somewhat over seven years. We can only guess at the number of guerrilla war fighters of the Vietminh and the Algerian national Liberation Front who lost their lives during those years, not to mention the number of civilian dead.

Of the two largest colonial empires, France and the UK, the decolonisation of the latter was the more peaceful. Of the three smaller ones, the Belgians transferred sovereignty extremely quickly once they had been asked, while the Portuguese were the most reluctant to give up their overseas possessions, although fighting was not very fierce on the whole. The French and Portuguese governments, confronted with conflicts in the colonies and problems at home, could not cope with the strain; partly as a consequence, the French Fourth Republic (1958) and the Portuguese successor to the Salazar regime (1974) collapsed.

Superpower involvement in conflict

As the Second World War progressed, it became increasingly evident that the distribution of power in the international system was bound to change. Germany, Japan and Italy would be forced to give up their big power status; France and the UK would have to accept a more modest role among the big powers. Indeed, in spite of a recognition of their big power status in some official arrangements, such as the composition of the UN Security Council, and much use of rhetorical terms like the 'Big Four' or the 'Big Three' in the early postwar period, in fact it was the USA and USSR – the 'Big Two' – who increasingly were the principal characters in world affairs.

Conflicts in two areas at the extreme ends of the Soviet Union marked the deterioration of the USA–USSR relationship in the early postwar years. One was at the Western border of the USSR, in Europe. In some of these border countries, governments dependent on Soviet support were imposed. Other countries linked themselves freely to the USA in a tightly integrated common defence organisation, or in a few cases were pressed to join that organisation. Germany became divided in this process of polarisation. That process was full of threatening crises, but was nevertheless without war. The other conflict was in the Korean peninsula near the eastern border of the USSR; here a war broke out (1950–3) in which, although the USSR and the USA did not directly confront each other massively in terms of military units, the war was nevertheless generally interpreted as a significant confrontation between the superpowers. Later on, tension between the superpowers fluctuated (Goldmann, 1973), but it has never been completely absent. The underlying conflicts on ideology, political and economic dominance and military power have not been solved.

In this context, each superpower has tried to create faithful allies, to keep them from fighting each other, and to deter the other superpower from meddling in their affairs. In short, both superpowers have created new empires: conglomerates of states where they could be the rule-makers, however different the rules may have been. Dominance relations in some parts of the world have been more outspoken and on occasion steadier than in others. The USSR has ruled in most of eastern Europe since the early postwar years. It has not been able to dominate China in the long run. The USA has maintained a very large influence in most of Central America and in the Caribbean. The early postwar dominance of the USA in western Europe (invited as well as sought) has not disappeared, but it has diminished as Western Europe has become more powerful, particularly in economic terms; and European–American relations are to some extent deteriorating.

In Asia, the Middle East, Africa and South America superpowers have tried to maintain stable allies, but this has proved difficult on the whole. Some of the steadier of these relations, like those of the USA and Saudi Arabia and of the USSR and India, leave the weaker party sufficient leeway to extricate itself from total domination. This can happen very quickly in different directions, as the Egyptian volte-face of 1973 (from USSR to US dependency) and the collapse of the Shah regime in Iran in 1979 and the subsequent cutting of links with the USA have demonstrated.

These efforts at building empires and maintaining them have often been accompanied by conflicts involving the two superpowers – sometimes against each other. The partition of Europe and the Korean war set the trend; how did it evolve during the whole postwar period?

In fact, on account of their immense resources and their global con-

Table 1.2 Direct military involvement of superpowers in war, 1945–80

	USA				USSR		
Location	Period	All military casualties	US casualties	Location	Period	All military casualties	USSR casualties
Korea	1950–3	2,000,000	54,000	Hungary	1956	10,000	7,500
Lebanon	1958	1,400	0	Angola	1975–80 (ongoing)	9,000	–
Vietnam*	1960–5	302,000	2,000	Ogaden	1976–80 (ongoing)	21,000†	–
Laos	1963–73	18,500	500				
Dominican Republic	1965	2,500	26	Afghanistan	1979–80 (ongoing)	10,500	2,500
Vietnam**	1965–75	1,216,000	56,000				
Cambodia	1970–5	156,000	500				

*South Vietnam, USA, National Liberation Front.
**Same parties, and also North Vietnam.
†Excludes victims of guerrilla movements.
Source: Small and Singer (1982).

cerns, there is some form of superpower involvement in most serious conflicts, be it diplomatic support, the rendering of political and military information, arms deals or logistic assistance. However, I want mainly to focus on the direct military involvement of superpowers in war. Small and Singer (1982) again have provided the data shown in table 1.2. I have considered the Cubans operating in Africa (Angola and Ogaden) to be part of a Soviet effort, although this is to an extent debatable. (For details of USSR–Cuban coordination, see Legum in Kaplan, 1981.)

There is some difficulty in comparing these data directly with the decolonisation wars enumerated in table 1.1. For instance, no battle deaths among the movements opposing the colonial government were taken into account in decolonisation conflicts. In table 1.2 all battle deaths have been counted apart from the Ogaden case. So from this perspective there are different criteria for including cases in the lists of wars in tables 1.1 and 1.2. However, if we use the data to examine the most serious conflicts of colonial powers (the French ones in Indochina and Algeria) and wars in which superpowers suffered comparable losses, we find that the number of cases is extremely low in both cases. Only the American casualties in Korea and the Vietnam war from 1965 onwards are of comparable size to the most serious conflicts on decolonisation. The losses of the USSR in Hungary could have been 'serious' if the war had lasted longer, and their losses in Afghanistan are serious, now that the war has continued for some more years.

During the period 1945–80 US forces have been involved in war more frequently and for a longer period than Soviet military forces, and they have suffered more battle deaths. One has to be aware that Small and Singer record the violence in Indochina in which the USA participated as four different wars; this may be disputed, but it does not significantly affect the conclusion.

US involvement in war has been concentrated in Asia: the two wars in which the USA had considerable battle fatalities (Korea, Vietnam) were both fought there. In these two cases general concerns about the presumed risks of giving in at one place and thereby causing other places to be endangered (e.g. the so-called 'domino theory') were probably more relevant than specific interests at stake in Korea and Vietnam. The most important involvements of the USSR (Hungary, Afghanistan) have presumably been motivated by more specific interests. Both are at the edge of the Soviet Union itself. The two African operations in the 1970s have been executed mainly by proxies. In this respect, the USSR has been the more prudent superpower. But this could change, as most of its war involvements have been more recent than the American ones.

In these wars an imperial superpower was involved in pursuing its own interests or those of its empire, but at the same time most of them were fought on battlefields of Third World state-makers, trying to establish and maintain viable political units. This goes for all of the wars except the Hungarian intervention by the USSR. Most superpower dominance has not been brought about, nor has it been maintained, by frequent direct military intervention. Superpowers have occasionally been involved in warfare, undoubtedly more than most states during the period, as has always been the rule for big powers in the international system – but by no means continually. As far as military pressure has been deemed necessary in the interests of superpower empires, it has probably been used far more often by way of threats or demonstrations or indirect assistance.

Because this volume is concerned particularly with the problems of nuclear armaments and nuclear warfare, I will extend this description of the conflict behaviour of the superpowers, the main repositories of military nuclear capabilities, to those forms of military conflict behaviour which have been less serious than war, on the assumption that any military involvement on their part bears some risk of escalating to a nuclear confrontation. For this purpose I use Blechman and Kaplan's (1978) and Kaplan's (1981) data on what they have called 'the political use of force'. Their lists of events cover moves or special manoeuvres or alerts of units of the armed forces of one of the superpowers in order to influence other states (sometimes the other superpower). In a few instances such activities only underlined attitudes of friendship and cooperation, but even so they could impress third parties in a less friendly way. In most cases they were meant to express a willingness to use coercive power if political preferences were opposed by other parties.

In figure 1.1 I have graphed the yearly number of these events for the USA and the USSR. The time frames differ slightly, but for the comparable time period (1946–75) the average yearly number of cases was 7 for the USA and 5 for the USSR. The USA is again somewhat more active in this respect, but there could be some underreporting, particularly for the USSR. Anyhow, differences are by no means extreme. The US use of armed force for political purposes reached unprecedented peaks in 1963 and 1964, possibly as a consequence of an upward trend from the late 1950s onwards, before coming down quite suddenly in 1965 and 1966 when large-scale war participation in Vietnam got under way. This sequence may be worth further exploration.

The USSR's use of armed force for political purposes has peaked about once a decade at much lower heights than the American culminating point. The activities of 1945 were meant to ensure that the satellite countries were brought under Soviet control after the Second World War. The 1956 peak was the result of activities intended to coerce loyalty to the USSR in Eastern Europe and culminating in the war involvement in Hungary mentioned earlier. In 1970 the extensive use of armed forces occurred in various parts of the world.

Figure 1.1 also indicates the years in which both superpowers partici-

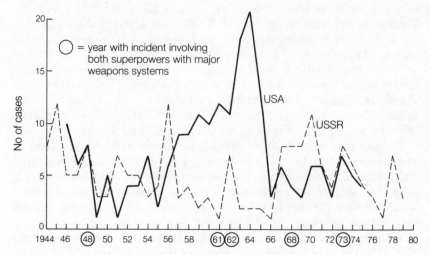

Figure 1.1 Frequency of political use of armed forces by superpower per year, 1944–80.
(*Sources:* Blechman and Kaplan, 1978; Kaplan, 1981)

pated in the same incident with major weapons systems. These were the incidents that could fairly easily have triggered the Third World War: the Berlin crises of 1948 and 1961; the Cuban missile crises of 1962; the seizure of the *Pueblo* by the North Koreans in 1968; the 1973 Arab–Israeli war. The first four were clear cases in which the territory and demarcation of superpower empires were at stake; the fifth one was primarily a consequence of a conflict between mutual client states. The first three were dominated by the superpowers from the start, the fourth and fifth were launched mainly by third parties. There may be a dangerous tendency to get entrapped in a situation more often by overzealous allies or overextended commitments than by anything else (Frei, 1983).

Based on the same information, table 1.3 shows the geographical distribution of the use of US and USSR armed forces for political purposes during three decades. The USA has always had its interests widely spread, and this is evident from its use of armed forces during the 30-year period. But the emphasis changes. The high frequency in Europe came to an end in 1955. After 1955 there was a relative increase in the Caribbean and Central America – the region the USA traditionally perceives as its sphere of influence, part of its empire proper. But Cuba moved to the other camp during those years, and this was accompanied by a lot of nervous sabrerattling in the area. After 1965 the emphasis changed again, now to the Middle East and North Africa. Israel and its Arab neighbours were very much at war from 1967 onwards, and indirect superpower confrontation was an important part of this regional conflict. Lacking comparable data

Table 1.3 Frequency of political use of armed forces by superpower, by region and decade (percentages)

	USA			USSR		
	1946–55	1956–65	1966–75	1946–55	1956–65	1966–75
North America	0	0	0	0	0	2
Caribbean and Central America	10	29	13	0	5	3
South America	6	8	0	0	0	0
Europe	40	13	15	67	57	37
Africa	2	6	2	0	7	14
Middle East and North Africa	17	15	32	10	12	29
Asia	25	29	38	23	19	16
Total	100	100	100	100	100	100
(No. of cases	48	119	47	48	42	63)

Source: Blechman and Kaplan (1978); Kaplan (1981).

for the years after 1975, I do not know if the SS-20 issue and the NATO dual-track decision of 1979 have again brought Europe to the fore.

Over the decades Asia (particularly the west coast of the Pacific from Korea to Indochina) has constantly been a major focus of American military diplomacy (as of war). The Western Hemisphere except for the Caribbean and Central America has had only faint attention in this respect.

The changes in the geographical distribution of Soviet political use of military forces are more straightforward. They show a secular downward trend in Europe and more interventions in the Middle East after 1965. These again are not matched with direct war involvements in the area. The early postwar concentration in Europe has been replaced by a more widespread pattern. According to these data (and they are corroborated by data on war involvements), the USSR has become more of a global power, like the USA, over time.

War-making and state-making in the Third World

Warfare which has not been connected with decolonisation or been dominated militarily by the superpowers has been a recurrent feature in many parts of the globe, but not in all parts and not everywhere to the same extent. Much of this was in support of state-making efforts in Third World countries. Various national elites competed violently for the levers of power within a state, with or without outside interference. Regional secessions were tried as a consequence of cultural and economic differences, or of efforts to secure or evade the national tax base, with political leaders riding a tide of inflamed xenophobia. Attacks were launched on neighbours for territorial gain. States interfered in the internal conflicts of others, often neighbours, in order to stabilise them, to help friends or to deter others from taking over (Tilly, 1981).

There is no doubt that most warfare since the Second World War has been of this type, and most lives lost in battle have been lost in this way. The four most severe wars were in China in 1946–50 (1 million battle deaths), in Nigeria in 1967–70 (also 1 million), in Pakistan in 1971 (500,000) and in Colombia over an extremely long period, 1949–62 (300,000). All of these were civil wars without major outside intervention. Small and Singer (1982) report the Indian intervention at the end of the 1971 war of secession in Pakistan as a separate event, victims of this war not being included in the preceding figure.

Small and Singer have listed 58 wars of this type during 1945–80. A few of them are really borderline cases, such as the 1956 war at the Suez Canal, where two core countries of colonial empires fought together with Israel against Egypt; they quickly pulled out when it became evident that the USA was not willing to support their intervention.

Table 1.4   Regional distribution of state-makers' wars, (1945–80), compared with the number of states in the region

	No. of wars	No. of countries
North America	0	2
Caribbean and Central America	7	14
South America	5	11
Europe	1	27
Africa	7	24
Middle East and North Africa	15	14
Asia	23	14
Oceania	0	5

Source: Small and Singer (1982).

These 58 wars were unevenly spread around the globe. Table 1.4 shows their regional distribution. None occurred in North America or Oceania and hardly any in Europe; the one European case concerns the Turkish intervention in Cyprus, a country that shares a colonial past with most of the Third World. The table also shows the number of countries in each region (averaged for 1945 and 1980), and it can be seen that this type of war occurs in the following ascending order of frequency: North America, Oceania, Europe, Africa, Latin America, Middle East, Asia. This under-estimates to some extent the frequency of war in independent Africa, since nearly all its countries attained their independence rather late, thus diminishing the chance for war to occur.

Table 1.5   Duration and severity of state-makers' wars in Third World regions

	Duration	*<5000* *battle deaths*	*≥5000* *battle deaths*
Latin America	< 3 months	5	0
	≥ 3 months	3	4
Africa	< 3 months	3	1
	≥ 3 months	0	3
Middle East and North Africa	< 3 months	4	2
	≥ 3 months	1	8
Asia	< 3 months	4	3
	≥ 3 months	1	15

Source: Small and Singer (1982).

Finally, in table 1.5 I have classified this type of war according to duration and severity for the four most relevant regions: Latin America, Africa, the Middle East and Asia. Very generally, there is a relation between duration and severity in all four regions, but there are also significant differences between regions as regards warfare patterns of this type. In particular, in Asia, but also in the Middle East, wars of this kind have been longer and more severe. In Asia they were not only more frequent but also lasted longer and resulted in more casualties.

It is by no means easy to account for these differences. One could think in material terms (availability of manpower and equipment), but possibly also in terms of warring traditions in several parts of the world. This should be further explored. Adding to the more or less indigenous war experience of Asia the very long and severe colonial war in Indochina and the deep commitments of the USA in Korea and Indochina, there is no escaping the conclusion that Asia, and Indochina in particular, have had a disproportionate share of warfare since 1945.

Conflict and nuclear arsenals

This final section is necessarily more speculative. What might have been the impact of new destructive technology, in particular nuclear weaponry and its surrounding paraphernalia, on postwar serious conflict? If one thing is clear about war theories, it is that one should be wary of single-factor explanations. Nuclear weapons will be but one in a set of factors determining the various dimensions of serious conflict. The question of where it ranks is to be answered mainly by making comparisons with a pre-nuclear world and also by comparing the conduct of nuclear and non-nuclear countries during the present period, keeping in mind, however, that these two kinds of countries may differ on other counts as well.

Small and Singer's data set covers the period 1816–1980 and thus makes comparisons with the pre-nuclear world feasible. Generally, their conclusion is that war has not become more prominent since 1816 if we take into account the expansion in the number of states. But some periods may have deviated widely from the 1816–1980 average. Is the postwar period one of these? Small and Singer have presented figures on wars for a sequence of 11-year periods. For my purposes the 1948–58, 1959–69 and 1970–80 periods, roughly the 1950s, 1960s and 1970s, are relevant.

Table 1.6   Relative frequencies of wars started and number of battle deaths during 1948–80 compared with 1816–1980

	1948–58	1959–69	1970–80	Means of all 11-year periods, 1816–1980
Wars per country	0.26	0.16	0.19	0.30
Battle deaths ('000s)	2344	3082	971	2662

Source: Small and Singer (1982).

Table 1.6 shows figures for the number of wars started during those periods divided by the number of states, and the mean of these figures for all 11-year periods since 1816. There is similar information for the number of battle deaths (without taking into account increase of population, military personnel or number of countries over time). On the whole, the figures for the postwar periods are somewhat or considerably below average, with the exception of the number of victims in the 1960s. If anything, the conclusion should be that nuclear weapons have had a limiting effect on warfare.

This may be in keeping with the fact that international wars in particular were less prominent while civil wars were relatively more frequent, for nuclear weapons would be expected to weigh more in the prevention of international than of intranational wars. On the other hand, the recent civil wars were rather more often marked by outside intervention (one in three, against one in five on average). It is not clear that this has anything to do with nuclear weapons, but perhaps it has to do with the general increase in the transportability of military power.

Nuclear weaponry may have had more specific consequences. Very few nations possess these weapons, and they have not fought each other directly since the Second World War; nor have their closest allies been engaged in war with the other superpower or its closest allies. It has often been said that one of the reasons for this is that the nuclear deterrent restrains and protects the superpowers – and in extended form their closest allies as well. In the commonly heard version of deterrence doctrine, threats and counterthreats have been of a general nature and it has been understood that considerable time lags between threats and their eventual execution may be allowed. Clearly, a deterrence policy has been pursued, but it does not follow that it has been successful. Its success can only be argued counterfactually – by virtue of what has not happened – which by its very nature is not very convincing. However, there have also been cases of immediate deterrences, with threats being specific and no long time lags being allowed. These cases can be evaluated empirically in terms of success rates; but the difference between immediate and generalised deterrence are fine.

Huth and Russett (1984) have evaluated 54 three-cornered historical cases of immediate deterrence with an attacker, a defender and a protégé. They cover the period since 1900. For these 54 cases two questions have been asked: (1) Under what conditions did counterthreats by the defender deter the attacker from executing his stated intentions against the protégé? (2) Under what conditions did the defender execute counterthreats, once the attacker had gone into action against the protégé?

Immediate deterrence is full of risk. Out of 54 cases of attempted deterrence only 31 were successful. Out of 23 unsuccessful, 15 ended in fighting. The figures show that attackers are to some extent restrained if they know that the defender possesses nuclear weapons – but only marginally so. Information on what precise threats of nuclear retaliation there have been is probably too unreliable to be incorporated into this type of analysis. Other factors influencing the success of deterrence have been the economic and military ties between defender and protégé, the local military balance, alliance bonds and the strength of the protégé. In conclusion, there is no reason to ascribe an overriding influence to the presence of nuclear weapons on the postwar pattern of warfare in the world, although they may have been relevant in particular cases.

The significance of these weapons lies elsewhere: it is in the social and technical dynamics that their presence sets in motion and in their ominous colouring of the future. Because they are so immensely powerful, there is the constant urge to keep them under control – the more so as they become more dangerous. They affect not only the societies of the possessor countries but also those of the other countries in which they have been installed. Moreover, technical developments mean they have invaded the commons of the globe, such as the oceans and space (Deudney, 1983). And although the chances of their use in each individual incident may be extremely small, the damage which they are able to inflict is so outrageous that risks are too large. It is a primary function of political units to provide some sort of social order; part of this is a modicum of stable expectations. Nuclear weapons unduly undermine this quest for stability.

References

Blechman, B.M. and Kaplan, S.S. (1978), *Force Without War: US Armed Forces as a Political Instrument*. Washington DC: Brookings Institution.

Chaliand, G. and Rageau, J.-P. (1983), *Atlas Stratégique: Géopolitique des Rapports de Force dans le Monde*. Paris: Fayard.

Deudney, D. (1983), *Whole Earth Security: a Geopolitics of Peace*, World-watch paper 55. Washington DC: Worldwatch Institute.

Frei, D. (1983), *Risks of Unintentional Nuclear War*. London: Croom Helm.

Goldmann, K. (1973), 'East–West tension in Europe 1946–1970: A conceptual analysis and a quantitative description', *World Politics*, 36, 496–526.

Huth, P. and Russett, B. (1984), 'What makes deterrence work? Cases from 1900 to 1980', *World Politics*, 26, 106–25.

Kaplan, S.S. (1981), *Diplomacy of Power: Soviet Armed Forces as a Political Instrument*. Washington DC: Brookings Institution.

Kende, I. (1978), 'Wars of ten years (1967–1976)', with an appendix listing wars since 1945, *Journal of Peace Research*, 15, 227–42.

Richardson, L.F. (1960), *Statistics of Deadly Quarrels*. Pittsburgh: Boxwood.

Singer, J.D. (1981), 'Accounting for international war: The state of the discipline', *Journal of Peace Research*, 18, 1–18.

Small, M. and Singer, J.D. (1982), *Resort to Arms: International and Civil Wars 1816–1980*. Beverly Hills: Sage.

Tilly, Ch. (1981), 'The sinews of war', in P. Torsvik (ed.), *Mobilization, Center-Periphery Structures and Nation-Building*. Oslo: Universitetsforlaget, pp. 108–26.

Weede, E. (1975), *Weltpolitik und Kriegsursachen im 20. Jahrhundert. Ein quantitativ-empirische Studie*. Munich: Oldenbourg Verlag.

CHAPTER 2

The Geopolitics of Deterrence

Patrick O'Sullivan

The geopolitics of deterrence are often presented in terms of a duopolistic competition between superpowers fearing each other's territorial ambitions and reacting with expansionism and policies of nuclear buildup. This chapter traces the history of this competition along with the evolution of the geographical perceptions which fuel it. These views of the world are at odds with the realities of geography. On the one hand, the friction of distance still operates to lend more security to the two superpowers than they appear to realise. This is especially so in the case of the USA. On the other hand, international relationships are not simply bipolar, but multi-lateral. If both of these facts of life were given fuller recognition, this would be a basis for decreasing fear between the superpowers.

Power and distance

The received wisdom in matters geopolitical reduces human intercourse to a two-sided fight. The maps of Mackinder and his successors are invariably of two classes of territory with a no-man's land between them. Whatever the source of this simplification of human affairs into a duality, its effect is to overemphasise the significance of the duopolistic competition between the USA and USSR, especially in the minds of their opinion formers and leaders. This obsession with each other has triggered the headlong race for superior capacity for nuclear destruction, which now threatens all of mankind.

What might relax the fear of each other's global ambitions, which has led to these terrible offensive arsenals, is a greater appreciation of the security which distance still affords against conquest or control. Boulding (1963) suggested that the relationship of power to distance could be characterised by a 'loss of strength gradient'. Power is greatest at home and declines in potency as distance from home increases. The further might is projected, the weaker it becomes. The advent of naval power, radio, aircraft, rocketry, nuclear weapons and satellites has diminished this gradient, and there are those who would dismiss distance as a factor in the balance of power (Wohlstetter, 1968; Bunge, 1973). However, the control of people's lives still rests fundamentally with power over the land on which they live (Gilpin, 1981, p. 37). Since to destroy the habitability of territory with nuclear weapons in order to conquer it makes no sense, nuclear weapons are militarily redundant. As a deterrent threat they do not signify in the competition for command over people's lives and minds. In the final analysis, the military capacity to control territory is still the measure of power. The heavy cost involved in long military supply lines was clear in the Falklands dispute and is the key issue in the why and wherefore of the US Rapid Deployment Force. The American declaration of its interests in the Persian Gulf could not be backed by the bluff of a nuclear threat to any other intruder: it required the real prospect of men on the ground to carry weight. Boulding laid emphasis on the logistic costs of such territorial power, especially when exercised from a distance. The potential for the exertion of economic clout must be dampened in a similar fashion, inasmuch as trade between nations does tend to attenuate with distance.

In addition to the frictional effect of distance, it is possible to think of other reasons why power should diminish with an increase in the radius over which it is exerted. If we think in terms of either an empire or a hegemony, the essence of its domination is that it exercises power over the occupants of territory. In the last resort, the military capacity to control territory is the measure of power. Hegemony implies not the complete political integration of a sphere of influence, but the capacity to exclude a rival and to dictate whose writ runs in the land. This means that the force to control the land must be available when it comes to the crunch. If the core of an empire or hegemony has limited capacity to deploy men and material, then, as the margins of its territorial ambitions expand, the same force must be spread more thinly and so will lose its potency. To put it another way, if the cost of control per unit area is the same everywhere, then, as the circumference of a circular empire expands, the total cost of controlling it will increase as the square of the radius. Whether or not there is a frictional effect, there will certainly be a thinning effect on military force with more far-flung ambitions or obligations. The same would apply to propaganda and subversion or economic aid.

In addition to the material friction of distance, there also seems to be a gradient of boldness which operates for individuals and groups. We can illustrate this with an analogy from the behaviour of animals. In his description of the territorial rites of the stickleback, Konrad Lorenz (1972) points to a loss of courage far from home as the cause of a falling off of power with distance. The boundary between the domains of two male sticklebacks is set by a series of attacks and counterattacks, with the resolve of each waning as he gets further from the nest he built. The battle wages to and fro with shallower attacks until a balance of their courage results in a stand-off along some intermediate boundary.

Any of these effects, or a combination of them, provides a process about which to theorise when it comes to the study of competition between poles of power for dominion over the globe. Changing capabilities, expansion and contraction, can be viewed in terms of spheres of influence composed of 'force fields' which diminish in intensity with distance from the projecting pole. This conception rests on the notion of a field-like phenomenon with spheres of influence determined by the rotation of continuous gradients about the axis of their cores. The picture it conjures up is of a collection of intersecting bell tents of differing heights. The analysis would proceed to establish dominance relations in the manner of central place or rent theory. The power pole with the greatest strength at any point in space dominates that part of the globe, just as the retail centre with the lowest delivered price or the crop with the highest bid rent function would. This would generate dominated territories, with the vast extent of hegemonic spheres separated by intervening independents, and possibly interrupted by isolated, autonomous states.

The idea of political force fields does focus on domination and the role of the superpower. In this it provides a possible insight into the geopolitical perceptions and behaviour of those who have steered the territorial and nuclear confrontation of the powers since the 1940s. It is to this interaction of world views and military decisions that we now turn.

Containment

Mackinder's model of a Eurasian heartland surrounded by peripheral crescents inspired the German school of Geopolitik which emerged in the mid-1920s (Parker, 1982). Whether this actually influenced Hitler's actions or not is debatable. In wartime London and Washington, however, these concepts were perceived to be at the heart of a Nazi plan for world conquest (Whittlesey, 1942). As a result, Mackinder's writings were resurrected and reworked in the 1940s. The 'world island' and 'heartland' came to figure in speeches and newsprint. Spykman (1944) reached back to the 1890s, and to Admiral Alfred Mahan's analysis of British naval power, to modify Mackinder's map. He placed greater emphasis on seapower and the significance of the 'rimland'. This was the key to power, and the alliance of Anglo-American seapower with Soviet landpower was ousting the Axis from control of the Eurasian shoreline. Spykman proposed that, when this task was complete, US policy should be directed to exclude Russia from power over the rimland.

In the same year, 1944, the American military began its preparation for a third world war against Russia. The Air Force purchased the long-range

B36 bomber, even though it would serve no purpose in a war in which the USA had established a firm foothold across the Atlantic.

In the 1930s Stalin had sought isolation and had consolidated Russian defences against an encircling, hostile world. Although he was a Georgian, his policy was Great Russian imperialistic nationalism. Even the zealotry of Marxism–Leninism had a precedent in the messianic tradition of tsarist Russia. With the defeat of Hitler, Stalin's main preoccupation was the creation of a broad cordon of defence under Russian control to fend off any Western effort to overwhelm the Soviets. Russia had been ravaged and had only 60 battle-weary divisions in Eastern Europe. The military and productive might of the USA was the most obvious fact of international politics. There were more American soldiers than Russian soldiers. At the close of the war Roosevelt and Churchill were willing to compromise with Stalin and to negotiate well-defined spheres of influence. However, with Roosevelt's death and Stalin's intransigence over Eastern Europe, there was a hardening of anti-Soviet attitudes in the West. By 1947 this distrust and fear had found expression in the Truman Doctrine, the Marshall Plan, the H-bomb programme and the Iron Curtain which Churchill drew figuratively across Europe.

In striving to keep Greece and Turkey within the sphere of the USA, the Truman Doctrine extended the potential for the conflict of American 'good' with Soviet 'evil' to the entire globe. The Marshall Plan was implemented, rebuilding Western Europe so that it could stand against Eastern pressure. In July 1947, George Kennan (writing as 'X') generalised these efforts into a policy of 'containment'. Although Kennan refused to acknowledge any debt to Mackinder, he was aware of the heartland notion, and his writing stressed the need to surround the threat of Russian landpower. The Soviet leaders saw these policies and actions as elements of an aggressive drive against their Eastern European security cordon. Stalin reacted by tightening the Soviet grasp, beginning with Czechoslovakia.

Nuclear confrontation

This jostling in the rimland was accompanied by the elaboration of nuclear weapons and strategies for their employment. In 1948 General Bradley announced the doctrine of 'massive retaliation'. The containment of Russia within Eastern Europe was to be achieved through the threat of nuclear devastation of the Soviet heartland as a penalty for further expansion. To counter any Russian advances, the USA stationed its forces so that it could strike at the heart of Russia with nuclear bombs carried in B36s and B50s. A small conventional force in Western Europe would provide a 'trip wire' to justify the response. By stumbling across these US troops in their expansionist drive, Russian columns would automatically call down nuclear fire on their homeland.

This threat lost its credibility in 1949, however, when the Soviets tested their first atomic bomb. By the mid-1950s the USA and USSR faced each other, both with the power to deliver nuclear bombardments across the oceans.

Shatterbelts and dominoes

At this juncture the competition between the USA and the remnants of European imperial power on the one hand and communist powers on the other had become truly global. Communist victory in China in 1949 drew the full attention of the US government to the Pacific rimland. In 1950 Dean Acheson laid down a 'last ditch' in the Pacific, running from the Aleutians to the Philippines, but excluding South Korea and Formosa. Subsequently the line of containment was pushed onshore to include South Korea, Formosa and Indochina. Lines of containment and spheres of influence were not well defined, either on the ground or in the minds of politicians and officials. In this space between the firmly established domains of the powers, there was room for indirect competition. Fairgrieve (1925) had used the term 'crush zone' to describe the belt of countries lying between the continental power and the sea powers. Whittlesey (1942) had called the states between Germany and Russia a 'shatterbelt'. In the early 1960s Cohen (1963) saw fit to present a geopolitical equilibrium, with core areas separated by shatterbelts. The nuclear duopoly made direct conflict too risky, and since the 1950s the competition between the USA and USSR for hegemony in the shatterbelts has been mostly indirect.

What came to be a widely held popular American view of the world, and a justification for diplomatic and military decisions, was first disseminated widely by William Bullit (1947). This conjured up the spectre of a monolithic power spreading communism outward from Moscow, engulfing first China, then South-East Asia and finally the world. The fear of the red tide powered by the combination of Russia and China was potent. Dulles talked belligerently of 'rolling back' this tide to 'liberate' territory in the Soviet sphere. In deed, however, he continued to contain Russia and China by establishing a US presence in South-East Asia and completing a ring of airbases around the opposition.

In 1953 Admiral Arthur Radford proposed to relieve the French in Dienbienphu with a carrier-based nuclear attack on the Viet Minh. He called for such action to stop the chain reaction of nations falling into the communist camp 'like a row of falling dominoes'. Eisenhower liked the catchy phrase; Kennedy in his term picked it up, and a simile became a theory. Nixon and Ford subscribed to it, as did Kissinger and now Reagan (O'Sullivan, 1982). This geographical phantom, and image of a duality of centre and periphery that goes with it, has haunted the words and deeds of American policy-makers for 30 years.

Coexistence

When Khrushchev gained the upper hand in the Soviet Union in 1953, he brought to bear a more aggressive and expansive view of the world than Stalin's. In military matters, however, he rejected as too risky the strategy of a pre-emptive strike to destroy the US threat before it could get off the ground. The military stance of the Warsaw Pact came to be similar to that of NATO. Ground forces were deployed for the forward, active defence. Greater mobility and firepower, including tactical nuclear weapons, were deployed to allow for fast strikes along a number of distinct avenues of central Europe. Medium-range missiles were developed to hit European targets. Scrambling to catch up in ability to drop nuclear bombs, the Soviets built a fleet of long-range bombers and defences to ward off bomber attacks on its cities.

Khrushchev seemingly had kept his faith in the inevitability of revolution and saw it as Russia's mission to undermine international capitalism. There was, however, no need to rush the process, and so he was willing to coexist with the protracted decay of the West, while gradually widening the Soviet sphere by indirect means. He injected a Russian presence into the Middle East, Africa and Latin America, filling power vacuums and encouraging 'wars of national liberation' to embarrass the Western alliance and outflank the USA. Khrushchev dismissed Stalin's doctrine of 'capitalist encirclement' by questioning who was surrounding whom? Eisenhower responded to these thrusts by extending the area of containment in 1957 to include the Middle East. There was little danger for Khrushchev of direct confrontation with the USA in all of this, since the USSR was not stirring political unrest but merely exploiting it where it existed.

Nuclear strategies

However, the direct competition in nuclear weaponry had gained a momentum of its own quite independent of the geopolitical circumstances by the end of the 1950s. In the USA, fear of a 'bomber gap' in the mid-1950s had led to the B47 and B52 programmes. Meanwhile, the Soviets had chosen to neglect bombers in favour of rockets. They proved that they could launch intercontinental rockets with Sputnik in 1957, and by 1960 the SS-6 was ready for use. Khrushchev established the Strategic

Rocket Force as the spearhead of deterrence, calculating that this force roughly balanced American nuclear might and thus allowed for a reduction in the massive conventional force which had hitherto been Russia's main deterrent. The US military establishment took a contrary view, regarding things as being out of balance. They perceived a 'missile gap' which might invite a Soviet surprise attack. Eisenhower was not convinced of Soviet ability to knock out the US bomber fleet, but the clout of the 'military–industrial complex' was strong enough to get the production of the Atlas, Titan, Minuteman and Polaris missiles underway. By 1961, when satellite sensors showed how few Soviet missiles were in place and the perceived gap vanished, it was too late. US rocketry rapidly outstripped Russia's. It was the imminence of US destructive superiority with Polaris and Minuteman which led Khrushchev to try to outflank the US early warning network geographically, by placing missiles in Cuba in 1962. Forced to back off in this endeavour, the Soviets turned to diplomatic means to decrease tension, seeking détente while offsetting their offensive inferiority by developing defences against bombers and rockets.

Once the USSR attained 'second-strike capacity', that is the theoretical ability to suffer a US attack and hit back, massive retaliation gave way to 'flexible response' as the nuclear doctrine of the USA. This strategy, requiring the ability to escalate step-by-step from the tactical to the global level of conflict for the last resort, involved the USA in building the firepower to destroy the USSR, China and their satellites as national societies after itself absorbing the worst possible attack. But the hope of defence against nuclear attack embodied in this strategy rapidly wore thin. Despite the theory, it became clear that, after the first shot, the reality of war would consist of blasting each other until one side's nuclear quiver was empty. Clearly, in such a fight there could be no victor. By 1962 the USSR and USA had enough nuclear explosive power to devastate each other beyond recognition. The realisation of this led to a view of nuclear weapons as the ultimate deterrent. The temptation to mount a surprise nuclear attack would be restrained by the certainty of retaliation in kind. The threat of a conventional strike by the Red Army would be blocked by the horror of an inevitable escalation through tactical nuclear weapons to all-out nuclear war. In order to work, this restraint of direct conflict between the two great nuclear powers had to be reciprocal. Neither side should have the slightest temptation to strike first.

The rapidity of technical advance made this a potentially uneasy balance of terror. Nevertheless, out of it arose the notion of global aggression held in check by the terrifying prospect of 'mutual assured destruction'. Each side was in a position to turn on an attack from the other with sufficient force to burn the fruits of victory to ashes. The balance, then, required the mutual perception of an invulnerable retaliatory force, thus removing the temptation to strike first. Any anxiety about vulnerability to a surprise attack carried with it the temptation to adopt a policy of 'launch on warning', carrying with it in turn an increased likelihood of an accidental holocaust. This menacing, terrorist strategy reduced nuclear weapons to utter military uselessness. Their only function was to remove the temptation to use them from others.

Since they were always trying to catch up in offensive force, the Soviets paid some attention to defences, to radar, surface-to-air missiles and interceptors. In the late 1950s they devised anti-ballistic missiles, some of which were in place around Moscow within a decade. When it became obvious by 1962 that these would be ineffective, the Soviet leadership began to show an interest in arms limitation. Despite evidence of the impotence of these defensive Russian weapons, the US government began the development of multiple war-headed weapons in order to overwhelm them.

The Soviet–Chinese split

In 1963 the world map of friends and foes got back to a more traditional arrangement as China and the USSR parted ways on ostensibly doctrinal grounds. The Chinese leadership denounced coexistence as the denial of a revolutionary faith which required armed struggle. In doing this they drew a new geopolitical image. The earth was being competed for by the true revolutionary spirit residing in China, by the Moscow revisionists and by the reactionaries led by the government of the USA. Around the core territories of these three powers the rest of the world was arranged into two zones: the first contained the peasant nations of Asia, Africa and Latin America; the second included industrialised Europe and Japan. Chinese attention was drawn to the first zone, the 'countryside of the world'. The myth of Mao's leadership of the revolutionary peasantry investing and swamping the cities of China in the 1940s was projected on to the global screen. For Mao, the impelling force of history was the violent antithesis of peasants and colonial powers. Any uprising was worth encouraging if it helped to demolish the structure of imperialism. Party cadres could then rapidly displace the inept factional elites which led such insurgency. Lin Piao (1965) enunciated this visionary schema. The 'cities of the world', namely those of North America and Western Europe, were surrounded by the 'countryside' of Asia, Africa and Latin America. The revolutionary failure of the urban proletariat passed the torch on to the peasants. Two-thirds of mankind should swamp US imperialism and its lackeys, the latter including the Russian revisionists who were seeking peaceful coexistence and gradual change out of a fear of nuclear weapons. True revolutionaries had no such fear, for the imperialists would be ashamed to turn such weapons against people's wars. Even if they did, Mao was willing to fight against those armed with nuclear weapons and conquer them by sheer numbers of survivors.

The Soviet leaders were torn by this challenge between appearing more militant than Mao or abandoning the role of violent revolutionaries. The latter path had the merit of reducing the risk of a direct clash with the USA and attracting a large following from the unaligned world. There has been a temptation to dump Marxist–Leninist doctrine and play the world power game as Great Russia. Although Brezhnev dabbled in disruption of the capitalist order far from Russia – in Africa, Asia and the Americas – he limited himself to inconsequential places, working for the status quo in the Middle East where there was a prospect of confrontation with the USA. The current entanglement in Afghanistan is an effort to retain control over what had been recognised as being within Russia's sphere of influence and was slipping away.

In China, too, since the death of Mao there has been a reversion to a more traditional world view, where importance varies with distance from the agricultural core of China rather than according to some revolutionary doctrine.

The nuclear spiral

While the world was changing in the mind's eye of the leaders of the USSR and China, the nuclear confrontation between the USSR and the USA continued to spiral upwards on a path determined by the detached logic of technology and combative posturing, and quite unrelated to the geography of political affairs.

In 1971 the Nixon administration continued to declare its innocence of the deed or intent of developing a first-strike force at a time when the USA was deploying multiple-warhead missiles. These upset the balance of terror. Each rocket could now kill several enemy rockets at their launching sites. As long as a missile had only one warhead, and given the probability of its failure, there was no advantage in using one rocket to attack another: the number of kills per rocket would always be less than one. But if the accuracy of guidance and the reliability of the weapons was high enough to give each warhead a reasonable chance of hitting a missile silo, the multiple-warhead rocket gave the advantage to the aggressor. It was a first-strike weapon. The USA tested it first in 1968 and had it ready for action in 1970. The USSR tested its first multiple-warhead missile in 1973 and had a number sited on land by 1975 and in submarines by 1979.

By 1980 the Soviet versions were considered by some military advisers to the US government to be opening the defensive 'window', i.e. increasing US vulnerability by threatening US land-based missiles. The MX missile was conceived as a means of closing this window. The appointment

of James Schlesinger as Secretary of Defense signalled the growing currency of a new attitude to nuclear weapons in the US corridors of power. In
September 1974 Schlesinger laid the foundation of the notion of winnable
nuclear war by disparaging US defences and describing a possible 'surgical' attack by the Soviets, knocking out US silos and killing only 800,000
civilians. This, he suggested, would cause any US president to capitulate.
Any attempted counter-stroke would be met by the extirpation of urban
America. It was suddenly possible to contemplate nuclear war, and outcomes of it, which were acceptable to one or other side. To gain the upper
hand in fighting a nuclear war, it was proposed that the USA should
develop the silo-busting MX. Russian denials that they could execute a
surgical attack, a more likely death toll of 20 million and the prospect that
this might well call forth a doomsday response from a president using the
bomber and submarine components of the USA triad did not impress the
exponents of the 'winnable war'.

In June 1979 Carter gave the go-ahead for the MX, a multiple-warhead
missile with the power and accuracy to destroy hardened Russian silos.
This was a political concession to the hawkish elements in Congress who
had been converted to Schlesinger's doctrine of 'counterforce capability'.
The new doctrine called for the building of weapons to match or outweigh
every element of the Soviet nuclear arsenal. Carter conceded this in the
hope of getting the Senate to ratify the SALT II treaty.

The only reason a power would want to be able to bust hardened silos is
if it is going to strike first. Although the MX was credited with 'second-
strike ICBM countersilo capability', this was only out of deference to the
US avowal that it would not launch a pre-emptive first strike. (US policy
continues to use the threat of first use of 'battlefield' nuclear weapons
against conventional forces.) Clearly, there is no point in smashing empty
silos. So the deployment of silo-busters makes sense only as preparation
for a pre-emptive strike against Soviet land-based missiles. These comprise 75 per cent of Russia's nuclear armoury. The Soviets could be
excused for viewing the MX as a first-strike threat, and they might
therefore be tempted into a hair-trigger 'launch on warning' policy and a
further spiral of the race to disaster.

If Schlesinger's proclaimed counterforce doctrine was to be given credibility, however, the MX would have to be treated as if it were not a
first-strike weapon but a retaliatory one. This logic would involve deploying it so as to withstand a Soviet first strike. It led to the elaboration of
a number of geographical subterfuges to ensure the survival of 100 missiles
with 1000 warheads. This was on the assumption that only half a force of
200 missiles with 2000 warheads would survive a Soviet attack. (By sheer
coincidence, 2000 warheads could knock out most of the Soviets' 1400
missiles in a first strike.) After investigating a variety of locational
strategems – deep emplacements, airborne launches and orbital bases –

Reagan finally ordered the placing of the MX, obscenely renamed 'Peace-maker', in 'superhardened' Minutemen silos. With the increasing accura-cy of missile aiming, no silo is safe, and this is the disposition of a first-strike weapon.

Beyond this, there has been speculation by the military on taking nuclear competition into space with the 'Star Wars' gadgetry of satellite launching platforms, killer lasers and particle-beams. The current collec-tion of weapons is militarily and geopolitically superfluous; never mind an escalation beyond the atmosphere.

Europe

The most likely place for the use of nuclear weapons is Europe. The USA has a commitment to extend its deterrent power to cover its NATO allies. The threat it poses is that, if the Warsaw Pact attacks Germany, the USA is willing to escalate the defence from conventional forces to tactical nuclear weapons to theatre weapons, such as the Pershing, up to the ultimate use of ICBMs aimed at Soviet missile silos. This is the policy of 'flexible response'. If US-based missiles are vulnerable to a pre-emptive Soviet strike this threat is empty. Nobody believes that a US president would use bombers and submarine-based missiles, which could only attack Soviet cities, and thus invite the killing of millions of Americans, in order to keep the Russians out of Germany and the Netherlands. NATO's perception of Soviet nuclear superiority is said to have led to the decision to place Pershing IIs and cruise missiles in Germany, the UK, Belgium, the Netherlands and Italy as a stopgap until the MX is deployed to close the 'window of vulnerability'. These are capable of reaching all of Eastern Europe and some of western Russia and are supposed to fill the breach between tactical and intercontinental weapons to assure its NATO allies that the USA will not take advantage of a missing rung in the 'ladder of escalation' to uncouple itself from a European fight and avoid an intercon-tinental exchange. No US president has, however, explicitly voiced will-ingness to risk urban America for the defence of the Ruhr.

All of this menace and the danger it holds is based on the belief that the hidden agenda of the Kremlin includes the conquest of Western Europe. Although Marxism–Leninism may have had some influence on the foreign policy of Khrushchev, Brezhnev and Andropov, there is little evidence of its imparting a strong direction to Soviet policy in recent years, never mind of its inspiring a master plan for world conquest. The USSR is having enough trouble with the satellites it has. The Kremlin has shown an increasing desire for stability and predictability in foreign affairs. The evidence suggests that Soviet intentions in Europe have been defensive since 1945.

The geographical myth of Soviet aggressive intent which continues to sustain the insanity of nuclear deterrence is, however, deeply embedded in the collective wisdom of the US political establishment. Some leaders and makers of opinion and decisions remain impressed with a Mackinder-like view of the world, which says that revolutionary violence emanating from the heartland must be contained for the sake of social stability. This is done by winning and holding the loyalty of governments in the surrounding rimland. This frame of mind finds expression in the continuing use of the domino motif, which puts every local conflict into a global context. Reagan's view of the world was formed in the 1950s, and he talks as a militant cold-warrior with a mission to conquer the 'evil empire' of communism. Everything is seen in terms not of local rights and wrongs but of a white camp and a red camp with a contested field of pink between. At a time when the rulers in Moscow and Beijing have returned to more traditional, nationalistic views of the world with local definitions of national interest, US foreign policy utterances and actions seem to draw from an ideological schema based on an excessively simple mental map of political geography.

The world network

The concentration by world leaders and media on those who dominate a continuous, force-field, spheres-of-influence image of the world has diverted attention from the way our world actually works and from changes in peaceful affairs. The reality of our daily reactions with one another on the face of the earth in politics, economics and social exchange is a matter of highly channelised flows, not of wave-like surges across widespread fields of energy. Our human numbers and the links between us are finite. The channels for interacting with each other are limited in number and extent. Although it has been characterised as a continuous envelope around the earth (Teilhard de Chardin, 1961), this realm of interacting human intelligence operates more nearly like a finite graph, especially when we consider transactions between states. There is a network of a limited number of connections joining some nodes of power to others. Interaction occurs over the links of this network via both direct and circuitous paths. To conceive of the world as a net joining nodes of power allows for a finer specification of the sources of political energy. The nodes in the network not only need to coincide with national governments, but also can represent interest groups within states or transnationally organised churches, parties and businesses.

This presents a picture of a more complex world, potentially more able to absorb local jolts to its stability by the dissipation of political energy. Such a model of the world offers no prospect of simple, comparative static analysis of the likely outcomes of perturbations to the system, such as the power-gradient formulation might provide. What it encourages is the search for complexity and the quantitative expression of relationships. This counters and demotes the impression of potentially catastrophic, duopolistic competition that is conjured up by spheres of influence. Such insight might have saved the USA a good deal of grief in Vietnam between 1961 and 1973. It is to be hoped that a network picture of the setting of foreign policy decisions would encourage the treatment of each case of conflict on its merits in terms of an explicit, rational notion of power transference. The notion of continuous spheres of interest seems to generate Pavlovian responses to any departures from the status quo within each hegemonist's definition of his or her turf. This is the view of the world which calls for nuclear deterrence and sustains the danger of a final holocaust.

References

Boulding, K. (1963), *Conflict and Defense*. New York: Harper & Row.

Bullit, W. (1947), 'A report to the American people on China', *Life*, 13 October.

Bunge, W. (1973), 'The geography of human survival', *Annals Association of American Geographers*, 63(3), 275–95.

Cohen, S. (1963), *Geography and Politics in a World Divided*. New York: Random House.

Fairgrieve, J. (1925), *Geography and World Power*. London: University of London Press.

Gilpin, R. (1981), *War and Change in World Politics*. Cambridge: Cambridge University Press.

Lin Piao (1965), *Long Live the Victory of the People's War*. Beijing.

Lorenz, K. (1972), *King Solomon's Ring*. New York: Signet.

O'Sullivan, P. (1982), 'Antidomino', *Political Geography Quarterly*, 1(1), 57–64.

Parker, W. (1982), *Mackinder: Geography as an Aid to Statecraft*. Oxford: Clarendon Press.

Spykman, N. (1944), *The Geography of Peace*. New York: Harcourt Brace.

Teilhard de Chardin, P. (1961), *The Phenomenon of Man* (trans. B. Wall). New York: Harper.

Whittlesey, D. (1942), *German Strategy of World Conquest*. New York: Farrar and Rinehart.

Wohlstetter, A. (1968), 'Illusions of distance', *Foreign Affairs*, 46(2), 242–55.

X (G. Kennan) (1947), 'The sources of Soviet conduct', *Foreign Affairs*, 25(5), 566–82.

CHAPTER 3

The Geography of Arms Dispersal

Tony Ives

East–West relations stand at the centre of any consideration of the geography of peace, but attention is increasingly being given to the multidimensional nature of the global buildup of arms, to regional arms races and to the phenomenon of conventional arms transfers between nations. The practical effect of the spread over the world's surface of advanced conventional weapons systems merits study. It is clear that tension between the great power alliances is not limited to their mutual geographical boundaries but extends to distant locations. Further, it is now readily recognised that the crisis which could lead to a nuclear exchange between the great powers might arise not directly between the major protagonists, but as a result of peripheral rivalries and instabilities between minor countries armed only with conventional weapons.

The potential tinder points are all too numerous. There have been at least 120 conflicts since 1945, and the number of people killed in conflict – possibly as many as 25 million – is comparable with the total of those killed in all theatres of the Second World War. An increase in the number of conflicts in recent decades has coincided with an upsurge in the rate of dissemination of major non-nuclear weapons systems.

The process of dissemination and conflict shows a clear geographical pattern. The great majority of the conflicts which have taken place since 1945 have occurred within and between the less developed countries, while most of the weapons used in such conflicts have originated in the developed or industrialised countries (see figure 3.1).

Although governments actively coordinate arms transfers, weapons are widely disseminated through conventional trading mechanisms. In a sense, the study of arms transfers can be seen as an examination of a traded commodity, a branch of commercial geography. Traditional geopolitics and geopacifics, grounded firmly in concepts of strategy, resources, race and balance of power, have tended to overlook the study of war *matériel* as a component of world trade. More surprisingly, the literature of development economics until recently gave only limited attention to a major component of the spending of less developed countries and to a factor

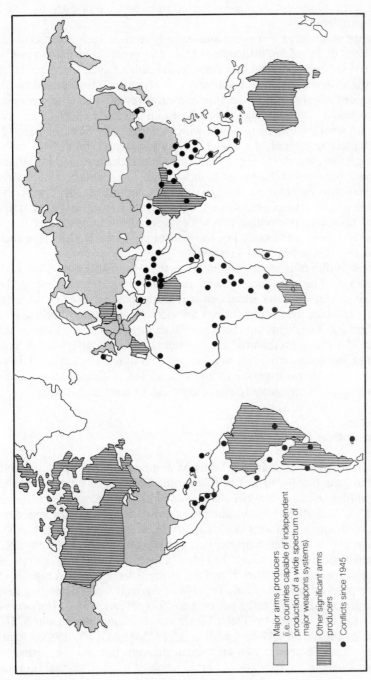

Figure 3.1 Arms producers and location of conflicts (Modified Gall Projection).
(*Source:* SIPRI, 1981, 1982; Sivard, 1983)

Major arms producers
(i.e. countries capable of independent
production of a wide spectrum of
major weapons systems)

Other significant arms
producers

● Conflicts since 1945

which some observers now consider contributes significantly to Third World problems.

As with other sectors of peace and security studies, facts about conventional arms dispersal are difficult to obtain and verify. Information can be restricted by both political and commercial sensitivity. Furthermore, in using the material which is available, close attention must be paid to the conventions adopted and to the omissions they reveal. Thus, for example, the Stockholm International Peace Research Institute (SIPRI) figures, which are most commonly used and which substantially form the basis for this chapter, relate only to 'major weapons systems' (military aircraft, tanks, missiles, warships, etc.). They therefore exclude several important categories such as small arms and ammunition; paramilitary, riot control or surveillance equipment; modified civilian equipment (such as Land Rovers); infrastructure, such as military airfield installations; or the training and maintenance programmes which normally accompany the transference of military hardware. The financial or political significance of such exclusions can scarcely be overstated.

If there is difficulty in assembling data, there is equally a problem with terminology. The term 'arms trade' refers to the major element in the dispersal of conventional arms, but it is inadequate to describe all arms movements since many transactions are effected as a form of military or economic aid. The distinction between aid and trade is often unclear in the context of various preferential arrangements. Accordingly, writers have preferred the term 'arms transfers' or even 'military assistance'. I have used the term 'arms dispersal' to embrace all forms of arms transactions and to emphasise the geographical dimension of arms movements.

The increasing rate of dispersal

The increase in levels of arms production and rates of dispersal since 1945 has been remarkable. Sivard (1983) estimates that the total volume of world military expenditures in 1982, at $660 billion, was at least 13 times that of the mid-1930s at constant prices. Most world military spending occurs within national forces. International arms transfers represent only a small fraction of world military spending (about one-tenth), but since 1945 they have risen more markedly than total military spending and the rate of increase of transfers to Third World destinations has risen most rapidly of all. As a proportion of the total, Third World armed forces' spending rose from 8 per cent in 1970 to 15 per cent in 1979 (SIPRI, 1981). Imports of major weapons systems by Third World countries increased from $7870 million in 1962–6 to $47,829 million in 1977–81 (SIPRI, 1982). Arms transfers have increased not only quantitatively but also in terms of quality. Whereas 30 years ago the arms involved in international transactions were usually secondhand or of relatively unsophisticated design, now the most advanced weapons are transferred.

There have been strong surges in the rate of dispersal. One followed the 1967 Middle East conflict, in part to replace the weapons lost in combat in that region. From 1973–4 onwards the rate of increase in arms transfers was even greater, this time largely owing to the rise in crude oil prices. The US and other governments encouraged the process of converting oil into arms as a means of recycling the surplus oil wealth, and at the same time as a way of cushioning the effect on arms industries of the end of the Vietnam war. In one year US arms sales doubled, from £3.9 billion in 1973 to £8.9 billion in 1974 (Sampson, 1977). The chief destination for US weapons at that time was the Middle East, with some two-thirds of all US arms exports in the period 1973–9 going to Iran, Saudi Arabia and Israel alone.

Producer regions and the 'push' factors

Relatively few countries are capable of design and development across the whole spectrum of conventional arms: they include the USA, USSR, France, West Germany, UK, Italy, Japan, Sweden and possibly China. Other industrial countries have a capability over a part of the spectrum only: Belgium, Spain, Czechoslovakia, South Africa and Israel. A further group manufactures conventional weapons but has to use imported technology under licence or make co-production agreements with corporations or governments among the major weapons-producing countries. This group includes not only developed countries such as Canada, Australia and Poland but also Third World countries such as India, Egypt, South Korea and Brazil.

Figure 3.2 shows the major arms-exporting countries. The 'push' factors encouraging arms dispersal from the producer regions are varied. The rivalry between East and West for strategic advantage in the Third World has been a constant motif in the dissemination of forces, weapons and instructors. Throughout the 1960s and 1970s, the USA was by a significant margin the major supplier of arms to Third World markets. Increasingly, arms were made available to friendly foreign countries as a substitute for the direct stationing of forces there or as a means of bargaining for strategic advantage. Around 1980, the USSR surpassed the USA as arms exporter. This reflected a temporary period of restraint during the Carter administration; also the apparent fall-back in direct US supplies was in part the result of a greater US willingness to enter into licensing agreements for local overseas manufacture. The USSR had begun to adopt the practice of Western producers in its search for markets, either assuming a commercial approach (to gain hard currency) or applying favourable terms for foreign policy objectives. SIPRI's characterisation of USSR aims could in fact relate just as well to all the exporting countries:

> Arms transfers serve as a means of establishing a presence in regions important to the Soviet Union . . . [they] often provide the opening wedge for a variety of other contacts which would otherwise have been difficult to achieve. An arms agreement with a developing country has been the point of departure for most Soviet advances in the Third World. . . . Arms transfers play a far greater role than economic aid or trade in this respect. . . . (SIPRI, 1982, p. 185)

Western Europe has long been a source of arms exports, but it entered the market strongly in the 1960s following postwar reconstruction. France in particular vigorously promoted arms transfers, largely to prevent the absorption of smaller Third World countries into the sphere of influence of the superpowers (Chirouf, 1981).

Among all Western producers, however, the production and export of arms is largely in the hands of private corporations, often with transnational links. For such companies, increased exports of weapons result naturally in higher turnover and profitability, and in longer production runs. The latter enables research and development costs to be spread and unit production costs to be reduced to a degree which can be critical in the highly competitive domestic arms markets, a factor which has been recognised and exploited by the military establishments of the developed countries.

Many transnational arms companies have sought to extend their influence by creating a Third World dimension to their production facilities. Kaldor (1982) describes the role of US and other firms in pre-revolutionary Iran:

> In addition to selling weapons, they were deeply involved in establishing an arms production base. Northrop owned 49 per cent of Iran's major aircraft industry. . . . Bell helicopters and the Italian firm Agusta were involved in the licenced production of various sub-systems and airframe components for helicopters. . . . (Kaldor, 1982, p. 106)

Other companies similarly involved in Iran included Grumman, Hughes Tool, Litton Corporation, British Aircraft and Vickers. With such strong commercial encouragement, the expansion of Iran's forces under the Shah, if all orders had been completed, would have left that country with more weapons than the UK or France.

Among the major producers with a wide range of competence in weapon development, only Japan and Sweden have not been large exporters of equipment to the Third World. Sweden has developed an advanced weapons capability largely springing from its own precepts of neutrality and independence from external pressure. Its reluctance to establish export or licensing links with other countries is the result of self-restraint rather than any disqualifying geographical factor. The pressure to offset development costs by exports is ever-present, however, and in the early 1970s Sweden did enter the race to build a new fighter aircraft type required by NATO and is now again promoting combat aircraft. But arms sales have represented only 0.6 per cent of Swedish exports, compared with 2.4 per cent for the UK, 3.1 per cent for France and 3.8 per cent for the USA (Sampson, 1977). The Japanese case is not unlike that of Sweden. Military production has risen to supply the defence force permitted by treaty, but the generally anti-militarist stance of Japan since 1945 has been reflected in low research and development budgets, in a low proportion of GNP spent on the military and in a negligible penetration of export markets. Nevertheless, the scale of Japanese GNP is such that its total military budget is the world's seventh largest, and recently there has been pressure both internally and from the USA for Japan to do more to meet the perceived defence requirements of the Far East. With the increasing use of electronic technology in weapons systems, more extensive Japanese intervention in the arms commodity market could result in a substantial shift in geographical patterns.

Increasingly, the 'technology-dependent' producers are participating in the arms export market, and exports from Third World manufacturers in particular are rising rapidly. Their success is based on a willingness to sell to any market and on a concentration of effort on a limited range of appropriate products (for example in the counter-insurgency field) as much as on low unit production costs. The total share of major weapons exports is still small, however. All arms exports from Third World countries in total are broadly equivalent to the exports of the UK alone (see figure 3.2).

Brazil is now by far the largest Third World exporter of arms. Its government originally established an arms manufacturing industry to produce relatively simple designs largely for import substitution, but it now produces 45.6 per cent of total Third World arms exports (Israel is the second exporter, with 21.1 per cent) (SIPRI, 1982). By 1980 it could make fighter and light aircraft, helicopters, armoured vehicles and military electronics, with exports exceeding $1 billion in 1981 (Sanger, 1982). Despite its intention to increase local content, Brazil still depends heavily on licensed technology and imported components, so that arms imports remain high ($371 million in 1978).

South Africa is the largest arms manufacturer in the Southern Hemisphere, producing more than Brazil. It has technical and licence links with

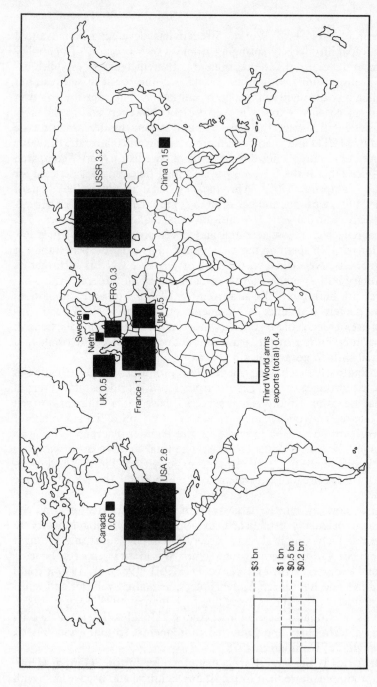

Figure 3.2 Principal arms exporters, 1981 (Modified Gall Projection). Figures are SIPRI trend indicator values for major weapons. All figures are in US$ billion at constant (1975) prices. Values include licences sold to Third World countries for major weapons production. (*Source:* SIPRI, 1984)

Israel, Taiwan, France and Italy but, unlike Brazil, hardly figures as a major exporter or importer; production is aimed at the establishment of self-sufficiency.

Consumer regions and the 'pull' factors

Figure 3.3 shows the principal arms-importing countries. The Middle East is clearly the largest importing region, reflecting both its oil wealth and its instability. South-East Asia also remains a significant market for arms.

Although still relatively small, the arms market of sub-Saharan Africa is one of the most rapidly growing. The geopolitical resonances of Africa's recent progress to independence are still being expressed in a high level of instability. Conflicts have stemmed from the process of independence itself, and from attempts to establish national identity in civil or intertribal war or in border disputes. Many African governments still have the radical and non-aligned attitudes of early post-independence and are willing to buy arms from all sources, East and West, and also to play off the great powers against each other. For their part, the great power alliances have been prepared to offer arms and military support in return for influence and bases. In the Horn of Africa, for example, where there has been longstanding tension between Ethiopia and Somalia, the superpowers have each, at various times, supplied military equipment to both of the protagonists with the objective of winning strategic positions close to the Red Sea.

Over large parts of Africa there remain strong political, economic and military supply links with the former colonial powers. France, in particular, maintains large forces in its former possessions, and gains advantages in training and weapons development.

Latin American territorial identities have been established longer than those of Africa, and although there are some remaining border disputes the relationships between states are generally settled. Thus the justification for large and growing military establishments relates often to internal problems. Arms purchases include much counter-insurgency and surveillance equipment. Supply links with North America remain strong but are no longer predominant. US reluctance up to 1970 to supply the most advanced weapons systems, together with the aggressive search for markets by Western European suppliers, resulted in the displacement of the USA as the major arms source. By contrast with Africa, however, Soviet bloc penetration of the arms market here has been very limited.

There are wide variations in the levels of imports and in the motivations of consumer countries, but clearly a potent factor in the growth of arms imports, especially in Africa and South-East Asia, has been the decolonisa-

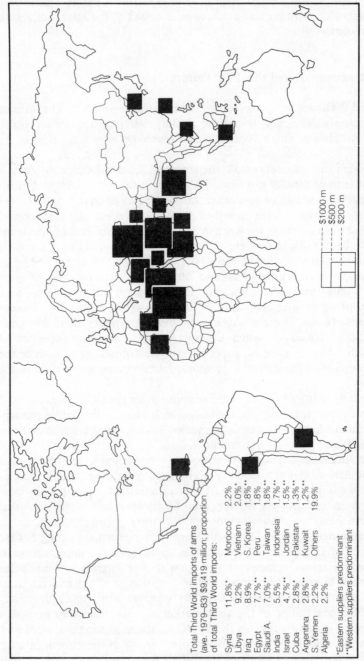

Total Third World imports of arms
(ave. 1979–83) $9,419 million; proportion
of total Third World imports:

Syria	11.8%*	Morocco	2.2%
Libya	9.2%	Vietnam	2.0%*
Iraq	8.9%	S. Korea	1.8%**
Egypt	7.7%**	Peru	1.8%
Saudi A.	7.0%**	Taiwan	1.8%**
India	5.5%	Indonesia	1.7%**
Israel	4.7%**	Jordan	1.5%**
Cuba	2.8%*	Pakistan	1.3%**
Argentina	2.8%**	Kuwait	1.2%**
S. Yemen	2.2%	Others	19.9%
Algeria	2.2%		

*Eastern suppliers predominant
**Western suppliers predominant

$1000 m
$500 m
$200 m

Figure 3.3 Average annual imports, principal Third World arms importers, 1979–83 (Modified Gall Projection). Figures are in US$ million at
constant (1975) prices.
(*Source:* SPIRI, 1984)

tion process, the establishment of many new nations and their subsequent militarisation. The new political units often inherited territorial limits which bore little relation to geographical, ethnic or cultural patterns. Colonial withdrawal left border disputes unresolved, and an apparent need to inculcate a sense of national identity in unwieldy territories. The armed forces in many emergent countries represented one of the few national institutions to transcend ethnic, religious or tribal divisions, and also one of the major repositories of skilled personnel and trained management. Military groups soon established dominant roles in a number of new nations, and it is now estimated that 56 countries in the Third World are under military control (Sivard, 1983). In the context of the Ethiopian revolution, inspired by discontented officers, Gutteridge (1979) refers to 'the dangers inherent in a military establishment which is dependent on its own growth dynamic'. The producer countries have been quick to exploit the resulting demand for equipment, although often, as Galal (1982) notes, 'the subsequent military build-ups have conformed more to the assessments of the military needs of the supplier than of the client'.

Trends and prospects in arms dispersal

Factors which have led to recent increases in arms dispersal seem likely to intensify. Among the 'push' factors, the increasing cost to the producer countries of weapons procurement will continue to encourage governments and companies to seek to reduce unit costs by increasing export sales. There will be an incentive to exploit a Third World market which is more dynamic than that of the developed world. (NATO's spending in constant price terms was less in the late 1970s than a decade earlier.) Competition between producer countries seems likely to result in even more positive marketing through such devices as trade fairs for advanced weapons. In 1983 the UK government even hired a ship as a form of floating trade exhibition to promote arms exports to the Middle East.

The 'pull' factors from the recipient countries also appear likely to continue undiminished, and there are now additional geographical factors which may increase instability and arms flows in the absence of coordinated steps to remove causes of tension. For example, whereas the first countries to gain independence were those most viable in political, defence and economic terms, the more recently independent countries have tended to be smaller and more vulnerable. The future of many such micro-states must be highly uncertain. Without regional agreements for protection, they may either fall prey to larger neighbouring states or have to devote disproportionate resources to the military. Some small territories, such as East Timor, have been subject to pressure from the outset; others, such as

Belize and Brunei, have had to depend on the deployment of overseas forces to maintain a semblance of independence.

Increasing tension may also stem from claims to exclusive zones of control over continental shelf resources and over the Antarctic, as well as from problems of fresh water supply and food production. Terms of trade and high interest rates continue to act to the disadvantage of Third World countries, increasing their burden of debt. While the theoretical effect of this should be to reduce the availability of resources for arms spending, in practice the result can be to lock many Third World countries further into the financial disciplines of international financial agencies, leading to authoritarian or military forms of government and to maintained levels of military spending.

As a corollary of the pressure from producer countries to increase their arms exports, licensing and co-production agreements may increase. Such agreements are often a key part of export arrangements. For the originator company or country, a licensing agreement may be seen as a way of avoiding export or import restrictions. In other cases, co-production may offer the possibility of cost-cutting for some components. Among Third World countries licensed production may be seen primarily as a means of import substitution, but also as a way to establish a degree of political independence. The trend in weapons research, however, is towards ever more complex forms of warfare systems using the latest information, space and laser technology. Such innovation implies not only that the cost of weapons systems desired by Third World countries will increase further, but also that technological dependence on a few advanced countries will be intensified. Thus, although Third World arms production (excluding China) rose from $1000 million in 1970 to $5000 million in 1979, it should not be assumed that autonomy is thereby increased. Countries like South Korea, Nigeria and Brazil may be able substantially to assemble the requirements of their own armed forces, but in order to stay equipped with the latest military equipment they will have to remain dependent on electronics and other components from the advanced countries.

The issue of technology transfer is related to that of nuclear proliferation. The use of nuclear weapons requires not merely the possession of the weapon itself but also suitable delivery systems. In the last two decades, the industrial countries have made advanced delivery systems and technologies available to many of the countries with nuclear potential, at least to the degree required to support regional warfare. Furthermore, the distinction in the weapons themselves between nuclear and conventional is becoming increasingly blurred so that, for example, the enhanced radiation/reduced-blast weapon, or 'neutron bomb', is seen by some NATO strategists as an anti-tank weapon. Sheehan (1983) describes how this and other battlefield weapons could be used 'to destroy units as they concentrated for attack . . . to destroy an attacking force's logistical support . . .

to modify terrain in such a way as to block the enemy's advance or force him to move into narrow areas where he can be attacked more easily'. These are all military objectives that might be desired in Third World battlegrounds. The possibility that weapons on this indistinct dividing line between nuclear and conventional might feature among arms transfers to Third World countries cannot be ruled out.

Only positive actions by governments can reverse these trends. There have been efforts to restrain arms transfers: the examples of Japan and Sweden have been referred to, and other countries such as Canada, the Netherlands and West Germany have exercised partial controls. The Carter administration attempted to limit arms exports to regions where conflict existed or might be exacerbated, to deny arms to human rights violators, to avoid using arms sales as instruments of foreign policy and to set a total ceiling on arms sales. The policy proved difficult to sustain. This was partly because of internal cost pressures, since longer production runs were seen as a way of reducing procurement costs for US forces, and partly because any niche in the market created by US restraint was rapidly filled by Western European competitors.

Political resistance to pressure for restraint has often been related to supposed employment loss, frequently in specific locations such as Barrow-in-Furness or Tyneside in the UK. Yet there has been little political commitment to research into the process of 'arms conversion', whereby local economies can successfully transfer from defence to civilian production.

Accepting that the dispersal of arms would be difficult to restrain, the Independent Commission on International Development Issues (1980) urged a form of financial levy on international arms transactions. It seems unlikely that such an approach would be effective. Costs would almost certainly be passed on to the consumer regions. Whynes (1979) accepts that defence spending is likely to continue to preoccupy less developed countries. While in no doubt about the net disbenefits of military spending, he investigates how the economic burden of defence could be minimised, for example by integrating the military more closely with the remainder of the economy through its participation in civilian development programmes or emergency relief. He also advocates mobilising the people of the Third World in forms of 'non-military defence' rather than continuing the present process by which, as SIPRI (1981) expresses it, 'an increasing number of armed forces throughout the world find themselves more or less adequately equipped with weapons designed for a war in Europe'.

Geographical significance of conventional arms dispersal

Clearly, the spread of major weapons systems employing the most up-to-date technology constitutes a spatial phenomenon of some importance. Two very significant perspectives are: first, the relationship between arms dispersal and the incidence of conflict with all its attendant geopolitical effects of economic disruption, population displacement, ecological disturbance, famine and disease; and second, the relationship between arms dispersal and prospects for economic development or welfare among the less developed countries.

It cannot be claimed that the increase in the number of Third World conflicts in recent decades is caused directly by the flow of weapons from industrialised countries; there are many contributing factors in each case. Nevertheless, recourse to armed conflict as a means of resolving internal or international disputes (in such cases as the Nigerian civil war, the Gulf War between Iran and Iraq and the Indonesian invasion of East Timor) has been possible only in the context of readily available supplies of major weapons systems to one or both sides.

Some regional conflicts have been called 'proxy wars' because of great power involvement in the background, particularly by the supplying of arms. Conflicts are rarely so simple in origin, but the great powers are certainly using the flow of arms to advance their own interests: to protect sources of raw materials, trade routes and (in the case of the West) investment and corporate interests. For the superpowers, 'national defence has come to have unlimited perimeters' (Sivard, 1983).

It has been suggested that the increasing role of the military in the Third World is related to arms dispersal as part of a cycle of repression aimed at perpetuating the political and economic interests of the industrialised countries. Thus, for example, the UK Committee on Poverty and the Arms Trade (COPAT) envisages a developing country facing an economic crisis, with resulting hardship and political turmoil:

> The military hierarchy . . . is in a powerful position to pose as the defender of the nation and insist that only the most vigorous repression of popular opposition will provide a solution. Repression requires further arms imports, and as the struggle becomes more violent pressure increases for both imports and even the local production of arms. The end result of this is the militarisation of the whole political process . . . the consequent state of severe repression is ideal for the increased penetration of the economy by outside interests. (COPAT, 1981)

The encouragement of military and other friendly governments by arms supplies from the great powers can be viewed (like the recent creation of the Rapid Deployment Force) as a means of substituting indirect long-range influence for direct stationing of military personnel in large numbers in distant territories. To that extent, the global spread of weapons systems is an expression of the East–West arms race and the term 'proxy war' can be justified. Gregory (1980) has emphasised that in many cases 'developed states become involved in the formulation and operation of the defence policy of developing states which is a far greater involvement than is suggested by the simple term arms sales'. Kaldor (1982) observes that 'the armament culture draws both military and industrial organisations into a complex interconnected global system'.

Yet producers can have exclusively commercial motives for arms sales, while consumers can be engaged in local or regional rivalries which have little to do with great power confrontation. (The 1983–4 Iran–Iraq conflict is a case in point.) Whatever the motive, the buildup of arms in one country has frequently been the cause of destabilisation in a whole region, provoking neighbouring countries to follow suit and leading to local arms spirals.

Perhaps more significant still is the issue of whether the arms build-up and military growth in the less developed countries contribute to or detract from the prospects for economic welfare or development. The picture is by no means straightforward. There are parallel and contradictory effects. Defence spending can have a beneficial local multiplier effect. D. K. Whynes concludes that in the Third World

> defence spending can generate some degree of regional multiplication and would, given an appropriate geographical location, serve as a policy tool in regional development programmes. However, the most pronounced multiplier effects can only be gained at those centres where industrial and infrastructural development is well advanced, and this constraint might run counter to the less-developed countries' desire for depolarisation. (Whynes, 1979, p. 53)

A multiplier effect can equally be expected from many forms of non-military investment; but in a developing country it has been argued that there might be particular benefits emanating from military spending, in the training and discipline of the workforce (reaching a wide cross-section of the population through national service) and the introduction of a 'modernisation ethic'. It is true that the dispersal of sophisticated weapons systems represents a transfer of technology from advanced to less developed countries, but this form of transfer carries its own costs in high maintenance and service demands which take up disproportionate amounts of money and trained manpower and frequently imply a continued political dependence on the supplier nation.

Most recent observers have concluded that growing expenditure on the

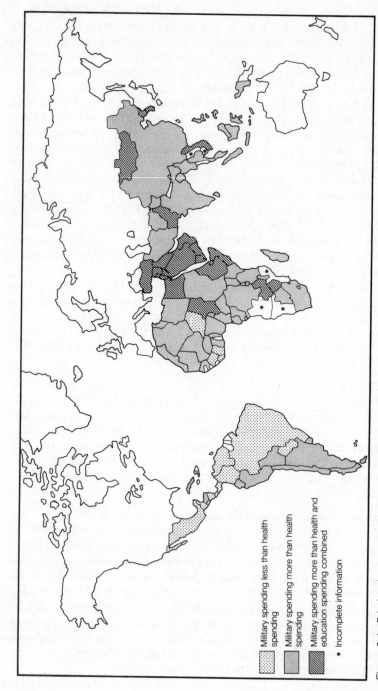

Figure 3.4 Priority given to military spending in Third World countries.
(*Source:* Sivard, 1983)

Military spending less than health
spending

Military spending more than health
spending

Military spending more than health and
education spending combined

* Incomplete information

military results in a net disbenefit to Third World economies and societies, through the channelling of funds into military procurement which could otherwise be used in civilian industrial or social programmes. Figure 3.4 illustrates the high priority accorded to arms spending in relation to other social needs by many Third World administrations. Those giving priority to arms spending include some countries with very low GNPs as well as the more wealthy OPEC countries. The Palme Report graphically demonstrates the disproportionate resource cost of arms dispersal for two poor countries:

> Ethiopia and Somalia spent more on arms imports in 1977–79 than did all the Nordic countries plus the Netherlands. Arms imports were worth less than 0.1 per cent of the national income of the six European countries but about 14 per cent of the national income of the two African countries. Their cost was equivalent to the income of 36,000 people in the European countries but of 5,000,000 people in the African countries. (Independent Commission on Disarmament and Security Issues, 1982, pp. 89–90)

Geographically, the effects of this microcosmic arms race in the Horn of Africa must relate to the wars and tensions there and to the subsequent patterns of famine, disease and ecological degradation.

Conclusion

The transfer of weaponry between nations has become a growing feature of the economic and political geography of the planet. The process has become associated with the acceleration of regional arms races and the availability of the most advanced conventional weapons and of delivery systems suitable for nuclear weapons in parts of the world hitherto not so equipped. The opportunity costs involved for the less developed countries contribute to the widening gulf in wealth between North and South. This, together with the propensity of the superpowers to use the flow of arms to pursue foreign and defence policy objectives, has helped to create a more complex spatial pattern of tensions, both North–South and within the South as well as East–West.

Arms dispersal is thus a geographical phenomenon of underrated importance. There can be no conclusive evidence to establish the effects of the great increase in arms dispersal, but it can reasonably be asserted that the increase has coincided with an upsurge of militarisation and a tendency to resort to European-style battleground conflicts to settle disputes. At a rate of growth of 6 per cent in military spending compared with 1 per cent for the more developed countries, the Third World forms the area of most dynamic militarisation on earth. Although the dissemination of arms is not exclusively an expression of the East–West arms race, the superpower blocs have political, strategic and economic interests in promoting the process. The consequent threat to world security and the waste of resources are increasingly recognised, but few substantive steps towards restraining the flow of weapons have been achieved.

Arms transfers constitute a central aspect of North–South relationships, as the Independent Commission on International Development Issues (1980) and the UN Expert Group on the Relationship between Disarmament and Development (see Sanger, 1982) have both shown. Despite some claims that arms transfers represent a spearhead of technical skills in poor countries, arms spending must divert skills and financial resources from welfare and development programmes. Arms growth and resource deprivation lock many less developed regions into a fateful downward cycle of conflict, further poverty and continued dependence. This cycle can be seen as one of the clearest geographical manifestations of the global obsession with arms systems rather than collective security through international law.

References

Chirouf, L. (1981), 'The French debate; arms sales', *Armament and Disarmament Information Unit Report*, 3, 4.

COPAT (UK Committee on Poverty and the Arms Trade) (1981), *Bombs for Breakfast*. London: Committee on Poverty and the Arms Trade.

Galal, E. (1982), 'Dynamics of the arms race: a Third World view', in J. Rotblat, *Scientists, the Arms Race and Disarmament*. London and Paris: UNESCO/ Pugwash Symposium.

Gregory, F. (1980), Arms sales involve more than the trade in weapons', *Armament and Disarmament Information Unit Report*, 2, 1.

Gutteridge, W. (1979), 'Disarmament, Development and Public Confidence', *Armament and Disarmament Information Unit Report*, 1, 3.

Independent Commission on Disarmament and Security Issues (1982), *Common Security: A Programme for Disarmament (The Palme Report)*. London: Pan Books.

Independent Commission on International Development Issues (1980), *North–South: A Programme for Survival*. London: Pan Books.

Kaldor, M. (1982), *The Baroque Arsenal*. London: André Deutsch.

Sampson, A. (1977), *The Arms Bazaar*. London: Hodder and Stoughton.

Sanger, C. (1982), *Safe and Sound: Disarmament and Development in the 1980s*. London: Zed.

Sheehan, M. (1983), *The Arms Race*. Oxford: Martin Robertson.

SIPRI (Stockholm International Peace Research Institute) (1981), *Yearbook*. London: Taylor and Francis.

SIPRI (Stockholm International Peace Research Institute) (1982), *Yearbook*. London: Taylor and Francis.

SIPRI (Stockholm International Peace Research Institute) (1984), *Yearbook*. London: Taylor and Francis.

Sivard, R.L. (1983), *World Military and Social Expenditures*. Washington: World Priorities.

Whynes, D.K. (1979), *The Economics of Third World Military Expenditure*. London: Macmillan.

CHAPTER 4

Propaganda Cartography

Alan Burnett

In one of the few academic papers published on the topic of propaganda
maps, Ager asserts, somewhat melodramatically, that 'maps like most
other means of communication can be deceptive and in the hands of
skilled manipulators they become subversive propaganda weapons' (Ager,
1978, p. 14). Once the exclusive domain of warring states or of those
making territorial claims, propaganda maps are now widely employed by a
disparate array of organisations and causes. Tyner rightly suggests that
'persuasive maps can be seen almost every day in our normal activities'
(Tyner, 1982, p. 140). To an extent, old-fashioned propaganda maps have
given way to what Ager calls 'non-cartographic maps' – those in which
stylised geographic outlines are used as a secondary background to other
graphics. Whatever sort of propaganda maps are used to spatially 'seduce'
the public, there is certainly no shortage of them in books, pamphlets,
newspapers and television. Thus, multinational companies use maps that
boast of the scale of their corporate domains and investment portfolios
to impress shareholders and potential investors; political parties include
maps in campaign literature to try to sway voters; and there are few
public inquiries where planners do not display maps to show the benefits
of proposed plans to those potentially affected. The use of maps in international airline advertising has been analysed by Fleming (1984).
    All this, of course, begs the question as to what is and what is not a
propaganda map. Does any map really 'tell the truth, the whole truth and
nothing but the truth'? Notwithstanding the fact that some cartographers
try to convey spatial information in an accurate and neutral manner and
others deliberately set out to lead or mislead, it is the use to which a map is
put that is a key factor in deciding if it can be defined as propaganda or
not. Tyner suggests that there is a continuum from the purely expository –
objective maps, in which the cartographer has attempted to portray geographical patterns truthfully – to the purely persuasive or propagandist,
where information has been manipulated in order to prove a point. The
stance that is taken in this chapter is as follows:

1   There are maps in which the cartographic elements are manipulated to make them more persuasive.
2   While the motives of cartographers and graphic artists do vary, even the 'purest' and most accurate of maps can be used for propaganda purposes.
3   There is no guarantee that the 'public information' maps produced by government agencies are less propagandist than the more overt political cartography of pressure groups.

Of course, maps are not the only or necessarily the most powerful way of conveying spatial information. Hall (1981) proposed a four-fold typology of geographical propaganda – numerics, semantics, technologies and graphics (a category comprising maps, graphs, tables, models and photomontages). However, maps are at least the most explicitly spatial form of propaganda and are clearly susceptible to geographical analysis. The techniques which are used in maps that set out to persuade are well known. They include choice of map projection and scale, the selection and omission of data, the use of certain symbols and colours, and the message incorporated in the title and accompanying caption.

This chapter focuses on propaganda maps relating to nuclear weapons. Recently there has been an upsurge in the production and installation of ever more powerful nuclear arsenals, particularly in Europe. In the plethora of publications which has accompanied the proliferation of nuclear arms in the early 1980s, 'one is struck by the extent and importance of maps. There are maps of bomb targets, nuclear explosions, arms dispositions, military aid, buffer zones, power blocs, boundaries, dominoes and war treaties' (Pepper and Jenkins, 1983, p. 206).

The aim of the chapter is to analyse and illustrate how such maps have been used. First, the governments of superpowers have used them to justify the development and deployment of additional nuclear weapons. These maps generally promote perceptions of threat, aggression and military superiority as between the USA and the USSR, and/or Western (capitalist) and communist blocs: Second, organisations who oppose the continued buildup of nuclear arms and argue for disarmament have also used maps; they commonly emphasise the pattern of nuclear bases and targets and the scale of destruction and death which would accompany any nuclear conflict, as well as the futility of civil defence. Having discussed the role of nuclear propaganda maps in general, and noted in passing the use of non-cartographic illustrations, the chapter presents a series of (1) *armament maps*, i.e. those which tend to argue for nuclear arms proliferation, and (2) *disarmament maps*, which have been drawn or used in the cause of nuclear disarmament.

Perspectives on nuclear propaganda in the Cold War

There is a role for geographers and cartographers to promote greater critical awareness among the public of what they are looking at when they are presented with maps and visual presentations of data on the Cold War and the arms race. Bunge's warning is clear: 'everyone but geographers knows what geographers do: they explore and map . . . wait until it [the public] realises that geographers are no longer exploring and mapping . . . if we do not do the job, others may take the job from us, or no-one will do the job' (Bunge, 1982, p. 209). Fishoff, Pidgeon and Fiske (1984) have noted the varied motives of social scientists for embarking on such studies. R. Douglas has analysed the process whereby Second World War allies became postwar enemies and each side built up its conventional and nuclear arsenals:

> In the middle phase of the Second World War official propaganda in the Allied countries was full of statements designed to persuade people that the 'Big Three' – Britain, the US and the Soviet Union – were united not merely in their determination to defeat the enemy, but also in their intention to cooperate closely in the post-war period. Yet within a year or two of victory, terms like 'cold war' and 'iron curtain' were in general use and many people believed that full scale military conflict between the erstwhile allies was likely within a short time. (Douglas, 1981, p. 1)

There is little doubt that it is the mutual distrust and antagonism between the USA and USSR and their allies which is the force that has fanned and fuelled the nuclear arms race since the 1940s.

Humphrey (1982) has referred to the existence of stereotypes in Western–Soviet relations. These are exploited by forces interested in increasing international tension and continuing the arms race. He claims that our perception of a situation depends upon our established expectations and that those expectations are heavily conditioned by what we have already seen. Thus, for example, where an 'unprejudiced' observer would see the last picture in the series in figure 4.1 as nothing other than the face of a bespectacled old man, an 'experienced' observer who has followed the series through will most likely persist in seeing it as a rat. Thus, while both the USSR and the West have changed beyond measure in the last 30 years, governments and the media of both sides inevitably find it difficult to escape earlier reality. Indeed, they actively resist any change of view and search for evidence which fits their perceived model. 'Bad news' from the other side of the Iron Curtain is widely reported and greeted with ill-concealed glee.

The rat's a rat for a'that

Figure 4.1
(*Source:* N. Humphrey, *The Guardian*, 29 March 1982)

In figure 4.2, the paranoia relating to world territorial hegemony by the USA and USSR is neatly portrayed by Ingram Pinn's illustration. The menace of a rapacious global capitalism is shown as being frightening to the Russian teddy bear, just as the cruel, powerful bear is frightening to a good-hearted and diminutive Uncle Sam. The encirclement and encroachment of Russian communism/American capitalism is highlighted by the arrow symbols.

The USA has long been preoccupied with the existence of Castro's communist regime in Cuba and its influence in the developing world. This has been seen as a threat to US hegemony in Central and South America. More recently, aid and assistance given to left-wing regimes in Africa, in the shape of military advisers and medical personnel (a mixed economic, military and humanitarian programme), has also been a subject of concern

Figure 4.2   Paranoia of the USA and the USSR.
(*Source:* Ingram Pinn, *Sunday Times*)

Cuba's Worldwide Sphere of Influence

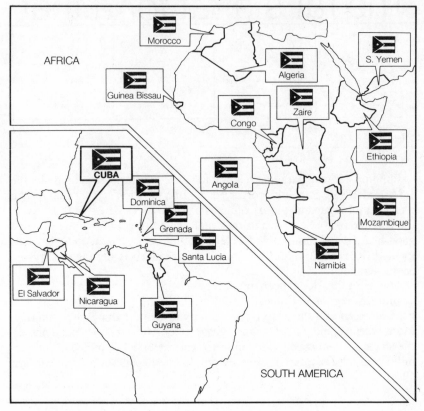

Figure 4.3
(*Source: Fortune Magazine*)

to Washington's foreign policy advisers. The caption of figure 4.3 refers to a 'world-wide sphere of influence', yet the map shows only Africa and South America. Furthermore, the Cuban flag symbols are not only of disproportionate size but are placed in such a way as to accentuate Cuban presence in those two continents. (Note the positioning of Dominica, Grenada and Santa Lucia.) Suffice to say that 40 years of Cold War propaganda have largely succeeded in creating and maintaining a state of tension between the superpowers, and that maps have certainly played their part in this process. As far as cartographic and other forms of propaganda relating to nuclear weapons and the dangers of nuclear war is concerned, three general points are worthy of note.

First, while there is a measure of mutual agreement as regards the end – a reduction in the chance of a nuclear war breaking out – there are sharp disagreements about the *means* by which the risk of such a catastrophe can be reduced. Thus, one side promotes nuclear weapons as a deterrent and the other promotes disarmament as a means of avoiding nuclear war or accidents in the testing and transport of nuclear weapons. However, each side may unwittingly adopt the hidden aspects of the opponent's image of the issue. For example, those arguing for a nuclear freeze or reduction by unilateral/bilateral policies assume the existence of a threat, even if they do not actually believe that the 'Russians are coming' in the first place. Likewise, the number and distribution of US bases in the UK, portrayed on many maps published by CND are interpreted as a threat (i.e. making us a target while we have little or no control over US weapons), but they do not have to be – they could be regarded as evidence that we are amply protected by our allies against possible Soviet invasion.

Second, estimating nuclear capacity in terms of megatonage or accuracy is an extremely complex problem, and calculating nuclear attack scenarios and the immediate and long-term impacts and casualties incorporates a degree of speculation. Given this complexity and uncertainty, it is hardly surprising that there is scope for manipulation of data in the furtherance of a particular political/military standpoint.

Third, relatively little is known about how policy-makers and ordinary people perceive, imagine, think about or otherwise hold images of the causes and consequences of nuclear war. Nor is it clear whether the barrage of propaganda, which has emanated from governments and peace groups in recent years, has had any appreciable effect on people of different nationalities, classes, sex, age or residential locations. Do pamphlets, books and television programmes really alter, or do they merely reinforce, deeply held views as well as more superficial opinions? And if any attitudes are thereby changed, is this reflected in political or any other sort of action? The evidence is uneven and incomplete.

One study reported by Fiske, Pratto and Pavelchek (1983) found, however, that the US public had a clear idea about the likely causes of death in any nuclear war. For example, a large majority thought that nearly everyone within a radius of five miles of ground zero would be killed. According to Zeigler and colleagues, location in space strongly influences perceptions: 'The people of Western Europe perceive the hazards of the nuclear arms race differently from North Americans because of their global location' (Zeigler, Johnston and Brunn, 1983, p. 85).

Of course, many people do hold definite views about nuclear weapons, and a minority take political action of one sort or another. But caution should certainly be exercised in investigating the links between cartographic propaganda and public attitudes and actions.

Non-cartographic illustrations

Before examining a range of nuclear 'propaganda' maps which portray different messages, it is worth noting, if only in passing, the widespread use of illustrations which have little or no cartographic component. Although maps do catch the eye and have, for many people, a solid 'trustworthy' image, they are not the only or necessarily the most effective way of illustrating arguments about nuclear arms. The Radical Statistics Nuclear Disarmament Group's pamphlet (*The Nuclear Numbers Game*) shows how statistics can be used to allow us to 'think about the unthinkable and justify the unjustifiable' (p. 7). Its point is, of course, that there is a whole battery of graphical means of illustrating the statistics of the nuclear age, including photomontages, cartoons and graphs. An excellent example of a publication which uses the gamut of types of illustrations with great clarity and sensitivity is *The Nuclear Casebook* (Phillips and Ross, 1983), a colourful guide issued by the medical campaign against nuclear weapons. Likewise, Garrison and Shivpuri's *The Russian Threat* (1983) incorporates a judicious selection of such illustrations.

Figure 4.4 compares the 'official' Home Office-predicted casualties of the 1980 defence exercise, after 131 warheads have reached selected targets in the UK, with the casualties predicted by independent observers. The contrast between the number of deaths and injuries (and by what means) are dramatically portrayed by figures and skeletons, each representing 1 million.

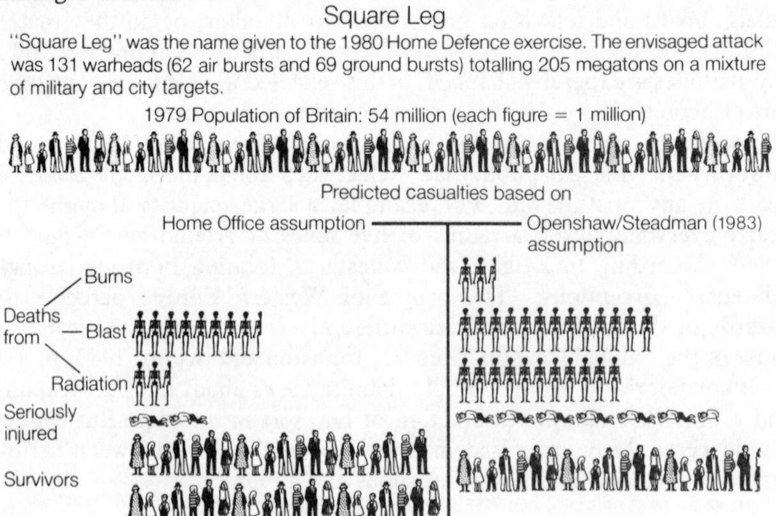

Square Leg

"Square Leg" was the name given to the 1980 Home Defence exercise. The envisaged attack was 131 warheads (62 air bursts and 69 ground bursts) totalling 205 megatons on a mixture of military and city targets.

1979 Population of Britain: 54 million (each figure = 1 million)

Predicted casualties based on

Home Office assumption ———— Openshaw/Steadman (1983) assumption

Deaths from — Burns / Blast / Radiation

Seriously injured

Survivors

Figure 4.4
(*Source:* Phillips and Ross, 1983)

American war deaths

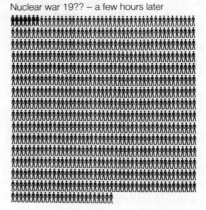

World Wars I and II

WW I
1914–1918

WW II
1939–1945

Nuclear war 19?? – a few hours later

The wars of this century have seen a trend
away from military casualties towards civilian
casualties. The ratio of military to civilian
deaths were:
World War I   20 :1 (ie 20 military deaths for
                                1 civilian death)
World War II 1:1
Korea   1:5
Vietnam   1:20
Nuclear War   1:100+

140 million (62% of population)

European war deaths

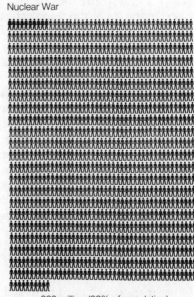

World Wars I and II

WW I

WW II

Nuclear War

| 👤 | = 200,000 soldiers |
| 🧍 | = 200,000 civilians |

In a nuclear war the majority of
civilians will be casualties.
Therefore, it is vital for each of
us to have a clear understanding
of the policies upon which our
lives depend.

200 million (38% of population)

Figure 4.5
(*Source:* Phillips and Ross, 1983)

The actual and predicted casualties in the two world wars, and a possible future nuclear war, are starkly demonstrated in figure 4.5 (as is the mix of civilian and military deaths). Perhaps more than anything else, the scale of civilian casualties is emphasised; this includes the elderly, children and pregnant women; Olympic athletes and refuse collectors; farmers and computer programmers; Californians, Catalans and Cumbrians.

Maps for nuclear armament

Before examining maps which aid the cause of disarmament, it is logical to present a few of many cartographic productions which support and encourage the possession and proliferation of nuclear weapons. The basic assumption of these maps is that the 'enemy' or the 'other side' has aggressive intentions and has been responsible for building up a superior nuclear stockpile which has to be matched in the interests of deterrence and defence. Soviet 'offensive' weapons are emphasised, and alleged superiority in numbers of nuclear arms – planned and already operational – are stressed by US sources, and vice versa. Sites, bases, flight paths, ranges, targets, radii of strike areas, global military power – all are shown in such a way as to give the impression of threat and vulnerability. Perhaps the best examples of this approach are *Soviet Military Power* (US Department of Defense, 1984) and *Whence the Threat to Peace* (USSR Ministry of Defence, 1982), jointly described by E. P. Thompson in his 1984 speech at the Oxford Union debate with Casper Weinberger as 'two of the most evil books of our time': each shows the other superpower as possessing and pursuing international nuclear military hegemony.

By careful selection and omission of data in the compilation of maps, and through choice of map projection, size, tone and design of symbols, the visual effect of 'who has the upper hand' is manipulated. For example, Mercator's Projection has been blamed 'for giving the impression of the Russian menace looming so large in people's minds' (Ager, 1978, p. 8). The spatial distribution of nuclear installations is deliberately portrayed to suggest encirclement and vulnerability. Basically, 'We are overstating the Soviet force and understating ours and we therefore greatly overstate the imbalance. Moreover, this is not something new, it has been going on for years' (Robert McNamara, former US Defense Secretary, in the *International Herald Tribune*, 15 March 1981; quoted by Garrison and Shivpuri, 1983, p. 12).

Other maps which misinform and mislead the public in the interests of those who arm and argue for deterrence include British Home Office plans and programmes (which include cartographic illustrations). These encourage of sense of efficacy in civil defence measures. The least damaging or

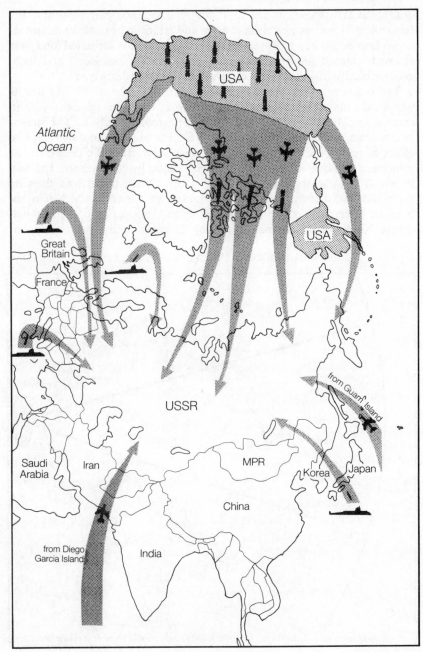

Figure 4.6
(*Source:* USSR Ministry of Defence, 1982)

deadly 'attack' scenarios are used for civil defence exercises, and the opportunities for 'escape' from injury and death are greatly overemphasised. Immediate and localised danger and destruction are noted (and, it is claimed, catered for by government plans), but longer-term and more geographically dispersed impacts are omitted or underplayed.

The message incorporated in figure 4.6 is clear: that the USA, and its worldwide network of bases and submarine force (as demonstrated in exercises held between 1970 and 1980), threatens the USSR. The stereographic map projection shows the USSR surrounded and also has the effect of increasing the size of those areas away from the centre of the projection while making the USSR look smaller by comparison. The way in which most weapons are pointing at the USSR, the arrows showing flight paths and targets within the country and, indeed, the placing of missiles seemingly 'on their way' all suggest nuclear encirclement and threat. No doubt such maps are used by the Soviet military establishment

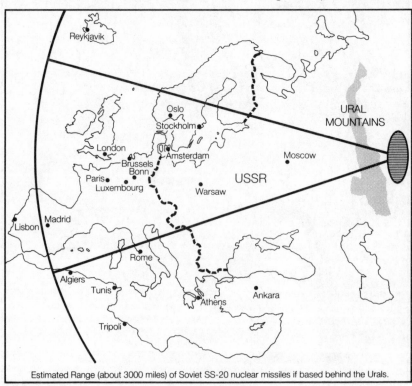

Either Side of the Urals – It's Still Target Europe

Estimated Range (about 3000 miles) of Soviet SS-20 nuclear missiles if based behind the Urals.

Figure 4.7
(*Source:* UK Ministry of Defence, 1982)

to justify further investment in naval strength and nuclear weapons. They also serve to remind the Western public of their own governments' extensive network of bases.

Figure 4.7 shows the UK Ministry of Defence's leaflet issued to counter the nuclear-free Europe movement. It claims that it is a 'fiction' that the world would be a safer place if all nuclear weapons were withdrawn from Europe. The pamphlet states: 'far from reducing the risk of war, a European nuclear-free zone would weaken the West's security and put at risk the peace and freedom that NATO's policy of deterrence has preserved in Europe for thirty years. Talk of a European nuclear-free zone is one-sided and naive. It ignores the realities of Soviet military power; it ignores the facts of geography'. The map shows that, even if the Russians pulled their SS-20 missiles behind the Urals (in the event of the creation of a nuclear-free Europe), most of Western Europe's cities would still be vulnerable. The map itself is accurate, but it is the emotive title that makes the point and the text which elaborates the argument.

The message of figure 4.8 is similar. As the caption states, 'a [nuclear] shadow is cast over all of Western Europe'. Clearly, the SS-20s are represented by disproportionately large symbols. The background map of Europe resembles a satellite image of Europe, and the dark shadow of the seven SS-20s casts a malevolent black hand over the brown land and blue sea of continent. The illustration appeared in *Fortune Magazine* at a time when a major American effort was being made to convince European

With a range of more than 3000 miles, the mobile, three-warhead SS-20 casts a shadow over all of Western Europe.

Figure 4.8
(*Source: Fortune Magazine*, 17 December 1979)

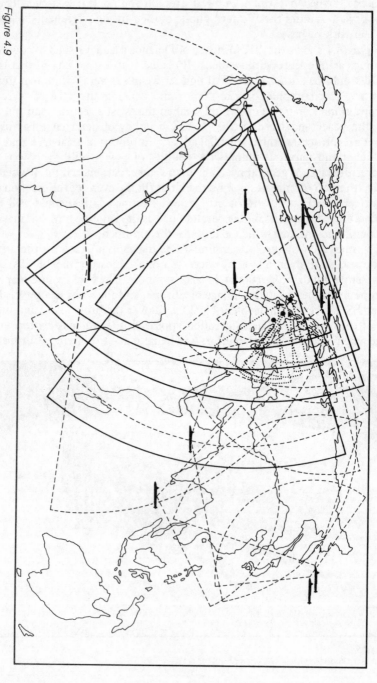

The Warsaw Pact View of the NATO Strategic Threat

Figure 4.9
(Source: Miller, Kennedy, Jordan and Richardson, 1983)

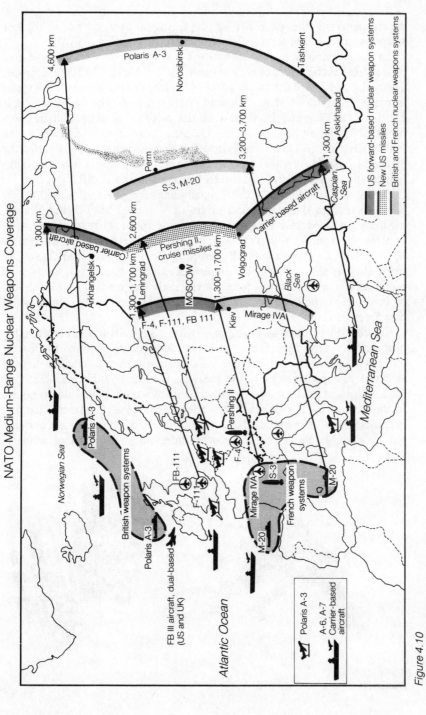

NATO Medium-Range Nuclear Weapons Coverage

Figure 4.10
(Source: USSR Ministry of Defence, 1983)

governments of the necessity of deploying a new round of nuclear weapons, namely cruise and Pershing II, to 'counter' the SS-20s.

The map projection used in figure 4.9 is of the Mollweide equal-area type. This has the effect of *not* exaggerating the size of USSR and Europe. Thus, the density of the target areas of Western nuclear weapons systems is more pronounced than it would otherwise be. The map, which is entitled 'The Warsaw Pact View of the NATO Strategic Threat',· was obtained by the authors from East German sources. As in figure 4.6, the multiplicity of NATO's missile threat is shown cartographically and the extent of 'spatial overkill' seen in the overlapping target zones is highlighted (for consumption in Eastern Europe and the USSR).

Figure 4.10 is from a Soviet English-language publication and shows Western readers the extent and origin of Western (NATO and France) medium-range nuclear weapons. Unlike the previous map (figure 4.9), only the Western section of the Soviet Union is shown to be threatened by sea- and land-based weapons. (By omitting the rest of the USSR, no doubt maps such as this – shown by the Soviet military to elite Moscow-based members of the Politburo – more convincingly suggest that roubles should be invested in nuclear arms – and not in canals, foreign aid, housing and consumer products.)

Figure 4.11 is a classic example of what Ager calls a non-cartographic propaganda map; i.e., the map background contains only the barest outlines – in this case of a rather misshapen and pseudo-satellite view of Western Europe. However, the message is clear enough: the USSR is sending 'peaceful' doves westward while it stockpiles its missiles at home. In the nuclear arms race, each side tries to convince its citizens that any proposals for disarmament, freeze or mutual surveillance are not genuine but are merely a tactic to lull the other side into a false sense of security,

Figure 4.11
(*Source: NATO Review*, vol. 32(2), 1984)

Westinghouse
Technology Applied to
Security

Today, Westinghouse airborne radar is one of
our first lines of defense around the world

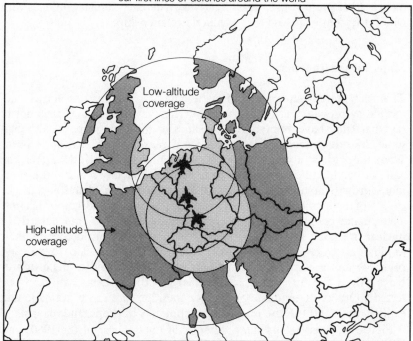

Figure 4.12
(*Source: Fortune Magazine*)

while the enemy behind the scenes is arming for nuclear supremacy.
Thus, the aim of official responses to unilateral nuclear arms control
proposals is always to impugn the motives of the other side and to
denigrate any suggestions which might lead to rapprochement.

In 1981 Pentagon payment for military-related contracts amounted to
over 30 per cent of the entire engineering output of the USA. Large US
defence-dependent companies, such as Boeing, Rockwell International
and McDonnell-Douglas, specialise in certain types of weapons systems
and are anxious to promote and sell their products. Governments are
persuaded to keep up with the latest and most sophisticated defence
technology. In figure 4.12 the Westinghouse Corporation is portraying the
coverage of its airborne radar system. The three inner circles, covering
West Germany, Switzerland and the Low Countries, with the Boeing 707
aircraft at their centres, are coloured in a bright yellow with the larger,

high-altitude coverage radii in a warm cream colour. Together they are shown as a 'safe' zone surrounded by 'unprotected' Europe shaded in brown. This map is unusual in that the armaments industry rarely appeals openly and directly to the public, as in this business magazine advertisement, rather preferring to deal directly with defence ministry officials with whom they enjoy a close and symbiotic relationship.

Maps for disarmament

This section reproduces and discusses maps which may be loosely described as propagating the cause of nuclear disarmament. That is not to say that they have been drawn specifically for that purpose, although some, like those from Bunge's *Nuclear War Atlas*, definitely have been. What they do, in a variety of ways, is to emphasise nuclear targets, the scale of death and destruction which would follow any attacks, the enormous growth of nuclear arsenals, the futility of civil defence, and the extent of opposition to nuclear weapons and support for disarmament. They make people aware of their own vulnerability to the hazards of nuclear weapons and attack. Some would not be considered by their originators to be propaganda maps in that they are said to be, and probably are, accurate representations of reality, devoid of distortion or bias. (Given the uncertainties noted earlier, these claims can rarely be tested.) Others disseminate an idea or message in a more dramatic and explicit way, and use the traditional techniques of propaganda maps.

Figure 4.13 represents the geography of nuclear war of the 1960s and 1980s, respectively. The former shows 400 pinheads, representing nuclear explosions, on cities in the USA and USSR of over 150,000 people. This scenario would result in the death of one-third of the entire population of each country. It gives a picture of a relatively sparse pattern of nuclear explosions. By contrast, the second map shows 16,000 pinheads, representing random explosions of the total number of strategic (intercontinental) nuclear warheads possessed by the USA and USSR in 1981. The legend shows that the radius of the map pinheads indicates 10 miles on the ground; thus, the overall impression is given of not only the vast increase in the number of Soviet and US nuclear missiles between the two decades but also of the fact that now few, if any, areas would remain unscathed in the event of a full-scale nuclear exchange.

The technique of standing two maps side by side is termed 'combination maps' and it is often used to portray the temporal change in state frontiers (e.g. the 'growth' of Israel). In this case, the huge increase in nuclear weapons over two decades is shown. The standard conic map projection employed highlights Europe's location between USA and USSR. Had a

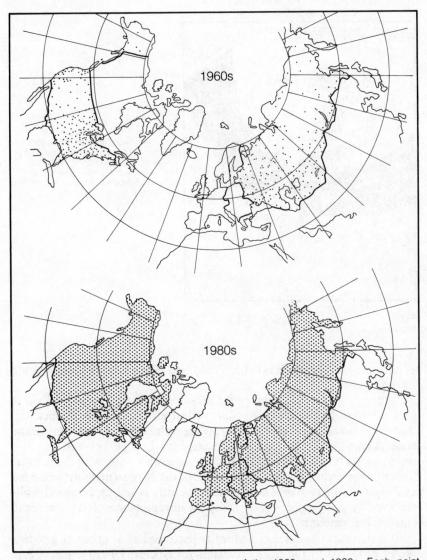

Figure 4.13 The geography of nuclear war of the 1960s and 1980s. Each point represents a radius of 10 miles on the ground.
(*Source:* Phillips and Ross, 1983)

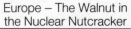

Europe – The Walnut in
the Nuclear Nutcracker

The courage of the people of Europe and
their good sense is to be universally
emulated. Literally millions of Europeans have
decided that they are not to be a ping pong
ball swatted back and forth by gigantic
nuclear paddles. They have taken to the
streets in numbers that only a mass threat to
life itself can evoke.

Figure 4.14
(*Source:* Bunge, 1982)

polar stereographic projection been used (see figure 4.6), this effect would
have been lost.

Figures 4.14 and 4.15 convey the message that certain places (albeit at
very different levels) are targets for nuclear attack, and (by implication)
that those living in or near such areas are vulnerable. At the continental
scale (figure 4.14), the 'central' location of Europe between the two
superpowers is again portrayed, this time in a cruder way with the familiar
'threatening' arrows being used. It is one of the 30 or so maps incorporated
in Bunge's *Nuclear War Atlas*. Its emotive title is self-explanatory, while
the caption gives a somewhat polemical interpretation of the European
anti-nuclear response.

At a more localised scale, Oxford is portrayed as a 'prime target' in a
poster produced by the city's Campaign for Nuclear Disarmament (figure
4.15). The background settlement pattern is produced in black and white,
and the concentric rings around ground zero in red and yellow. These are
dominant colours which give prominence to the extent of area affected by
blast and burning should a nuclear bomb explode on the city. Again, the
legend expresses the message of the map explicitly.

Figure 4.15
(*Source:* Oxford CND)

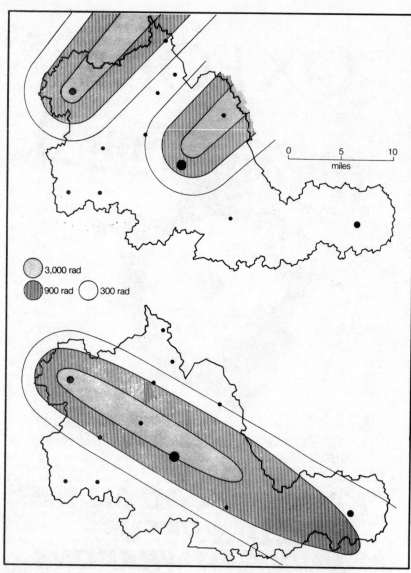

Figure 4.16   (a) Idealised fallout contours of the accumulated dose 24 hours after two 1 MT groundbursts, assuming a south-westerly wind of 15 mph; (b) idealised fallout contours of the accumulated dose 24 hours after two 1 MT groundbursts, assuming a west–north-westerly wind of 15 mph.
(*Source:* Qasrawi, Wellhoefer and Steward, 1982)

Unlike the proximate contours shown on this map, the information contained in figure 4.16 is precise and accurate, and is presented in an objective manner. It is a scientific assessment of the fallout contours over the West Midlands, showing the accumulated dose of radiation 24 hours after two 1 megaton groundbursts, assuming (1) south-westerly and (2) west–north-westerly winds of 15 miles per hour. These maps are deemed propaganda maps only in the sense that they are incorporated as 'ammunition' in a pamphlet produced by a local anti-nuclear group. The same applies to figure 4.17, except that, as with Bunge's earlier map (figure 4.14), the caption is implicitly propagandist; but this is a difference of degree only. Many accurate and objectively drawn maps are contained in anti-nuclear books, pamphlets and films. In the sense that they are used to illustrate a particular argument (generally in favour of disarmament by portraying the extent of death and damage), they may be deemed to be

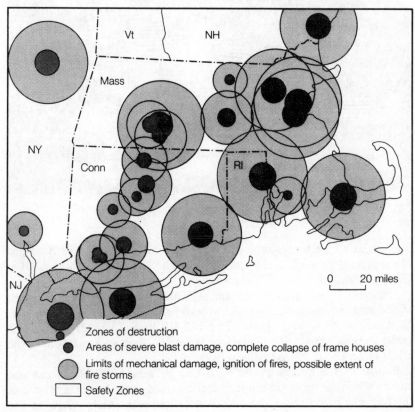

Figure 4.17
(Source: Bunge, 1982)

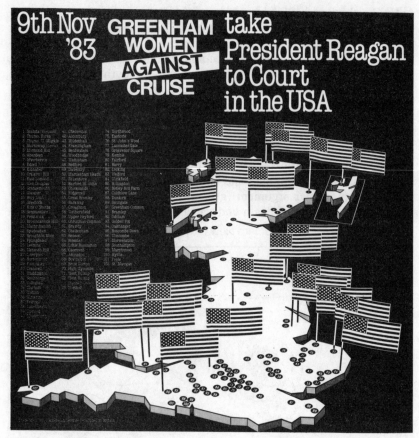

Figure 4.18
(*Source:* Greenham Women Against Cruise)

propagandist (see for example Thompson, 1983, p. 19; City of Bradford Metropolitan Council, 1983, pp. 13, 14 and 15; Szulc, 1981, p. 108; Greene et al., 1982, pp. 37, 41, 47).

Figures 4.18 and 4.19 show maps of Britain (Ireland has been omitted) which emphasise the number and widespread distribution of US bases in England, Scotland and Wales. The 102 US bases (with 27,000 service personnel) are shown. The overlarge symbols – flags and stars – have the effect of accentuating the pattern of bases.

Figure 4.18 is a large poster with four colours, blue, black, red and white. While the bases are numbered and named in the key, it is the use of the flag which comprises the major distortion in the map. 'Gaps' in the distribution of bases are covered by the stars and stripes in such a way as to give the impression of a dense and even distribution of foreign military bases; in reality, they are concentrated in south–central England and East Anglia. The use of flags also emphasises the fact that these bases are not British and make the point that cruise missiles are under the control of US military authorities and, ultimately, the US president, and not the UK government. However, to some supporters of NATO and Anglo-American military cooperation, the presence of so many bases may well be seen as a source of comfort rather than concern. That this was not however the aim of the organisations which produced them is clearly shown by the

Figure 4.19
(*Source:* CND)

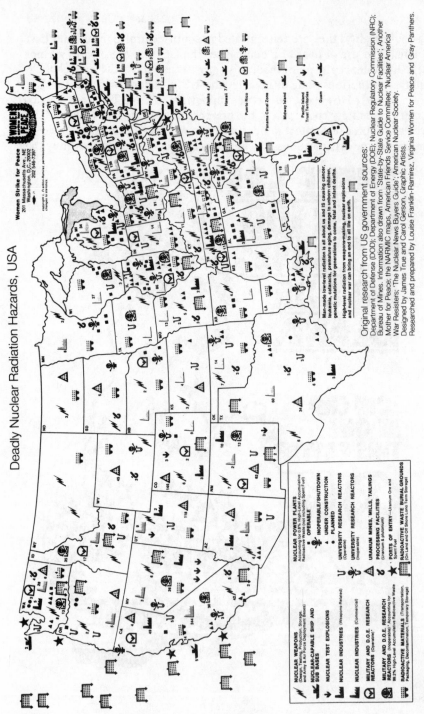

Figure 4.20

(*Source:* Women Strike for Peace, 1983)

captions, which (in 1983 and 1984) urged the British public to support legal action and take direct non-violent steps against American nuclear bases.

The map in figure 4.20 does not restrict itself to nuclear weapons, but shows the distribution of a whole range of nuclear 'hazards' including reactors, test explosions, power plants, uranium mines, processing plants and radioactive dumping grounds in the continental USA. Produced by an organisation called 'Women Strike for Peace', it is designed to give an impression of the widespread incidence of 'noxious' nuclear facilities of one sort or another. Some facilities, such as radioactive waste burial grounds and military and research reactors, are shown by symbols which given an exaggerated idea of the size and associated risk. The seemingly arbitrary positioning of maritime hazards – Panama Canal zone, Alaska and Guam, all off East Coast seaboard – also enhances the crowdedness of possible sources of nuclear radiation. The title leaves little doubt as to the message being portrayed by this map.

Suggestions for additional disarmament maps

Below, a number of suggestions are made for maps which could be drawn by geographers, cartographers, graphic artists or, indeed, members of peace groups, with a minimum of skills. They cover a variety of scales and topics.

1   To combat the many armament maps which deliberately exaggerate the enemy's superiority in nuclear weapons of one sort or another, maps which show 'asymmetrical equality' – each 'side' being superior in different aspects of nuclear capabilities – are needed. The total nuclear arsenals of the USSR and the USA should be disaggregated in terms of whether they are land- or sea-based, their accuracy, radius of operation, vulnerability to detection and interception, etc., and the respective weaknesses of each side should be documented and emphasised.

2   Although the Iron Curtain is now a fact of Europe's political geography, there is scope for maps which show the enormous range of transactions that bridge this barrier in both directions, and the spatial integration between East and West, whose economies are increasingly interdependent. Fortunately, no single missile has yet crossed the borders of countries at which it is aimed, but broadcasts and signals, television and plenty of oil and gas, wheat, orchestras, tourists, scientists, satellites and merchant shipping have done so.

3   Also, at any scale one could use colour to differentiate actual or potential nuclear-free zones. A map of the missile and bomb-infested Europe of 1985 could be contrasted with one of a future continent painted in warm 'safe' colours. A similar exercise could be done for sub-

continental areas such as the European Community, Balkans, Nordic states or, indeed, the two Germanys. National or intranational nuclear-free zones could similarly be portrayed, although whether any single continent, country or city could resist the realities of nuclear war is a moot point.

4   Although there is no shortage of potential nuclear attack impact maps (see figures 4.13, 4.15–4.17), and many local maps of varying degrees of sophistication have been prepared by peace groups and academics, still more could be drawn. Every town, city and region should have its 'who would be killed and injured, where, when and how' map(s), if possible accompanied by texts which describe in detail the destruction of familiar places, and fatalities among friends and neighbours, and the young and old. The technical task of measuring the spatial extent of blast, heat, radioactive fallout, etc., of a 1 megaton bomb is well documented, and OS base maps are readily available. The neighbourhood, village, town and city are the scales at which everyday life is lived. The horror of nuclear war has to be brought down to that level in maps drawn by students, scientists and even sixth-formers. These need not be restricted to what Bunge calls the 'one-city–one-bomb type', but could show the pattern over wider areas.

5   The appalling and apparently endless nature of the escalation in the cost of maintaining and expanding nuclear arsenals is another message which, when portrayed in terms of family budgets and the provision of essential services, surely makes an impact. Again, maps could be drawn which either show how much specific nuclear bases and facilities cost to equip and run, or the location of much-needed services which could be provided if funds were diverted from spending on nuclear weapons. Maps showing a wide range of facilities – nursery schools, clinics, bypasses, sixth-form colleges, all-weather sports pitches, law centres, etc. – could be provided. Additionally, a map of actual or threatened cutbacks and closures which could be prevented by diverting a fraction of the cost of the Trident programme could be constructed. The nebulous 'security' that is proffered by those who urge further expenditure on nuclear weapons ought to be contrasted to the tangible benefits to be derived from investing in education, the health and social services, and the improvement of our environment. This can be achieved by the use of 'combination maps' – one with bases and missiles, and another with public service facilities of comparable cost. A similar exercise could be undertaken on a global scale for a world which is, for the most part, 'either arming itself to death or being starved to death' (Garrison and Shivpuri, 1983, p. 8).

6   Although the growth of nuclear stockpiles has been amply documented, there is still further scope for showing present-day trends cartographically. This includes a series of maps showing the spatial diffusion of nuclear military installations. Twelve of the 60 countries possessing some

sort of nuclear capacity have refused to sign the Nuclear Non-proliferation Treaty, and Argentina, Brazil, Pakistan and South Africa are close to having their own nuclear weapons. Similarly, our nuclear stockpile now stands at 16 billion tons of TNT-equivalent. Garrison and Shivpuri (1983) have estimated that it would take 4600 years if we exploded one Hiroshima-type bomb every day to get rid of this ever-growing arsenal.

There is a host of ways in which maps could be drawn and used to work for disarmament. A useful exercise would be to consider how the techniques employed in every propaganda map encountered might be used for peaceful purposes. In particular, the imaginative efforts of graphic artists employed to boost the profits of multinational corporations are worth emulating. Bunge's *Nuclear War Atlas* has set a valuable precedent.

Conclusion

In the introduction to their study of *Britain after the Nuclear Attack*, Openshaw, Steadman and Greene (1983) rightly state that the subject of their book is *intrinsically geographical*, and yet it is an area which geographers, in their professional capacity, have largely ignored. The evidence of this chapter is that nuclear mapping is, indeed, alive and flourishing. In the UK, both the Ministry of Defence and national and local peace groups construct and use maps and other graphic illustrations, but for different purposes. There is mapping for armament as well as disarmament. These propaganda maps do not necessarily distort and mislead, but each, if considered with the titles and accompanying texts, puts over a particular message. Many of the traditional methods of propaganda cartography are employed, such as selecting a 'kindly' map projection, the judicious use of certain colours and, in particular, the careful choice of size and distribution of symbols.

Perhaps the most urgent task of cartographers is to use their skills to try to portray accurately and clearly the 'real' size of national nuclear armouries, and to imprint on the consciousness of ordinary people the horrific scale of death and destruction which would, inevitably, follow any nuclear war, however 'localised' it might be at the outset. Because conflict involving nuclear bombing is so inconceivable, it seems that one obvious task is to convey such an eventuality in terms of the realities of everyday life. The task of calculating the spatial impact of a nuclear attack on any city in the Soviet Union, Western Europe, North America and elsewhere is relatively simple (see Katz, 1982, and Greene et al., 1982, appendices 1, 2 and 3). Perhaps the day will come when public and school libraries, the waiting rooms of doctors' surgeries and health centres and, indeed, every home will contain leaflets which have at least one map showing the extent of destruction to life and landscape. Future ministries of defence may publish White Papers incorporating maps which portray their plans for unilateral or multilateral disarmament. When this day arrives, those pressure groups and political parties that revel in the Cold War, and the arms industries that profit from it, will really be on the defensive.

Acknowledgements are made to Andrew Harrison, Peter Collier and the editors for their advice and assistance

References

Ager, J. (1978), 'Maps and propaganda', *Society of University Cartographers Bulletin*, 11, 1–15.

Bunge, W. (1982), *The Nuclear War Atlas*. Victoriaville, Quebec: The Society for Human Exploration.

City of Bradford Metropolitan Council (1983), *Bradford: The Day After*. Bradford: City Metropolitan Council.

Douglas, R. (1981), *From War to Cold War 1942–48*. London: Macmillan.

Fishoff, B., Pidgeon, N. and Fiske, S. (1984), 'Social science and the politics of the arms race', *Journal of Social Issues*, 39, 161–80.

Fiske, F., Pratto, F. and Pavelchek, M. (1983), 'Citizens' images of nuclear war', *Journal of Social Issues*, 39, 41–65.

Fleming, D. (1984), 'Cartographic strategies for airline advertising', *Geographical Review*, 74, 76–93.

Garrison, J. and Shivpuri, P. (1983), *The Russian Threat: Its Myths and Realities*. London: Gateway Books.

Greene, O., Rubin, B., Turok, N., Webber, P. and Wilkinson, G. (1982), *London After the Bomb: What Nuclear Attack Really Means*. Oxford: Oxford University Press.

Hall, D. (1981), 'A geographical approach to propaganda', in A. D. Burnett and P. Taylor (eds), *Political Studies from Spatial Perspectives*. Chichester: John Wiley, pp. 313–30.

Humphrey, N. (1982), 'The rat's a rat for a' that', *The Guardian*, 29 March, p. 9.

Katz, A. (1982), *Life after Nuclear War: the Economic and Social Impacts of Nuclear Attacks on the US*. Cambridge, Mass: Ballinger.

Miller, D., Kennedy, W., Jordan, J. and Richardson, D. (1983), *The Balance of Military Power*. London: Salamander Books.

Openshaw, S. and Steadman, P. (1983), 'Predicting the consequences of a nuclear attack on the population of Britain: models, results and implications for public policy', *Environment and Planning, C*, 1, 205–21.

Openshaw, S., Steadman, P. and Greene, O. (1983), *Doomsday: Britain After Nuclear Attack*. Oxford: Basil Blackwell.

Pepper, D. and Jenkins, A. (1983), 'A call to arms: geography and peace studies', *Area*, 15(3), 202–8.

Phillips, C. and Ross, I. (1983), *The Nuclear Casebook: an Illustrated Guide*. Edinburgh: Polygon Books.

Qasrawi, A., Wellhoefer, F. and Steward, F. (1982), *Ground Zero: the Short-Term Effects of a Nuclear Attack on the West Midlands*. Milton Keynes: Scientists Against Nuclear Arms.

Szulc, T. (1981), 'The unthinkable', *The Washingtonian*, 106–11.

Thomas, A. and Lowe, B. (1984), *How Britain was Sold. Why the US Bases Came to Britain*. Nottingham: Peace News/Housemans.

Thompson, D. (1983), *Over our Dead Bodies: Women Against the Bomb*. London: Virago.

Tyner, J. (1982), 'Persuasive cartography', *Journal of Geography*, 84(4), 140–4.

US Department of Defense (1984), *Soviet Military Power*. Washington DC: US Government Printing Office.

USSR Ministry of Defence (1982), *Whence the Threat to Peace?* Moscow: Military Publishing House.

USSR Ministry of Defence (1983), *Disarmament: Who's Against?* Moscow: Military Publishing House.

Zeigler, D., Johnston, J. and Brunn, S. (1983), *Technological Hazards*. Washington DC: Resource Publications in Geography for Association of American Geographers.

CHAPTER 5

The Geography of Arms Manufacture

Charles H. Anderton and Walter Isard

Introduction

The world community spent approximately \$0.66 trillion in 1983 for military purposes. The USA accounts for about 30 per cent of this total; as we approach the mid-1980s, US military expenditures may reach even higher levels. A recent study estimates that real military spending for 1984–8 will increase at about 7.2 per cent annually (Congressional Budget Office, 1983, p. 3). As figure 5.1 shows, this would amount to the largest levels of real US military spending in the postwar era.

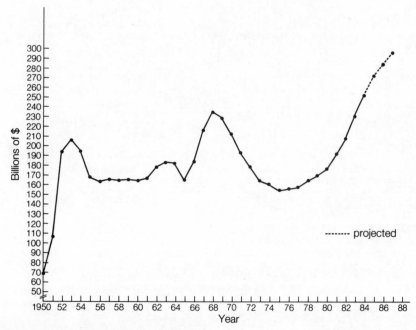

Figure 5.1 US defence spending, fiscal years 1950–88 (in fiscal year 1983 \$ billion). (*Source:* Congressional Budget Office, 1983)

Such high expenditures have significant economic effects in the regions in which they are spent. The purpose of this chapter is to discuss the issue of regional economic dependence on arms manufacture in the USA. Although we do not analyse nations other than the USA, we do raise issues applicable to any country engaged in arms manufacture. (For analyses of regional economic dependence on arms manufacture in the UK see Short, 1981; Todd, 1981; and Law, 1983.)

Regional economic dependence on arms manufacture

The massive reductions in unemployment that occurred during the early years of the Second World War left many people with the impression that defence spending was a necessary component of a healthy economy. This view has been heralded by Marxist and non-Marxist critics as evidence that the US economic system is fraught with contradiction, but it is used by political leaders to attack those who advocate reductions in defence spending. The view is unfounded, however, because it does not consider that *alternative* government expenditures, for such services as schools, hospitals, roads, recreation, etc., could be substituted for defence spending and thereby provide as many or more jobs, along with positive social benefits. This controversy over jobs lies at the heart of the issue of regional economic dependence on arms manufacture.

By regional economic dependence on arms manufacture we mean the regional employment and financial rewards to profit-making and non-profit-making institutions that result directly and indirectly from arms manufacture. This definition implies that, in the absence of adequate transition planning, particular occupations, industries and geographical areas would suffer severe short- and medium-term damage from significant reductions in arms manufacturing activities. Evidence for this is provided in tables 5.1–5.3.

Table 5.1 shows the significance of defence activities for employment levels in various occupations. The first column lists the number of people devoted to defence work in the Department of Defense and defence-related industries, by occupation. The second column gives the number of employees devoted to defence work as a percentage of total employment (defence and non-defence) by occupation. For example, 31,000 aero-astronautic engineers were employed in the Department of Defense (DoD) and defence-related industries in 1981; these employees represent 47 per cent of the total aero-astronautic engineers employed throughout the USA. As table 5.1 shows, 11 occupations had more than 10 per cent of their workers employed in the Department of Defense and defence-related industries in 1981.

Table 5.2 presents some industries affected by the defence effort in

Table 5.1   Civilian employment in the Department of Defense and defence-related industries, by occupation, 1981

Occupation	No. employed ('000s)	Proportion of occupation total (%)
Teachers, vocational ed.	17	61.0
Aero-astronautic engineers	31	47.0
Mathematicians	4	30.3
Physicists	5	24.4
Electrical engineers	60	18.3
Industrial technicians	5	15.8
Mechanical technicians	8	15.7
Lawyers	11	14.2
Mechanical engineers	26	12.2
Computer programmers	26	11.3
Electrical and electronic technicians	38	10.9
Industrial engineers	11	9.7
Civil engineering technicians	3	9.6
Metalworking crafts workers	84	9.3
Metalworking operatives	141	8.6
Assemblers	140	8.5
Metallurgical engineers	1	8.4
Civil engineers	12	7.7

Source: Congressional Budget Office (1983, p. 27).

Table 5.2   Industries affected by defence effort, calendar year 1980

Industry	Share of industry's 1980 gross output induced by defence purchases (%)
Ordnance	60.9
Transportation equipment	15.9
Aerospace	39.3
Shipbuilding	54.2
Electrical equipment components	11.2
Mining	6.7
Instruments	6.2
Primary metals	5.8
Iron and steel	5.2
Nonferrous metals	6.5
Petroleum	5.6
Transportation/communications	3.4
Fabricated metals	3.3
Machinery	2.7
All industry	3.2

Note: Shares include production of finished goods for defence and intermediate goods to be used for production of those finished goods.
Source: Congressional Budget Office (1983, p. 13).

Table 5.3 Distribution of military prime contract awards over $10,000 and total defence spending by region and state, 1981

States	Prime contracts ($ million)	Prime contracts ($ per capita)	Total defence ($ million)	Total defence ($ per capita)
New England	10,357.1	832.3	12,296.0	988.1
Maine	475.0	419.3	713.0	629.4
Vermont	166.9	323.7	208.0	403.4
New Hampshire	392.0	418.6	750.0	800.9
Massachusetts	4,596.2	796.2	5,276.0	914.0
Rhode Island	234.8	246.6	490.0	514.7
Connecticut	4,492.2	1,433.5	4,859.0	1,550.5
Mid-Atlantic	11,157.7	302.6	14,902.0	404.1
New York	6,480.7	368.2	7,473.0	424.6
Pennsylvania	2,374.5	200.0	4,081.0	343.8
New Jersey	2,302.5	311.0	3,348.0	452.2
E. N. Central	7,637.8	183.3	11,799.0	283.2
Illinois	1,155.1	100.8	2,552.0	222.6
Indiana	1,713.3	313.3	2,289.0	418.6
Michigan	1,735.3	188.5	2,365.0	257.0
Ohio	2,436.4	226.0	3,780.0	350.6
Wisconsin	597.7	126.1	813.0	171.5
W. N. Central	7,091.7	411.3	9,960.0	577.7
Iowa	311.5	107.4	445.0	153.4
Kansas	1,007.9	423.1	1,658.0	696.0
Minnesota	1,158.8	283.0	1,400.0	342.0
Missouri	4,349.1	880.1	5,312.0	1,075.0
Nebraska	105.8	67.1	559.0	354.4
N. Dakota	104.2	158.4	361.0	548.7
S. Dakota	54.4	79.2	225.0	327.7
S. Atlantic	12,482.6	330.6	30,248.0	801.2
Delaware	236.3	394.9	406.0	678.5
Washington DC	594.7	942.5	1,321.0	2,093.5
Florida	3,094.4	303.9	6,515.0	639.8
Georgia	1,245.1	223.4	3,470.0	622.5
Maryland	2,373.2	556.7	4,167.0	977.5
N. Carolina	825.1	138.6	2,865.0	481.3
S. Carolina	434.1	137.0	2,131.0	672.8
Virginia	3,590.9	661.3	9,164.0	1,687.7
W. Virginia	88.8	45.5	209.0	107.1
E. S. Central	2,832.5	192.4	6,772.0	459.9
Alabama	790.6	201.8	2,183.0	557.2
Kentucky	371.7	101.5	1,337.0	365.0
Mississippi	1,168.2	461.7	2,158.0	852.9
Tennessee	502.0	108.8	1,094.0	237.1

Continued Overleaf

Table 5.3 Distribution of military prime contract awards over $10,000 and total defence spending by region and state, 1981 *(Continued)*

W. S. Central	11,016.9	450.2	18,932.0	773.7
Arkansas	153.9	67.0	675.0	293.8
Louisiana	2,826.1	656.0	3,990.0	926.2
Oklahoma	620.9	200.3	1,899.0	612.7
Texas	7,416.0	502.2	12,368.0	837.6
Mountain	3,057.9	261.5	7,407.0	633.4
Arizona	1,123.3	402.1	2,083.0	745.7
Colorado	935.3	315.4	2,184.0	736.5
Idaho	28.0	29.2	217.0	226.6
Montana	42.0	52.9	199.0	250.5
Nevada	78.4	92.8	421.0	498.4
New Mexico	383.0	288.4	1,040.0	783.1
Utah	404.0	266.0	1,063.0	700.0
Wyoming	63.9	129.9	200.0	406.7
Pacific	20,246.0	623.8	33,661.0	1,037.1
Alaska	323.4	785.2	841.0	2,042.0
California	16,629.8	687.3	25,622.0	1,059.0
Hawaii	590.7	602.2	2,223.0	2,266.4
Oregon	113.7	42.9	403.0	152.0
Washington	2,588.4	613.8	4,572.0	1,084.2

Sources: Department of Defense (1981) and Bureau of the Census (1983).

calendar year 1980. As this table shows, a number of industries, such as ordnance, transportation equipment, aerospace, shipbuilding and electrical equipment/components, are substantially affected by the defence effort. Such patterns of economic dependence on arms manufacture will most likely stay strong, at least in the near future. For example, according to Data Resources Inc., defence purchases will account for nearly half of the growth in the aerospace industry through 1987 (Steinberg, 1984). The slow-growing primary and fabricated metals industries can expect nearly 20 per cent of their new demand to come from defence (Steinberg, 1984).

Table 5.3 presents the distribution of DoD prime contract awards of over $10,000 and defence spending by region and state, in total and per capita terms. (A 'prime contract' is a contract between the government and a profit or non-profit institution for defence work involving the following types of procurement: research, development, test and evaluation (RDT&E); other services and construction; and supplies and equipment.) As it shows, there are significant regional differences in the distributions of prime contracts and total defence dollars; for example, West Virginia received $45.5 prime contract per person while Connecticut received $1433.5 in 1981.

In figure 5.2 we show the percentage distribution of prime contract awards of over $10,000 by region. This distribution changes significantly over time. For example, the Mid-Atlantic and East North Central regions have had significant declines in their percentage shares of prime contract awards since the early 1950s, while the Pacific, West South Central and South Atlantic regions have had significant increases. Part of the shifts may be due to the specialisation of regions and changing technological requirements of arms manufacturing. The heavy industry requirements for arms manufacturing have been giving way to more sophisticated

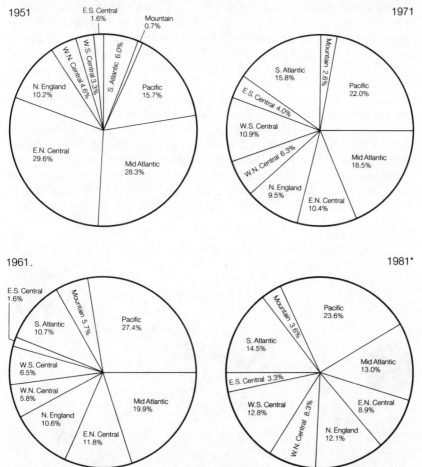

Figure 5.2 Percentage distribution of prime contract awards of over $10,000, by region, 1951–81. *Figures for 1981 do not total 100 owing to rounding. (*Source:* US Department of Defense, 1981)

weaponry requiring computer technology. This is at least a partial explanation for shifts in arms manufacturing activities from the Mid-Atlantic and East North Central regions to the Pacific region.

The process of subcontracting is important in evaluating the distribution of arms manufacturing activities and in the analysis of local impact. It has been estimated that as much as 50 per cent of all prime contracts are eventually subcontracted. Figure 5.3 presents confidential subcontracting information that was available in 1960 for a South West prime contractor. While presenting out-of-date data, the figure none the less illustrates that subcontracting can drastically change the regional pattern of arms manufacturing impact. Note that the map is partitioned into two sections: the top section shows the percentage shares of a particular firm's subcontracts going to various states located in the North, Mid West and Eastern parts of the United States; the bottom section shows percentage shares going to Texas, Arizona and California.

Malecki (1984) presents state-wide data that also show that the regional pattern of arms manufacturing impact can be significantly affected by subcontracts. These data are reproduced in table 5.4. As the table shows, only 14 out of 50 states have above-average per capita levels of subcontracts. It also shows that 15 states have above-average per capita levels of prime contracts (9 above-average for prime contracts and subcontracts, 6 above-average for prime contracts only). In 1981, 18 states had above-average per capita levels of prime contracts. Table 5.4 also indicates that,

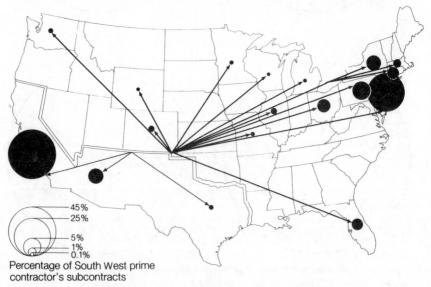

Figure 5.3 Subcontracts from a south-west prime contractor, by states.
(*Source:* confidential, 1960)

Table 5.4 States with above-average per capita levels of prime contracts and subcontracts, fiscal year 1979

State	Subcontracts ($)	Prime contracts ($)
Above-average for prime contracts and subcontracts		
Connecticut	447.71	476.52
Vermont	264.15	234.62
Massachusetts	160.50	314.43
California	138.52	460.86
New Hampshire	134.58	262.98
Arizona	119.98	204.06
New Jersey	80.66	256.83
Washington	73.90	388.91
Maryland	71.36	215.33
Above-average for subcontracts only		
Utah	181.45	153.79
New Mexico	101.46	0.39
Indiana	99.49	122.80
New York	77.19	178.10
Ohio	76.67	176.35
Above-average for prime contracts only		
Missouri	39.61	609.08
Virginia	30.68	221.65
Florida	48.78	221.44
Colorado	52.30	213.19
Texas	38.61	210.24
Maine	18.23	192.06

Source: Bureau of the Census (1981).

of the 14 states with above-average per capita levels of subcontracts, 9 have above-average per capita levels of prime contracts also. Thus, not only are subcontracts concentrated (in terms of being above-average on a per capita basis) in fewer states than prime contracts, but they tend to concentrate in states where prime contracts are also concentrated. This has led some analysts (i.e. Peterson and Muller, 1980; Riefler and Downing, 1968; Weidenbaum, 1974) to argue that subcontracts lead to a greater overall concentration within the defence industry than prime contract data would indicate. This means that the disparate regional pattern of arms manufacturing impact found in prime contract data is reinforced when one takes subcontracts into account.

Figure 5.4 presents location quotients by states for the year 1983. The location quotient here is the ratio of defence spending per capita for a state to defence spending per capita for the nation as a whole (Isard and Karaska, 1963). For example, if the location quotient for a state was 1.5 (or 0.5), this would imply that the state was the recipient of 50 per cent more (less) defence expenditures than could have been expected on the average over the nation on the basis of population alone. The location quotients can also be calculated for Standard Metropolitan Statistical Areas, counties, and regions; in all cases they reflect an uneven distribution.

Tables 5.1–5.3 and figure 5.4 highlight the *direct* influence of defence activities across occupations, industries and regions. Figure 5.3 and table 5.4 show that subcontracting results in a very important indirect regional impact. There are also other important indirect impacts that result from arms manufacturing activities. When a defence firm is contracted to produce goods and services it must purchase inputs (e.g., a defence firm producing tanks would need to purchase steel, aluminium, plastics, etc. as well as machinery, tools, computer products and other equipment) and pay employees in order to produce the goods. The defence firm purchases thus become defence-related income for input suppliers, who in turn buy inputs and pay their employees. The employees purchase haircuts, food, trips to the cinema and a whole host of non-defence goods. The industries producing these goods are receiving income that is indirectly tied to the initial arms manufacturing activities. The end result is a wide circle of employees and businesses tied directly and indirectly to defence expenditures. This tendency for $1 in one type of expenditure to lead to more than

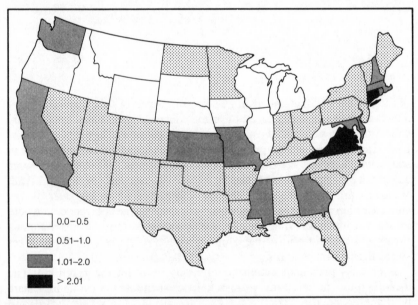

Figure 5.4 Location quotients for defence spending per capita, by state, fiscal year 1983. Location quotients for Alaska and Hawaii are 2.16 and 2.61, respectively. (*Source:* Bureau of the Census, 1984)

$1 in overall income is called the *multiplier effect*. When Sunseri analysed the impact of the military sector in Iowa, he concluded, somewhat conservatively, that each Pentagon dollar coming into that state results in $1.56 being generated into the Iowan economy (Sunseri, 1977, p. 161). In a broader national study, the Regional Science Research Institute estimated a defence spending multiplier of 3. Isard and Langford (1971, pp. 151–202) concluded that the direct impact of fiscal year 1968 Vietnam war expenditures in the Philadelphia area was $284 million. The indirect impacts for this same year totalled $999.5 million, giving a total impact of $1283.5 million.

The multiplier effect can also work in reverse. If a region faces a decline in Pentagon dollars used to finance arms manufacture, the result will be a direct loss to the firms and employees dependent on the defence contracts. Indirect losses spread throughout the region as the direct losers purchase fewer goods and services from others, who in turn purchase less, and so on in a downward spiral. Politicians at all levels of government are aware of the regional economic dislocation that may result from reductions in arms manufacturing. During the 1972 presidential campaign, Spiro Agnew reminded the employees of McDonnel–Douglass (direct losers) and the people of St Louis (indirect losers) that their economic livelihood was endangered by the McGovern defence proposals:

> While he [McGovern] has gone around the country deploring present rates of unemployment he is apparently oblivious to the fact that his defense proposals would throw an estimated 1.8 million Americans out of work. But I'm sure the people of St Louis and the employees of McDonnel–Douglass are not unaware of the fact, especially since the Senator has specifically stated that he would cancel the F-15 as part of his defense cutbacks. (Nincic, 1982, p. 44)

Direct and indirect spending and employment are not the only economic variables affected by arms manufacturing. Cumberland (1973) has discussed regional economic impacts that cause dynamic change. Spending for defence products *may* result in increased productive capacity owing to capital growth in existing firms. (Later we discuss the argument that defence production leads to decreased capacity and a smaller infrastructure.) This increases the size of the local economy. Defence spending may also bring new kinds of industry to a regional economy as well as changing the production functions of industries within the region.

Many people think that the income, employment and dynamic benefits that result from arms manufacturing activities are significant. A lapel button worn by some employees of a West Coast defence firm summed up many people's feelings about regional economic dependence on arms manufacturing. It said, 'Don't Bite the War that Feeds You' (Udis, 1973, p. 1). In the following section we discuss alternatives to this view.

Is arms manufacturing a necessary component of regional economic health?

The Public Interest Research Group in Michigan and the Center for Defense Information conclude that military spending is not an effective method of job creation (Nincic, 1982). Their results are presented in tables 5.5 and 5.6. These tables offer evidence that there exists a number of public expenditure options that have a greater job-creating potential than defence spending. Table 5.5, for example, indicates that $1 billion of public expenditure devoted to the Job Corps would create approximately two-and-a-half times the number of jobs as devoting $1 billion to defence. Table 5.6 shows that government programmes such as public service employment and anti-recession aid to state and local governments have a significantly greater job-creating potential than defence spending.

Table 5.5   Number of jobs created by $1 billion of public expenditure

	No. of jobs
Job corps	145,000
Teachers	76,000
Nurses	85,000
Police	73,000
Fire	70,000
Defence (military personnel)	58,000

Source: PIRGIM (1974).

Table 5.6   Number of jobs created by $1 billion of expenditure

	No. of jobs
Public service employment	98,000
Anti-recession aid to state and local governments	71,000
Civilian production	53,000
Defence spending	45,800

Source: Center for Defense Information (1977, p. 3).

Gold (1980) compared the employment impact of the MX missile with six alternatives and concluded that each would do better than the MX at creating jobs (see table 5.7, and also Nincic, 1982). For example, the number of jobs created directly and indirectly by $1 billion of public expenditures on day care is more than double the direct and indirect jobs created by spending $1 billion on the MX missile.

Steinberg (1984) states that defence spending will create around 1.2 million new jobs between 1984 and 1987 but that the same investment in the civilian economy could produce roughly 25 per cent more jobs. The Congressional Budget Office (1983) concluded that additional spending on

Table 5.7 Number of jobs directly and indirectly created by $1 billion of public expenditure

	Direct + indirect employment
MX missile	53,248
Solid waste treatment	65,859
Railroad construction	54,220
Day care	120,496
Solar energy/energy conservation	65,079
Solar energy	57,235
Mass transit	79,300

Source: Gold (1980, p. 4).

defence and non-defence purchases of goods and services appear to have equal expansionary effects on employment in the short run.

Other studies support the conclusion that alternative public expenditures are at least as effective as defence spending at creating jobs. This implies that, with adequate planning (i.e. proper mix and timing of offset programmes, such as temporary education, retraining, employment service and financial assistance programmes for displaced workers and businesses, coordinated with monetary and fiscal policies), regions are not necessarily economically dependent on arms manufacturing activities. Thus, a transition to lower levels of arms production can be smoothed for the employees and industries that are currently supplying our defence needs. The resources freed from defence could be assigned to such activities as job training, education, housing, public transport or tax cuts to individuals or industry. Some or all of the freed resources could be used to lower the federal budget deficit, which would tend to lower interest rates and inflationary pressures. Agreement on priorities would be far from unanimous. However, if defence activities could be reduced without jeopardising national security, then the burden of establishing priorities would be a better alternative than not having an opportunity to do so.

Up to now we have established that arms manufacturing activities are not a necessary component of regional economic health, given adequate offset programmes. Some people have argued that defence spending in general may be harmful to the economy. Thus, a Cabinet coordinating committee concluded that the cost of the Vietnam war had been a 'load for the economy to carry – not a supporting prop' (Udis, 1973, p. 2). Spending for defence leaves fewer resources that can be devoted to capital investment, education, health services and other activities. Lower capital investment leads to smaller capital stocks and infrastructure and lower economic growth. For example, economic growth in Japan and West Germany has been significantly higher than that in the USA and the UK on average over the last 25 years; one argument proposed to explain the differing growth rates is that Japan and West Germany devote a smaller proportion of their GNP to defence than the USA and the UK, thus leaving more resources available for building productive capital equipment and infrastructure. In 1983, for example, the USA devoted 5.6 per cent of its GNP to the military while the UK devoted 5.2 per cent; on the other hand, West Germany and Japan devoted only 3.2 and 0.9 per cent respectively of their GNPs to the military (Sivard, 1983).

An additional point regarding the harmful economic consequences of defence spending can be seen if we consider the East North Central region of the USA. Figure 5.2 indicates that military production in this region was relatively high in 1951. If during the early 1950s there had been less military production in the region (as a result, say, of smaller national military expenditures), alternative programmes could have resulted in more investment in roads, schools, hospitals and other urban and regional infrastructure. It follows from this that a larger labour force would have been at work providing services for, and maintaining, this infrastructure. Consequently, the low level of military production that occurred in the East North Central region in the 1970s and 1980s would not have led to as high a level of unemployment as it did, because a larger urban and regional infrastructure would have been in place supporting a larger number of jobs. Thus, although heavy military production in the East North Central region in the 1950s did mean high employment there, it turned out to have a double-edged negative impact; for not only were and are residents of this region suffering some employment problems arising from the shift in military production to other regions: they (as well as other US citizens) are also forgoing considerable amounts of goods, services and jobs because a larger urban and regional infrastructure is not in place.

Conclusions

Although a thorough statement of the regional impact of arms manufacture should dig more deeply into the effects on sectors, firms, subsets of the labour force, communities, institutions and other diverse groups, our brief enquiry covers the general type of findings that can be anticipated.

We have shown that regional economic dependence on arms manufacture is significant in the USA. This dependence is distributed unevenly over regions in total and per capita terms. Further, while subcontracting and multiplier effects make it more difficult to assess the regional impact of arms manufacturing, it is nevertheless highly uneven. An important consideration, and one that is often overlooked by policy-makers, is that proper offset programmes can alleviate negative regional impacts arising from reductions in arms manufacturing activities. Studies have shown that other government expenditure programmes create as many or more jobs than defence expenditures, both directly and indirectly. Some analysts have further argued that arms manufacturing activities lead to more regional economic damage than benefit. In so far as arms manufacturing uses resources that could have been devoted to health services, education, roads, etc., then urban and regional infrastructures and welfare are provided at a lower level than they might have been.

References

Bureau of the Census (1981), *Shipments to Federal Government Agencies, 1979*, Current Industrial Reports MA-175(79)-1. Washington DC: US Government Printing Office.

Bureau of the Census (1983), *Federal Expenditures by State for Fiscal Year 1981*. Washington DC: US Department of Commerce.

Bureau of the Census (1984), *Federal Expenditures by State for Fiscal Year 1983*. Washington DC: US Department of Commerce.

Center for Defense Information (1977), 'Jobs and the Pentagon: Is military spending good for the economy?', *The Defense Monitor*, September–October, pp. 1–80.

Congressional Budget Office (1983), *Defense Spending and the Economy*. Washington DC: Congress of the United States.

Cumberland, J.H. (1973), 'Dimensions of the impact of reduced military expenditures on industries, regions and communities', in B. Udis (ed.), *The Economic Consequences of Reduced Military Spending*. Lexington, Mass.: Lexington Books, pp. 79–147.

Department of Defense (1981), *Military Prime Contract Awards by State: Fiscal Years 1951 to 1981*. Washington DC: Washington Headquarters Services.

Gold, D. (1980), 'MX and the American economy', *Arms Control Today*, February, pp. 3–5.

Isard, W. and Karaska, G. (1963), *An Atlas On United States Military Contracts*. Philadelphia: World Friends Research Center.

Isard, W. and Langford, T.W. (1971), *Regional Input–Output Study*. Cambridge, Mass.: MIT Press.

Law, C.M. (1983), 'The defence sector in British regional development', *Geoforum*, 14, 169–84.

Malecki, E.J. (1984), 'Military spending and the US defense industry: regional patterns of military contracts and subcontracts', *Environment and Planning C: Government and Policy*, 2, 31–44.

Nincic, M. (1982), *The Arms Race*. New York: Praeger.

Peterson, G.E. and Muller, T. (1980), 'Regional impact of federal tax and spending policies', in V.L. Arnold (ed.), *Alternatives to Confrontation*. Lexington, Mass.: D. C. Heath, pp. 207–24.

PIRGIM (Public Interest Research Group in Michigan) (1974), *The Empty Pork Barrel*. Lansing, Michigan: PIRGIM.

Riefler, R.F. and Downing, P.B. (1968), 'Regional effect of defense effort on employment', *Monthly Labor Review*, 91, 1–8.

Short, J. (1981), 'Defence spending in the UK regions', *Regional Studies*, 15, 101–10.

Sivard, R.L. (1983), *World Military and Social Expenditures*. Leesburg, Virginia: World Priorities.

Steinberg, B. (1984) 'The military boost to industry', *Fortune Magazine*, 30 April, 42–8.

Sunseri, A.R. (1977), 'The military–industrial complex in Iowa', in B. F. Cooling (ed.) *War, Business and American Society*. Port Washington, NY: Kennikat Press, pp. 158–70.

Todd, D. (1981), 'Regional variations in naval construction. The British experience, 1895–1966', *Regional Studies*, 15, 123–42.

Udis, B. (1973), *The Economic Consequences of Reduced Military Spending*. Lexington, Mass.: Lexington Books.

Weidenbaum, M.L. (1974), *The Economics of Peacetime Defense*. New York: Praeger.

PART II

The Geography of Nuclear War

CHAPTER 6

Doomsday Revisited

Stan Openshaw and Philip Steadman

Introduction

We have recently published an extensive series of estimates of likely casualties in a nuclear attack on the UK, in the book *Doomsday* (Openshaw, Steadman and Greene, 1983). These estimates were made using a computer model (Openshaw and Steadman, 1983), and they take account of deaths and injuries from the three principal short-term effects of nuclear explosions: thermal radiation, blast and local fallout. Although we believe that these calculations remain plausibly realistic and fairly comprehensive, a number of extensions and elaborations are possible, two of which we describe in this chapter.

The *Doomsday* predictions were presented first for the country as a whole, and then by counties in England and Wales, and by regions in Scotland. An obvious next step is to break those figures down further into smaller local areas – although the numerical values become somewhat less meaningful than at the higher levels of aggregation. Indeed, estimates of the local effects of attack are already being made manually for a number of purposes – by civil defence workers, medical 'war planners' and peace campaigners – and a disaggregation of the *Doomsday* computer forecasts would perhaps be useful to all of these groups. In the first part of this chapter the previous county-level forecasts are disaggregated to the district level.

The second topic investigated here is the general question of the uncertainties involved in calculations of this type. Broadly speaking, they are of two kinds. Some are to do with the assumed patterns of attack: what numbers and types of weapons are used, against which targets, and with what degree of accuracy. These may be termed 'scenario effects'. Others are to do with difficulties and approximations involved in predicting the physical and medical effects of nuclear explosions.

Both areas of uncertainty are discussed at length in *Doomsday*, to which interested readers are referred. Assessments of likely scenarios of attack obviously depend on a whole series of military and strategic considerations. The principal conclusions reached in the book were that, should the UK be subjected to nuclear attack by Warsaw Pact forces in the near future, that attack would be likely to involve at least 200 and possibly up to 350 megatons or more, directed against military and industrial targets – not against cities as such. (One megaton is the explosive equivalent of 1 million tons of TNT.) Of Soviet longer-ranged nuclear forces allocated to Europe, between 700 and 1000 warheads, with a total explosive power of between 500 and 700 megatons, are now likely to be targeted against the UK. These figures are calculated from the two standard sources, SIPRI (1982) and IISS (1982). Making generous allowances for missile failures and bombers being intercepted, it is clear that an attack of the order of 200 megatons lies towards the lower end of the range of likely scenarios. Many factors make smaller, more limited attack patterns very improbable – with the possible sole exception of a retaliatory (Mutually Assured Destruction, or 'MAD') attack, in circumstances where the majority of Soviet weapons have been destroyed in a US/NATO first strike.

In *Doomsday* the question of 'scenario effect' was addressed by constructing a graduated series of some 11 attack patterns, labelled 'A' to 'K', ranging in explosive power from 40 to 350 megatons. The purpose of looking at the smaller attacks was to examine in a systematic way the cumulative consequences of adding in more targets and more weapons – not that the smaller attacks were considered to be at all probable. By the stage at which strategically plausible levels of attack were reached, with scenario 'H' (219 megatons), the total predicted short-term casualties totalled 42½ million; and by attack 'K' (350 megatons), these had risen to 48½ million (out of a total mainland UK population in 1971 of 54 million).

The first reaction of any person of normal sensibilities to these figures would surely be that further refinement of the calculations is pointless, not to say morbid. Any concern as to whether the predicted casualty rate might be precisely 82 instead of 82.5 per cent, say, would be academic in the worst sense. The figures above refer, after all, just to *short-term* casualties caused in the first 14 days. If longer-term and secondary effects are considered, especially those on agriculture, let alone the newly revealed prospect of a 'nuclear winter' (see chapter 7 below), then the outstanding conclusion is that human and most animal life in the UK would simply be exterminated after nuclear exchanges of this magnitude.

Unfortunately, as this is a highly political subject, the issue of casualty estimates is still a hotly debated one. Home Office and civil defence spokesmen have criticised figures such as those presented in *Doomsday* and earlier papers by the authors on two main counts. First, they have questioned the military and strategic considerations on which the attack scenarios rest. Soviet intentions are unknowable or uncertain, it is said, and the quantity of weapons which might be used is impossible to predict. Civil defence plans should be prepared against attacks with conventional bombs only, or with one or two nuclear weapons. 'All-out' nuclear war is the least likely eventuality.

It is not our purpose to address these strategic issues here. To such critics we would simply cite the many distinguished military analysts who have concluded that any war in Europe in present circumstances will be almost certain to escalate to nuclear war; and that, even if nuclear war were confined to European territory, the UK would be bound to suffer massive nuclear bombardment. These experts include Lord Mountbatten (1979), Field Marshal Lord Carver (1980), three other Chiefs of UK Defence Staff (see Zuckerman, 1982, pp. 70–2), members of the authoritative Palme Commission (Independent Commission on Disarmament and Security Issues, 1982) and, most recently, the architect of NATO's European strategy of 'flexible response' himself, former US Secretary of Defense Robert McNamara (1983).

Until 1981 at least, the standard assumption which the Home Office itself made for civil defence planning purposes was a 200 megaton nuclear scenario (Home Office, 1977, 1981). By contrast, more recent official pronouncements have suggested that very limited or conventional attacks are now the major threat. These have not however been accompanied by any explanation in terms of, say, some supposed changes in Soviet strategy. The USSR has of course been *increasing* the number of warheads carried on its medium-ranged missiles deployed for use in Europe, notably the SS-20, over this period. Indeed, it is difficult to see this recent volte-face by the Home Office as anything other than a rather desperate attempt to scale down the imagined problem to the point where present civil defence plans might arguably have more than marginal effect.

The second kind of argument criticises the *Doomsday* figures on the basis of the undeniable uncertainties inherent in the calculations of weapons effects and of the resulting casualties themselves. It is argued that such predictions involve huge extrapolations from the observed effects of the two bombs on Hiroshima and Nagasaki, and from the measurements made of the American above-ground test explosions before 1963. Nuclear weapons in the megaton range have never been used on cities, or in large numbers simultaneously.

In view of such doubts, it might be argued that total short-term casualties in a 200 megaton attack could prove in the event to be nearer to say 20 million than 40 million. The corresponding implications for civil defence would clearly be very different. In 1981 the Home Office published some official calculations made by using a computer model similar in structure to our own, but incorporating very different values for certain critical parameters. These indeed showed something just over 20 million killed and injured in an attack with 193 megatons (Butler, 1982). For most people this lower figure would still be, in the words of a recent minister for civil defence, 'grotesquely unacceptable'. But suppose there was even the possibility that, under very extreme circumstances, some government might actually contemplate running this kind of risk when weighing the option of using nuclear weapons in the country's 'defence'? The importance for such a decision of having the best possible estimates of the resulting consequences for the UK scarcely needs emphasising.

Many of the assumptions built into the Home Office model have been heavily criticised, by ourselves (see *Doomsday*, chapter 9), by the British Medical Association (1983) and by others (e.g. Greene et al., 1982). As a result mainly of the BMA's criticisms, the Home Office has withdrawn its previous figures and is now (1984) in the process of revising its model. However, general arguments about the difficulty and unreliability of any calculations are still being made – for example about whether figures for the vulnerability of typical US houses to blast damage are applicable to houses in the UK (Hurd, 1983). It is these questions which we take up in the second section of this chapter.

Our calculations show in fact that making reasonable allowance for many areas of uncertainty in the *Doomsday* figures does *not* open up the possibility that predicted casualty totals might err on the side of overestimates. On the contrary, those figures, particularly in relation to fallout casualties, are probably excessively conservative. The basic reason is very simple. The amount of explosive power involved in a scenario of the magnitude of attack 'H' (219 megatons) represents such a massive level of 'overkill' that, if people do not become casualties of the effects of either heat, blast or fallout, they carry a high probability of suffering death or injury from some other effect. Only at much lower levels of attack would this cease to apply – and these, as we have said, are militarily very unlikely.

Disaggregating the Doomsday forecasts

In principle, the task of producing district instead of county or regional level forecasts is straightforward. We have chosen to present figures here for the *Doomsday* attacks 'H' and 'K'. In attack 'H' 342 warheads are used, whose exact total yield is 219.2 megatons. The total number of predicted deaths is 37.5 million, and of seriously injured a further 5.1 million. In attack 'K' 485 warheads are used, with a total yield of 347.6 megatons. Predicted deaths total 45.3 million and seriously injured, 3 million.

The forecasts can be geographically disaggregated because the computer models make calculations by 1 kilometre grid-squares throughout the country. Predictions are made separately for all 152,000 inhabited grid-squares in mainland Britain. (Northern Ireland is excluded.) The figures published in *Doomsday* were obtained by aggregating these 1 kilometre square forecasts to counties. A disaggregation of the results to district level required only a change of the relevant boundaries. A set of computer-readable district boundaries is available, and these were used to assign each 1 kilometre square automatically to the appropriate district. However, the quality of these data is best described as poor, so there was a risk that districts of small size might be missed. This risk was avoided by processing smaller districts first.

The results for all 458 districts in England, Scotland and Wales are given in figures 6.1 and 6.2. They are presented as casualty rates: that is,

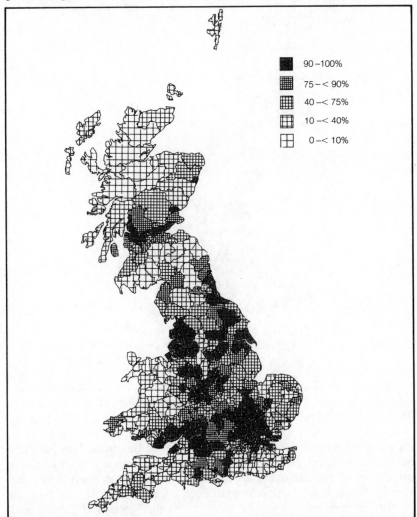

90–100%

75 – < 90%

40 – < 75%

10 – < 40%

0 – < 10%

Figure 6.1   Estimated two-week casualty rates for attack scenario 'H', by district (percentages of the original population).

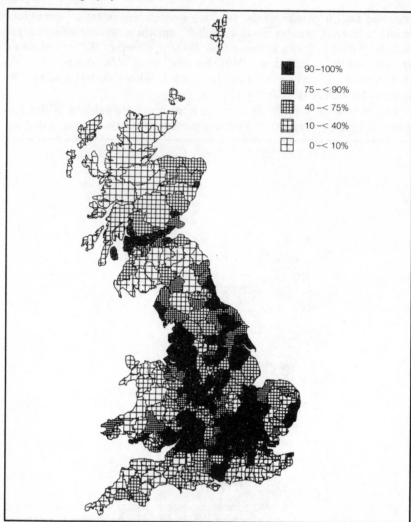

Figure 6.2   Estimated two-week casualty rates for attack scenario 'K', by district
(percentages of the original population).

the number of people seriously injured or killed by burns, blast or early
fallout, in the two weeks following the attack, expressed in each case as a
percentage of the original population. In many of the major cities the
survival rate is zero or only a few per cent, even in attack 'H'. Most of the
short-term survivors, it will be seen, are in the Scottish Highlands and
Border counties, in North Wales, in parts of the West Country and, by a
slight freak of the targeting pattern, in East Sussex. Many military bases

and other high-priority targets in Britain are unfortunately sited near to or within areas of high population density, and it is for this reason that casualties are concentrated in the conurbations. (Centres of population are not targeted in their own right in these scenarios.)

Some care should be taken nevertheless in interpreting the local results, since the geographical accuracy of the model predictions at this scale is more open to question. The spatial patterns of thermal radiation and blast damage will be affected in reality by physiographic features, whereas the models assume a perfectly flat and featureless ground plane. The techniques used for predicting fallout patterns involve some simplifying assumptions, by which the total *area* affected can be reasonably well estimated, but the *shape* of this region – which might cover thousands of square kilometres – is highly schematised. The positions and sizes of even these schematic fallout plumes depend entirely on the assumed speed and direction of the wind. (The fact that East Sussex escapes relatively lightly in the results for scenario 'H' is largely a function of an assumed south–south-westerly wind direction.)

Another factor is that the census data which are used provide in effect a night-time, 'at-home' distribution of the population; surprise attack in working hours, or an attack with some warning given, could find a rather different local population distribution. Some of these problems are discussed further in the next section.

Incorporating the effects of uncertainty into casualty forecasts

A statistical approach

The casualty forecasts just described are conditional on the computer models and data used. The models themselves involve a series of empirically derived weapon–effect relationships and casualty rules, with a small number of key parameter values – for example, the percentages of the population assumed to be killed and injured at different levels of blast pressure, or the assumed wind speed and direction in relation to fallout. The choice of values depends on the assumptions that are made, as discussed in the following section. A simple but effective means of estimating the consequences of these assumptions is to vary the critical model parameters systematically, and to relate changes in these parameters to changes in the casualty predictions obtained. This approach has already been used in various sensitivity analyses described in Openshaw and Steadman (1983). It works best when only one or two parameters are changed with the remainder held constant.

A more comprehensive approach is simply to allow the values for the uncertain parameters to vary probabilistically according to specified distributions and within specified ranges, and then to use Monte Carlo simulation to represent the effects of the assumed levels of uncertainty (Openshaw, 1979). The distribution of different outcomes can be used to provide a statistical summary of these effects. A similar approach has been widely used to estimate the variability in the consequences of reactor accidents owing to uncertain meteorological conditions (Clarke and Kelly, 1981).

The method used here is to generate a random sample of 100 sets of casualty forecasts for a given attack scenario (attack 'H') by simultaneous randomisation of the principal uncertain model parameters and selected data assumptions. The distribution of results can then be processed to give an expected value for each county (a mean or median), and the range of possible casualties found by computing measures of dispersion (standard deviations, and percentiles). If required, a Monte Carlo significance testing procedure could be used to test any relevant hypotheses against the null hypothesis represented by the random simulations.

The problems with this approach are basically two fold. First, there is a possible tendency to underestimate the levels of variability in the model parameters, resulting in too narrow a range of results. Second, the extent of the computational load is imposed by the need to run a suite of casualty estimation models 100 times for each set of assumptions about parametric uncertainty. (A single set of 100 simulations requires about 25 hours of central processing time on an IBM 370/168.)

Assumptions about levels of model and data uncertainties

The most important practical question concerns the choice of model parameters for randomisation, and the nature of the uncertainty assumptions that are made. There are few or no empirical data to provide guidance, and so recourse has to be made to what may be termed 'pragmatic pessimism'. The aim is to identify extreme ranges within which the parameters could conceivably vary, but at the same time to ensure that the values do not go beyond the bounds of realism. In practice, we have chosen to make two sets of runs, one in which the assumed uncertainties are generally 'low', the other in which they are 'high'.

The first area of uncertainty concerns the accuracy of targeting of weapons. In the model each weapon is normally assigned a precisely located ground zero. For the present experiments it was assumed that errors in targeting of up to 1 kilometre ('low') or 2 kilometres ('high') might be expected, these errors being random and normally distributed about the desired ground zero. Either assumption could be sustained by reference to published figures for the 'circular error probable' (CEP) values of different Soviet weapons. For the medium-range land-based missiles currently targeted on the UK, these range from 300 to 2300 metres; so the chosen error values seem suitably realistic.

No allowances were made, on the other hand, for the complete failure of missiles, which might be expected to affect perhaps 20 per cent of warheads, or for bomber aircraft being intercepted. Our argument here is that attack ' H', although involving as much as 219 megatons, lies at the *lower* end of *likely* scenarios in terms of megatonnage; and that these factors have in effect already been allowed for in the basic scenario design.

Other uncertainties have to do with the effects of weapons, and the resulting casualty rates. In the case of thermal radiation and the burns injuries resulting from direct exposure to the fireball, these uncertainties are especially great. The key parameter here is the assumed percentage of the population out of doors or at windows, and hence exposed to radiant heat. This could vary greatly with time of day, time of year, whether any warning was given, and whether or not weapons exploding in the same general area were detonated simultaneously.

US studies have taken figures for the percentage exposed ranging up to 25 per cent (Office of Technology Assessment, 1980). The Home Office previously made the assumption that warning of attack would be completely effective, and hence that casualties from this cause could be ignored (Butler, 1982). Similarly, for the present exercise it was decided to omit burns; not because these would be unlikely to occur, but because to do so is obviously conservative. Calculations published in *Doomsday* showed that in any case the omission of burns has the effect of reducing total casualties in attack 'H' from 42.5 million for 5 per cent exposed to 42.3 million for none exposed – i.e. a reduction of 200,000. The reason for this being such a small reduction will become clear.

As regards blast effects, the model follows the Office of Technology Assessment (OTA) in distinguishing five critical blast overpressure ranges: more than 12 psi (pounds per square inch), 5–12 psi, 2–5 psi, 1–2 psi, and less than 1 psi. The distance ranges are computed using empirical relationships obtained from actual weapons tests. Figures are given in Glasstone and Dolan (1977) for a 1 kiloton explosion, from which ranges can be scaled for other yields. (One kiloton is the explosive equivalent of 1000 tons of TNT.) These data are widely used but may involve uncertainties to do with measurement errors, with the approximations which are made in scaling, with varying weapon design and, perhaps most important, with the effects of a non-flat ground surface, since physiographic features such as hills and valleys may offer shelter in some circumstances, or may funnel the blast wave in others.

These range estimates, which are nevertheless generally regarded as fairly reliable, are then related to blast casualty rates. The rates used here are again those of the OTA, which derived them in turn from the US

Department of Defense. The OTA describes its figures as 'relatively conservative'. Nevertheless, the precise mechanisms of injury and death are undoubtedly complex, highly variable and not fully understood. What is more, different forms of building will offer varying levels of protection.

The Home Office has argued that US blast casualty rates cannot necessarily be applied directly to the UK, because of these differences in house construction. It has suggested, for example, that the OTA figures refer to wood-frame buildings. (See British Medical Association, 1983, p. 67; this is not in fact the case.) It is certainly possible that there might be small systematic differences in the blast resistance of houses between the two countries; however, in the absence of more detailed research, it is not obvious which country the comparison would favour. Houses built in the UK since the war are of rather lightweight construction, often with large areas of glass. High-rise and prefabricated buildings would be particularly vulnerable.

It should be emphasised that the extremely large differences between the OTA blast casualty rates and those formerly used by the Home Office (see Bentley, 1981) are in any case not accounted for by allowances for differing forms of house construction. They occurred because the Home Office was using data not from nuclear explosions, but from the effects of conventional high explosives in the Blitz. These are not remotely comparable, however, even allowing for the huge differences in explosive power between typical-sized conventional and nuclear weapons. (See *Doomsday*, chapter 9, for a discussion.)

One further factor concerning blast casualties is that of overlap of the areas of blast damage from adjacent explosions, which would occur extensively in an attack of the size of 'H'. It is reasonable to suppose that buildings might be weakened by a first explosion, and that casualties would therefore be greater at the same overpressure from a second or subsequent explosion. This possibility of cumulative blast damage is not allowed for in the casualty rates.

It is clearly desirable, then, to allow for some levels of uncertainty in the blast model, but how much and where is a matter of judgement. The easiest variables to randomise are the blast overpressure ranges. It can then be assumed that this allows for uncertainties in the blast ranges themselves, and simultaneously for uncertainties in the blast-to-casualty conversion rates. On this assumption the blast ranges are taken for this exercise to have random, normally distributed errors with a standard deviation of ± 2.5 and 5 per cent for the 12 psi and above range; ± 5 and 10 per cent for the 5–12 psi range; ± 7.5 and 15 per cent for the 2–5 psi range; and ± 10 and 20 per cent for the 1–2 psi range. The two values represent the 'low' and 'high' levels of uncertainty in each case. The errors are made to increase with distance from ground zero, because as the severity of the blast effects diminish, so the variable factors discussed will arguably have an increasing influence.

A final area of uncertainty concerns the fallout calculations. The main problems here are in the assumptions made about meteorological conditions at the time of attack, principally about wind speed and wind direction. It is normally assumed for these purposes that the speed and direction of the wind are the same for all weapons. This is arguably a conservative assumption, since a variable wind direction could spread fallout over a larger total area.

Other difficulties are inherent in the structure of the fallout model itself, which uses the standard idealised elliptical contours for representing fallout distribution patterns, as already mentioned (cf. Glasstone and Dolan, 1977, pp. 422–33). More sophisticated models exist which use actual wind data to predict changes in the direction and speed of the fallout cloud in detail, hour by hour (see Schmidt, 1975; Atmospheric Science Associates, 1981). The difficulty with this, of course, is that there is no knowing what the precise meteorological conditions might be at the time of attack. What is more, it can be expected that one effect of detonating so many megatons of nuclear weapons in a short period will itself be to transform local weather patterns in quite unpredictable ways. This in turn could have consequences for casualties, for example through rain acting to wash out fallout particles.

We have decided to allow for these uncertainties simply by randomising wind speed and wind direction. The effective wind speed is assumed to be uniformly randomly distributed between 13 and 72 kilometres per hour, which is the maximum range over which Glasstone and Dolan's (1977) unit-time reference dose-rates can be computed. Wind directions are randomly selected through 360 degrees.

The last step in the fallout calculations is to relate total accumulated radiation doses to the consequences for injury and death from radiation sickness. The question of the level of mean lethal radiation dose, or 'LD-50' value, for humans is a particularly controversial one, and has been much discussed in the recent medical literature (for a summary, see British Medical Association, 1983, or *Doomsday*, chapter 6). Values have been cited, for doses received to surface tissues in a few hours, of between 350 and 600 rads. For doses received over longer periods the values could be higher. The Home Office, acting on advice from the Medical Research Council (MRC), was in 1981 using an effective LD-50 for one-week doses (to surface tissues) of 900 rads (Bentley, 1981); although it now seems that the MRC is having second thoughts about this advice and its application to casualty calculations. The model used here takes an LD-50 of 450 rads for two-week doses.

To these problems may be added major uncertainties about the levels of protection against radiation provided by buildings and shelters – their 'protection factors'. This is another complex and controversial topic, not to be entered here. Certainly the most crucial issue is the extent to which blast damage to buildings will reduce their radiation protection factors. The Home Office made no allowance whatsoever for this effect in its previous calculations of fallout casualties, even for areas where buildings would have roofs off, doors and windows removed, or even would be demolished altogether. This is plainly absurd, and is the main reason – together with the use of a high LD-50 value – for the Home Office having predicted less than 1 million deaths from fallout sickness in a 200 megaton attack (Butler, 1982), when the equivalent *Doomsday* estimate would be closer to 15 million.

Given all these uncertainties, and other doubts about the precision of the radiation dose estimates, an arbitrary assumption was made for the present experiments of a normally distributed random error in the accumulated dose values of $\pm$ 12.5 per cent, or $\pm$ 25 per cent. This uncertainty factor is calculated separately for each of the 1 kilometre grid-squares treated in the model.

It should be noted that, apart from this last calculation, each warhead is considered separately and independently. This is not entirely realistic, because for weapons which detonate on the same target, presumably at very nearly the same time, it may very well be that different wind speeds and wind directions are assumed.

The effects of uncertainty

The results of 100 complete simulations can be analysed to yield information about the spectrum of forecasts produced by the uncertainties in the various areas just identified. Attention is again focused on the short-term survival rate. The expected value for this rate is given by the mean, while the range of results can be measured as the difference between the minimum and maximum values recorded for a county or region. Another measure of spread is given by the standard deviation (σ). Table 6.1 shows the results for the 'low' set of uncertainty assumptions, and table 6.2 the results for the 'high' values.

Table 6.1 includes a column showing survival rates for a standard run of the model on attack 'H' without uncertainty assumptions. The outstanding feature of the results of incorporating uncertainties, by comparison, is a *dramatic reduction in survival rates throughout*. These figures imply a very small number of short-term survivors over the country as a whole. It is simply not the case, then, at least on this analysis, that the undeniable difficulties which exist in fixing values for the more critical model parameters are likely to lead to overestimates of casualties, as some critics have suggested.

Table 6.1   Short-term survival rates for attack 'H' under low uncertainty assumptions

| County | Survival rates | | | σ | Survival rates without uncertainty assumptions |
	mean (%)	min. (%)	max. (%)		
Scotland					
Borders	1.38	0.0	64.72	7.07	99.87
Central	1.07	0.0	13.44	2.41	13.12
Dumfries & Galloway	1.20	0.0	22.35	3.32	87.25
Fife	0.89	0.0	19.17	2.93	6.87
Grampian	4.74	0.0	30.13	6.53	35.68
Highland	11.14	0.0	57.50	13.73	93.71
Lothian	0.93	0.0	7.68	1.58	13.55
Strathclyde	0.37	0.0	2.36	0.54	9.89
Tayside	1.61	0.0	22.68	3.29	32.81
Islands	26.68	0.0	64.53	21.00	76.18
East Anglia					
Cambridgeshire	0.03	0.0	0.89	0.11	5.76
Norfolk	0.26	0.0	9.98	1.26	43.36
Suffolk	0.05	0.0	1.71	0.19	45.73
East Midlands					
Derbyshire	0.03	0.0	1.69	0.16	24.42
Leicestershire	0.13	0.0	5.01	0.62	16.59
Lincolnshire	0.05	0.0	1.21	0.15	31.73
Northamptonshire	0.00	0.0	0.19	0.02	35.38
Nottinghamshire	0.03	0.0	0.84	0.10	13.76
North					
Cleveland	0.20	0.0	3.10	0.53	1.59
Cumbria	0.83	0.0	8.80	1.78	28.51
Durham	0.31	0.0	7.44	0.93	25.91
Northumberland	1.53	0.0	21.30	3.30	25.61
Tyne & Wear	0.26	0.0	3.33	0.62	1.37
North West					
Cheshire	0.02	0.0	0.62	0.08	16.89
Greater Manchester	0.07	0.0	2.59	0.28	1.78
Lancashire	0.30	0.0	3.20	1.02	0.84
Merseyside	0.04	0.0	1.25	0.15	0.96
South East					
Bedfordshire	0.00	0.0	0.15	0.02	0.09
Berkshire	0.02	0.0	1.91	0.18	41.49
Buckinghamshire	0.01	0.0	0.29	0.03	12.48
East Sussex	0.04	0.0	3.16	0.30	99.74
Essex	0.11	0.0	5.57	0.56	16.23
GLC	0.00	0.0	0.07	0.01	9.01
Hampshire	0.02	0.0	0.38	0.05	15.39
Hertfordshire	0.00	0.0	0.25	0.02	0.40
Isle of Wight	0.18	0.0	6.16	0.89	87.96
Kent	0.11	0.0	0.98	0.23	55.71
Oxfordshire	0.05	0.0	4.36	0.41	10.06
Surrey	0.01	0.0	0.20	0.03	42.04
West Sussex	0.04	0.0	3.15	0.30	80.85

Continued Overleaf

Table 6.1 Short-term survival rates for attack 'H' under low uncertainty assumptions
(Continued)

South West
Avon	0.02	0.0	0.60	0.07	43.23
Cornwall	2.93	0.0	49.95	7.45	76.95
Devon	0.24	0.0	4.62	0.65	57.88
Dorset	0.13	0.0	7.02	0.71	27.59
Gloucestershire	0.07	0.0	5.19	0.49	1.08
Somerset	0.09	0.0	1.32	0.24	74.77
Wiltshire	0.03	0.0	1.50	0.16	14.11
West Midlands					
Hereford & Worcester	0.03	0.0	1.99	0.19	39.0
Salop	0.17	0.0	7.41	0.77	35.74
Staffordshire	0.04	0.0	1.39	0.18	4.02
Warwickshire	0.01	0.0	0.43	0.04	12.04
West Midlands	0.01	0.0	0.31	0.03	1.40
Yorkshire & Humberside					
Humberside	0.08	0.0	1.10	0.21	4.50
North Yorkshire	0.13	0.0	1.74	0.30	20.67
South Yorkshire	0.14	0.0	7.81	0.76	9.47
West Yorkshire	0.07	0.0	3.22	0.33	38.85
Wales					
Clywd	0.12	0.0	5.81	0.59	89.91
Dyfed	0.41	0.0	5.23	0.92	71.95
Gwent	0.02	0.0	0.55	0.08	7.63
Gwynedd	0.34	0.0	21.60	2.22	89.32
Mid Glamorgan	0.02	0.0	1.47	0.15	51.27
Powys	0.22	0.0	20.70	1.91	69.49
South Glamorgan	0.02	0.0	1.45	0.14	0.44
West Glamorgan	0.11	0.0	4.02	0.49	15.68

Note: The 'survival rate' measures the numbers of people surviving uninjured from the immediate effects of heat, blast and fallout, expressed as a percentage of the pre-attack population. The extreme right-hand column shows survival rates according to the standard version of the model, without uncertainties, for comparison.

It might be objected that taking *higher* levels of uncertainty has the effect of *increasing* the expected rates of survival, as table 6.2 demonstrates (although these are still well below the values for the standard run of the model). This result, however, is itself a consequence of the fact that in both experiments, with either 'high' or 'low' values, the casualty totals are close to the total population of the country. There is such an excess of destructive power in an attack of this magnitude that the real constraint on the numbers killed and injured is placed not so much by any one of the effects of the weapons, as simply by *the number of people present*. With 'high' uncertainty values, it is to be expected that 'maximum' survival rates will be raised somewhat by comparison with the 'low' uncertainties. However, the 'minimum' survival rates obviously can never go below

Table 6.2   Short-term survival rates for attack 'H' under high uncertainty assumptions.

County	mean (%)	min. (%)	max. (%)	σ
		Survival rates		
Scotland				
Borders	2.27	0.0	32.41	5.70
Central	1.51	0.0	20.94	3.17
Dumfries & Gallway	1.27	0.0	22.14	3.75
Fife	1.94	0.0	25.99	5.04
Grampian	6.88	0.01	27.02	6.55
Highland	15.54	0.60	66.53	13.08
Lothian	1.21	0.0	8.77	1.53
Strathclyde	0.66	0.0	3.16	0.70
Tayside	2.23	0.0	19.90	3.32
Islands	38.96	8.18	64.10	12.89
East Anglia				
Cambridgeshire	0.05	0.0	2.61	0.26
Norfolk	0.25	0.0	5.83	0.91
Suffolk	0.13	0.0	1.72	0.30
East Midlands				
Derbyshire	0.04	0.0	1.36	0.15
Leicestershire	0.07	0.0	1.48	0.21
Lincolnshire	0.05	0.0	0.48	0.10
Northamptonshire	0.03	0.0	2.65	0.26
Nottinghamshire	0.04	0.0	1.03	0.14
North				
Cleveland	0.31	0.0	5.18	0.69
Cumbria	1.05	0.0	10.92	1.80
Durham	0.99	0.0	9.75	1.92
Northumberland	2.24	0.0	25.98	4.00
Tyne & Wear	0.32	0.0	2.95	0.54
North West				
Cheshire	0.04	0.0	1.24	0.14
Greater Manchester	0.15	0.0	4.99	0.56
Lancashire	0.12	0.0	1.41	0.24
Merseyside	0.04	0.0	2.38	0.25
South East				
Bedfordshire	- 0.01	0.0	0.35	0.04
Berkshire	0.00	0.0	0.20	0.02
Buckinghamshire	0.01	0.0	0.42	0.04
East Sussex	0.11	0.0	8.37	0.82
Essex	0.19	0.0	4.17	0.60
GLC	0.00	0.0	0.16	0.02
Hampshire	0.03	0.0	0.68	0.10
Hertfordshire	0.03	0.0	0.68	0.11
Isle of Wight	0.22	0.0	10.19	1.07
Kent	0.31	0.0	5.23	0.81
Oxfordshire	0.00	0.0	0.16	0.02
Surrey	0.01	0.0	0.16	0.03
West Sussex	0.03	0.0	0.71	0.12

Continued Overleaf

Table 6.2 Short-term survival rates for attack 'H' under high uncertainty assumptions
(Continued)

South West				
Avon	0.04	0.0	0.73	0.12
Cornwall	5.09	0.0	47.32	9.05
Devon	0.75	0.0	23.96	2.76
Dorset	0.04	0.0	1.58	0.17
Gloucestershire	0.04	0.0	1.04	0.14
Somerset	0.25	0.0	11.18	1.12
Wiltshire	0.02	0.0	0.29	0.04
West Midlands				
Hereford & Worcester	0.00	0.0	0.12	0.01
Salop	0.12	0.0	1.91	0.28
Staffordshire	0.04	0.0	1.47	0.16
Warwickshire	0.01	0.0	0.26	0.03
West Midlands	0.01	0.0	0.31	0.05
Yorkshire & Humberside				
Humberside	0.09	0.0	1.49	0.21
North Yorkshire	0.28	0.0	3.60	0.53
South Yorkshire	0.09	0.0	1.34	0.24
West Yorkshire	0.09	0.0	2.36	0.34
Wales				
Clwyd	0.14	0.0	3.00	0.44
Dyfed	0.71	0.0	7.42	1.36
Gwent	0.03	0.0	1.44	0.15
Gwyredd	0.11	0.0	2.77	0.32
Mid Glamorgan	0.04	0.0	1.65	0.18
Powys	0.07	0.0	2.29	0.28
South Glamorgan	0.03	0.0	0.72	0.10
West Glamorgan	0.22	0.0	7.01	0.80

The results for each county or region are computed independently. That is to say, the maximum and minimum values relate to the sample of 100 runs for that *county*. This means that care is needed in interpreting the complete tables. For instance, the minimum survival rates of zero in all cases in table 6.1 do not mean that the UK minimum survival rate as a whole is zero and that casualties amount to 100 per cent. They mean only that for each region or county a zero survival rate has been encountered during the computer simulations at least once.

zero. So the effect is for the mean survival rate also to be shifted upwards by the higher uncertainties.

It seems probable that the results seen in the tables can be attributed very largely to the randomisation of wind direction. This has the effect of producing a more uniform spread of fallout throughout the country, and hence causing many more casualties from radiation. Protection factors of buildings will have been reduced by blast damage in some areas which previously escaped fallout, and here the additional casualties will be especially numerous. It is only in parts of the country which are hundreds of kilometres from any groundburst explosions – as in the Scottish Highlands and Islands – that mean survival rates remain much above 1 or 2 per cent. (Mean wind speeds have also been increased somewhat over the standard run, and this too would result in a small increase in casualties.)

As already noted, it is certainly unrealistic to assume *completely* random wind conditions, as we have done here, for different explosions in the same scenario. This will result in the notional fallout plumes running in quite different directions in the same local area; and many plumes will actually cross each other. On the other hand, these experiments undoubtedly show that the assumption, by contrast, in fallout calculations of a single fixed wind direction over the entire country is likely to lead to serious underestimates of radiation injury rates. In reality, fallout would tend to be spread in a much less spatially concentrated pattern than those calculations imply.

The effects on mean survival rates of the other uncertainty assumptions are probably small by comparison with the effects of wind direction, especially as they could act either positively or negatively. Interpretation is not easy, and the conclusions might have been clearer if a large number of simulations had been performed – perhaps with the effects of wind direction separated from other uncertainties. The practical computing problems here have already been discussed.

Conclusion

For the UK, nuclear war means national suicide. This has been established, we believe, as a virtual certainty, by the *Doomsday* calculations and the experiments reported here. The next step is to ensure that politicians and decision-makers are left in no doubt whatsoever about the likely outcome. Only then may they gain sufficient political and moral conviction to bring about the reversal of the international growth of nuclear terror, which seems necessary to ensure our survival into the twenty-first century. The 'nuclear winter', constituting as it does a kind of ultimate 'doomsday machine', might itself seem to be a sufficient reason for turning away from the madness of nuclear 'defence'. But even if those prospective horrors of climatic trauma are set completely on one side, there remains the overwhelming evidence presented here.

Quite simply, the effects of even large uncertainties in both weapons data and model parameters are insufficient to question the conclusions of the earlier *Doomsday* studies. For most areas of the UK the resulting variations in numbers of predicted casualties are fairly small, as indeed is only to be expected. They are small because of the level of 'overkill' implicit in the attack scenario considered (despite its being at the lower end of the range of likely attack patterns). For many people who will become casualties there are potentially multiple causes, either different effects from the same weapon, or combined effects from two or more weapons. This is a consequence of the high concentration of population in the UK, the close proximity of that population to many targets of military importance, the great spatial range of the effects of nuclear weapons, and above all the grotesque excess of explosive power which is represented by weapons now deployed.

References

Atmospheric Science Associates (1981), *DNAF 1: an Analytical Fallout Prediction Model and Code*. Washington DC: Defense Nuclear Agency.

Bentley, P.R. (1981), *Blast Overpressure and Fallout Radiation Dose Models for Casualty Assessment and Other Purposes*. London: Home Office (Scientific Research and Development Branch).

British Medical Association (BMA), Board of Science and Education (1983), *The Medical Effects of Nuclear War*. Chichester: John Wiley.

Butler, S.F.J. (1982), 'Scientific advice in home defence', in F. Barnaby and G. Thomas (eds), *The Nuclear Arms Race – Control or Catastrophe?* London: Frances Pinter, pp. 135–63.

Carver, Field Marshal Lord (1980), statement in *Hansard*, House of Lords, 23 April, p. 834.

Clarke, R.H. and Kelly, G.N. (1981), *MARC – the NRPB Methodology for Assessing Radiological Consequences of Accidental Releases of Activity*, National Radiological Protection Board Report 127. London: HMSO.

Glasstone, S. and Dolan, P.J. (eds) (1977), *The Effects of Nuclear Weapons* (3rd edn). US Department of Defense and US Department of Energy; published in UK by Castle House, Tunbridge Wells, 1980.

Greene, O., Rubin, B., Turok, N., Webber, P. and Wilkinson, G. (1982), *London After the Bomb*. Oxford: Oxford University Press.

Home Office (1977), *Training Manual for Scientific Advisers*. London: Home Office (Scientific Advisory Branch).

Home Office (1981), *Domestic Nuclear Shelters: Technical Guidance*. London: HMSO.

Hurd, D. (1983), Minister of State at the Home Office, interviewed on ITV's *World in Action*, 12 December.

IISS (International Institute for Strategic Studies) (1982), *The Military Balance 1982–83*. London: IISS.

Independent Commission on Disarmament and Security Issues (1982), *Common Security: A Programme for Disarmament* (The Palme Report). London: Pan Books.

McNamara, R.S. (1983), 'The military role of nuclear weapons: perceptions and misperceptions', *Foreign Affairs*, Summer, 59–80.

Mountbatten, Earl (1979), speech on the occasion of the award of the Louise Weiss Foundation Prize to the Stockholm International Peace Research Institute in Strasbourg, 11 May.

Office of Technology Assessment (OTA), Congress of the United States (1980), *The Effects of Nuclear War*. London: Croom Helm.

Openshaw, S. (1979), 'A methodology for using models for planning purposes', *Environment and Planning A*, 11, 879–96.

Openshaw, S. and Steadman, P. (1983), 'Predicting the consequences of a nuclear attack on Britain: models, results, and implications for public policy', *Environment and Planning C: Government and Policy*, 1, 205–28.

Openshaw, S., Steadman, P. and Green, O. (1983), *Doomsday: Britain After Nuclear Attack*. Oxford: Basil Blackwell.

Schmidt, L.A. (1975), *Methodology of Fallout-risk Assessment*. Washington DC: Institute for Defense Analyses.

SIPRI (Stockholm International Peace Research Institute) (1982), *Yearbook 1982*. London: Taylor and Francis.

Zuckerman, Lord (1982), *Nuclear Illusion and Reality*. London: Collins.

CHAPTER 7

Climatological Effects of a Large-Scale Nuclear Exchange: a Review

Derek Elsom

Introduction

The climatological disturbances which may occur in the weeks, months and years following a large-scale nuclear exchange may so profoundly damage the biological base that sustains human life that the consequences to mankind may be as serious, or even more serious, than the immediate effects (blast, heat, ionising radiation) of the nuclear exchange itself. Survivors from the immediate effects of a nuclear war may have to face months of subfreezing temperatures, low sunlight levels, severe storms in coastal regions, a reduced amount of increasingly acid precipitation, excessive air pollution (ionising radiation, particulates, toxicants, photochemical oxidants) and several years of increased ultraviolet radiation. Such a climatological scenario is very different to that postulated by pre-1982 research studies because those studies have now been shown to have suffered from major omissions and underestimations.

Early studies and their limitations

Before 1982, climatologists generally believed that a large-scale nuclear exchange involving tens of thousands of nuclear detonations – totalling the equivalent of 5000 or 10,000 million tons (megatons) of TNT – would have a significant, but small effect on the global climate. The report by the National Academy of Sciences (1975) estimated that the surface dust injected into the stratosphere during a 10,000 megaton nuclear exchange would be comparable to that from a large volcanic eruption such as that of Krakatoa in 1883 (approximately 20 cubic kilometres of ejecta). Consequently it was concluded that a large-scale nuclear war might have a climatic impact similar to a large volcanic explosion. At most, an average global temperature reduction of 0.5 degC lasting a few years might be expected, but that is well within the statistical noise of natural climatic variability. However, recent research points to the inadequacies of the report, in its consideration of the nature and quantity of the dust which would be generated by nuclear explosions and the extent to which a volcanic eruption is an appropriate analogy. An even more serious defect of the report is its complete neglect of the effects of the particulate pollution produced by the extensive fires which would be started by nuclear explosions (Crutzen and Birks, 1982; Turco et al., 1983a, 1983b).

The inappropriateness of the volcanic eruption analogy is demonstrated by recent research, which suggests that the long-term climatic impacts of volcanic eruptions are attributable to the sulphuric acid aerosols formed chemically from the sulphur compounds released during the eruption, and not from ejected mineral dust and ash (Rampino and Self, 1982; Toon and Pollack, 1980). The fine mass fraction of the total solid ejecta from volcanic eruptions which reaches the stratosphere to become climatologically significant appears to be very low. By contrast, the efficiency with which dust is injected into the stratosphere by megaton-yield nuclear explosions is close to unity (Turco et al., 1983b). This means that 1000 megatons of nuclear surface or near-surface detonations can inject approximately the same quantity of fine dust into the stratosphere as the Tambora eruption of 1815 (150 cubic kilometres of magma, rock and soil were removed), which caused a 1 degC fall in global temperature. In other words, it is likely that only the largest historical eruptions (1000 cubic kilometres or more of ejecta) can have produced effects comparable to those which would be associated with the dust of a full-scale nuclear war.

An alternative analogy for comparing the effects of the dust generated by a nuclear exchange is that of the dust which would be raised by an asteroid striking the earth (Pollack et al., 1983). Alvarez et al. (1980) and Alvarez et al. (1984) have suggested that a 10 km diameter impacting asteroid or comet nucleus generated such extensive dust clouds, causing a rapid and drastic global cooling, that mass species extinction occurred at the Cretaceous–Tertiary geological boundary, 65 million years ago.

Surprisingly, the 1975 National Academy of Sciences report (and Batten, 1966) ignored the potential climatic effects of the massive quantities of smoke which would be released from fires initiated by nuclear explosions. Following a nuclear exchange, widespread fires would be expected in urban areas, forests, grasslands, and oil and gas production fields (Broido, 1960; Crutzen and Birks, 1982; Glasstone and Dolan, 1977; Lewis, 1979). The experiences at Hiroshima and Nagasaki revealed that nuclear explosions (13 and 22 kiloton weapons, respectively) initiate fires in two ways. First, the intense pulse of thermal radiation ignites exposed flammable material over a large area – the extent of which depends upon the size and height of the nuclear detonation, surface conditions and atmospheric attenuation. Second, as an indirect effect of the destruction caused by the blast wave, fires can be started by broken fuel lines, electrical short-circuits, and upset stoves, water heaters and furnaces

(Glasstone and Dolan, 1977). The blast wave also damages water mains and fire fighting equipment, blocks streets and causes injuries to expert personnel, so preventing effective fire fighting (Lewis, 1979). Widespread urban and rural fires would be expected to generate enormous quantities of fine, dense, sooty smoke whatever the season and weather conditions at the time. Such smoke, composed of a complex mixture of oils, tars and graphitic (or elemental) carbon, is highly absorbing of solar energy compared with soil dust, which is typically non-absorbing (Turco et al., 1983b). Further, sooty smoke is composed primarily of submicron particles while soil particulates are mostly micron-sized or larger, so the former remain in the atmosphere for longer. Thick clouds of sooty smoke in the troposphere, together with smoke injected into the lower stratosphere by firestorms, would strongly absorb incident solar radiation, so warming the upper atmosphere. By contrast, the surface and lower atmosphere, deprived of its solar energy, would cool rapidly by radiating infrared energy through the smoke clouds into space. With thousands of smoke-generating fires throughout the middle latitudes of the Northern Hemisphere, continental surface temperatures in those regions may be expected to fall dramatically, resulting in what has become termed a harsh 'nuclear winter', regardless of the season in which a nuclear war began. With marked changes in the heating patterns which drive the general circulation of the atmosphere, changes which earlier studies have not considered may also take place in this circulation.

The failure of earlier studies to consider the heavy particulate loadings of the atmosphere arising from widespread urban and rural fires mean that they underestimated radioactive fallout levels. The increased particulate loadings generated from nuclear-induced fires would increase the scavenging of radionuclides. Local (or prompt) radioactive fallout could be significantly increased, so increasing those areas receiving lethal doses of ionising radiation in the first few days and weeks following a large-scale nuclear exchange. Turco et al. (1983b) calculate for their baseline 5000 megaton scenario that about 30 per cent of the land in northern latitudes could receive a short-term dose of greater than 250 rads – half the human lethal dose – while 50 per cent would receive a long-term dose greater than 100 rads. Both doses are approximately ten times larger than those previously estimated. Since doses of 100 rads can affect the immune system, the radiation would increase the probability of infectious disease, cancer and genetic and embryonic effects.

Changes in the general circulation of the atmosphere arising from the presence of thick smoke clouds in the Northern Hemisphere may also affect global (or delayed) fallout. The National Academy of Sciences' (1975) suggestion that the appearance of radioactive debris in the Southern Hemisphere would be delayed by at least six months may not be valid. Unprecedented quantities of particulates released into the atmosphere may so alter interhemispheric circulation patterns that radioactive debris may be rapidly transported to the Southern Hemisphere. Consequently, parts of the Southern Hemisphere may quickly receive large doses of ionising radiation even though the nuclear exchange was confined to the Northern Hemisphere.

One consequence of a large-scale nuclear exchange which was predicted by earlier studies, and which has not been recently disputed, concerns stratospheric ozone depletion. Nuclear fireballs from detonations larger than about 1 megaton, heating a large volume of air to several thousand degrees Kelvin, generate and inject considerable amounts of nitric oxide into the stratosphere – which, by way of complex chemical reactions, removes ozone (Foley and Ruderman, 1973). Confirmation of this predicted process has been sought through analyses of the effects of the nuclear weapons tests of the 1950s and early 1960s. These are claimed to have reduced stratospheric ozone by up to 5 per cent (Chang, Duewer and Weubbles, 1979; Johnston, Whitten and Birks, 1973; Reinsel, 1981). However, such a small reduction lies within the year-to-year variability of ozone levels, and the question of confirmation remains controversial (Angell and Korshover, 1973; Bauer and Gilmore, 1975; Goldsmith et al., 1973; Turco et al., 1981).

For a 10,000 megaton nuclear exchange involving 5000 1 megaton weapons and 500 10 megaton weapons uniformly distributed between 20 and 60°N, the National Academy of Sciences (1975) estimated that the ozone column would be reduced by 30–70 per cent in the Northern Hemisphere and 20–40 per cent in the Southern Hemisphere. Calculations for 10,000 megaton scenarios by Whitten et al. (1975), Crutzen and Birks (1982) and Turco et al. (1983b) produce similar results. Such ozone depletion would lead to increased ultraviolet radiation reaching the earth's surface, with a many-fold increase in the biologically active ultraviolet UV-B wavelengths (280–320 nm) lasting for several years. Increased UV-B would suppress the immune systems of man and other mammals, so increasing the likelihood of disease and skin cancer. It would impair the vision systems in mammals, and disrupt oceanic and terrestrial ecosystems (Westing, 1982). At first, the increased UV-B would be absorbed by the increased particulates present in the troposphere, but as the particulate loading decreased so the excessive UV-B doses would reach the surface.

The key factor in calculating the amount of nitric oxide entering the stratosphere, and the consequent removal of ozone, is the stabilising height of the nuclear mushroom cloud. The cloud height is related to the weapon yield and the height of the tropopause, such that, for the mid-latitude tropopause, clouds from weapons having yields greater than about 1 megaton reach the stratosphere (Crutzen and Birks, 1982). This explains why limiting the explosive power of all individual nuclear weapons to approximately 0.5 megaton would effectively eliminate the possibility of

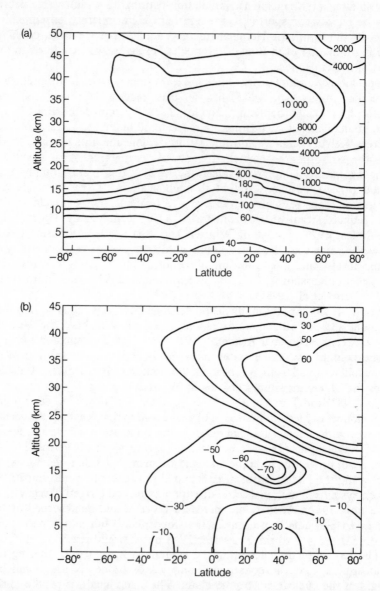

Figure 7.1   (a) Ozone mixing ratios (ppbv) in the present atmosphere as calculated by a two-dimensional model; (b) ozone depletion (%) 50 days after the beginning of a 10,000 MT nuclear exchange scenario. Negative values indicate ozone increases; they show how oxides of nitrogen injections have opposite effects on ozone in the upper and lower regions of the atmosphere.

(*Source:* Crutzen and Birks, 1982)

any significant damage to the stratospheric ozone layer (Openshaw, Stead-man and Greene, 1983; Teller, 1983). As arsenals are modernised with low-yield multiple warheads, the threat of large ozone depletions becomes less likely. For example, Crutzen and Birks (1982) employ a 5750 megaton nuclear exchange scenario in which most of the weapons have yields of less than 1 megaton and they estimate that most of the nitric oxide is deposited in the troposphere, so causing no significant depletion of stratospheric ozone. The appropriateness of their nuclear weapon scenario may be questioned, as current estimates suggest that 7000 megatons out of the world's 12,000 megaton total of strategic and theatre nuclear weapons are accounted for by warheads exceeding 1 megaton (Turco et al., 1983b). Crutzen and Birks (1982) provide estimates of the effects of an alternative, 10,000 megaton nuclear exchange scenario (as employed by the National Academy of Sciences, 1975) involving larger weapons. They show that this would cause 65 per cent ozone depletion in the Northern Hemisphere and up to 20 per cent in the Southern Hemisphere (figure 7.1). Additional ozone depletion, not taken into account by any model to date, might arise if significant quantities of oxides of nitrogen were introduced into the stratosphere by urban firestorm plumes penetrating the tropopause.

Estimating the severity of the nuclear winter

Research by Aleksandrov and Stenchikov (1983), Covey, Schneider and Thompson (1984), Crutzen and Birks (1982), Thompson et al. (1984) and Turco et al. (1983a, 1983b) highlight that it is the presence of the enor-mous quantities of smoke released by nuclear-induced fires, rather than the dust raised by nuclear explosions, which would cause surface tempera-tures to plunge to subfreezing levels in the weeks following a large-scale nuclear exchange. For example, for their baseline scenario of a 5000 megaton exchange, Turco et al. (1983b) calculate that 75 per cent of the initial increased atmospheric opacity that would follow would be due to tropospheric smoke and only 25 per cent to stratospheric dust. It is only after two to three months that dust would come to dominate the atmos-pheric optical depth, as the smoke became largely depleted by rainout and washout processes.

Given the importance of tropospheric smoke in producing the nuclear winter, it is essential to obtain realistic estimates of the quantity and nature of the materials likely to be burned in urban and rural fires; the quantity of smoke emitted; the duration and extent of the fires; the particle-size distribution of the smoke; the height to which smoke would be injected; the residence time of the smoke and its solar radiation absorp-tion properties. However, there are large uncertainties in quantifying and modelling these parameters. In cities the spread of fires depends upon the interaction of blast and fire, the extent of the blast damage, the amount of combustible material in a given area, the closeness and combustibility of the buildings, topography and the weather conditions at the time. How fires burn is also important, because under some conditions the many individual fires may coalesce into firestorms. In a firestorm many fires merge to form a single convective column rising from the burning area, with fire-induced hurricane-force centripetal winds burning virtually everything combustible within the firestorm area (Lewis, 1979). Firestorms may have an important climatic impact by injecting smoke via their rapidly rising convective plumes into the stratosphere up to 19 kilometres, where it will have a long residence time and a potential for amplifying the magnitude and duration of the surface cooling. Further research is needed to assess the likelihood of such firestorms. Present simulations, such as those undertaken by Turco et al. (1983b), appear conservative in estimating that firestorms would account for only 5 per cent of urban fires.

One-sixth of the world's urban area (50 per cent of the buildings) is assumed to be partially burned following the detonation of weapons yielding 1000 megatons on high-priority military and industrial targets near or within towns. They estimate that in addition 500,000 square kilometres of forest, brush and grassland would be burned. Again, this figure appears conservative, given that Crutzen and Birks (1982) suggest that 1 million square kilometres of forests may be expected to burn. Turco et al. (1983b) calculate that, together with particulate emissions from oil and gas production well fires, the total smoke emission for their 5000 megaton scenario would be approximately 225 million tons released over several days, of which 5 per cent would reach the stratosphere. Of the total smoke emission, urban/suburban fires account for 52 per cent, firestorms for 7 per cent, wildfires for 34 per cent, and long-term fires for 7 per cent.

To evaluate the effect on atmospheric temperatures of both the smoke and the dust produced by nuclear explosions, Turco et al. (1983b) employ a series of physical models including a one-dimensional annually averaged radiative–convective model. This uses calculated atmospheric smoke and dust loadings and particle-size distributions to derive visible and infrared optical properties, light fluxes and air temperature as a function of time and height. Such a model represents an extreme simplification of the behaviour of the real atmosphere (Elsom, 1984; Maddox, 1984). It averages out all horizontal variations and considers that quantities such as temperature and aerosols vary only as a function of altitude and time (Covey et al., 1984). Separate simulations were made for land and ocean surfaces, so the temperature reductions predicted for landmasses by this model do not include any ameliorating effect arising from the oceans; therefore, the surface temperature perturbations shown in figure 7.2 for several nuclear exchange scenarios should be considered to apply to the

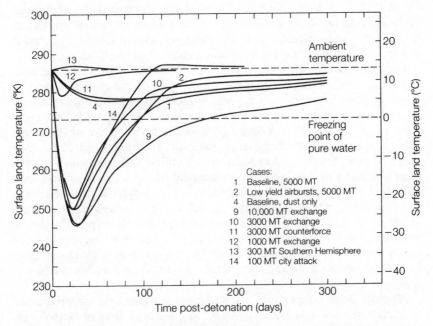

Figure 7.2 Average surface temperature variations for the Northern Hemisphere following selected nuclear exchange scenarios. Predictions do not take into account the effects of oceanic amelioration, and temperatures generally apply to the interior of continents.
(*Source:* Turco et al., 1983b)

interior of continental landmasses, and even there some oceanic amelioration may be expected.

Turco et al. (1983b) suggest that, if oceanic amelioration is taken into account, actual temperature decreases may be approximately 30 per cent smaller than they predict in continental interiors, and 70 per cent smaller in coastal regions. Even with these qualifications, their results point to many of the nuclear exchange scenarios producing subfreezing temperatures within three to four weeks. For the 5000 or 10,000 megaton scenario, continental interior temperatures of the Northern Hemisphere may fall as low as −15 to −25 °C (with little or no diurnal cycle) as the earth's surface is deprived of over 90 per cent of its solar radiation for several weeks. The abrupt onset of subfreezing temperatures and darkness would probably cause widespread severe damage to natural and agricultural ecosystems, particularly in the mid-latitudes of the Northern Hemisphere. The impact of drastically reduced temperatures and light levels would depend on the season in which they occurred, their duration and the tolerance limits of the species. For example, a spring or summer war might kill or damage virtually all crops in the Northern Hemisphere. By contrast, a nuclear war in the autumn or winter would probably have a lesser effect on vegetation if normally cold-tolerant plants had time to develop freezing tolerance before lethal temperatures were reached (Ehrlich et al., 1983).

Even nuclear exchanges less severe than 5000–10,000 megatons (cases 4, 11 and 12 in figure 7.2) would cause temperature decreases of 5–10 degC – which is enough to turn summer into winter. The relative importance of tropospheric smoke as opposed to stratospheric dust is indicated by a comparison of cases 10 (a 3000 megaton countervalue exchange involving urban targets and generating large quantities of smoke) and 11 (a 3000 megaton counterforce exchange involving military targets, which injects large quantities of dust into the stratosphere from surface explosions but only limited quantities of smoke into the atmosphere from nuclear-induced fires), which reveals the smoke to be the cause of a sudden dramatic cooling while the fine stratospheric dust is responsible for a prolonged but lesser cooling. The sensitivity of the climate to large quantities of smoke is demonstrated in the 100 megaton city attack scenario (case 14), which reveals a cooling comparable to much larger nuclear exchange scenarios.

Whereas large temperature reductions over continents are predicted, the reduction over oceans is likely to be only 2–3 degC because of the large heat capacity of oceans and the rapid mixing of surface waters. Consequently, the ameliorating effect of the oceans will considerably offset

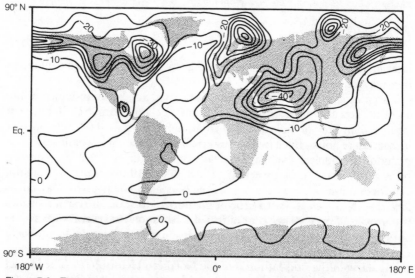

Figure 7.3 The predicted change in surface temperature (degC) 40 days after a nuclear exchange of approximately 6000 MT. Isotherms are at 5 degC intervals. (Source: after Aleksandrov and Stenchikov, 1983)

cooling in coastal regions, as suggested by Turco et al. (1983b) and shown by MacCracken (1983) using a two-dimensional (latitude–height) model. However, only three-dimensional general-circulation models can adequately reveal regional variations in the temperature reductions which are likely to result from a large-scale nuclear exchange. In addition, many more research studies employing general circulation models are needed to validate the predictions by Turco et al. (1983a, 1983b) that a nuclear winter would indeed follow a large-scale nuclear exchange. Initial confirmation came from Soviet research conducted by Aleksandrov and Stenchikov (1983), who found that 40 days after a large-scale nuclear exchange the Northern Hemisphere would experience an average temperature drop of approximately 13 degC, and the Southern Hemisphere a drop of 3 degC. Regional variations would be profound, with temperatures in parts of North America falling by 40 degC, in Scandinavia by over 45 degC and in parts of the USSR by over 40 degC (figure 7.3). Even the Arabian Peninsula and Plateau of Iran, in low latitudes, would experience temperature reductions of over 40 degC. By contrast, ocean temperatures would decrease much less.

A more sophisticated general circulation model, developed by the US National Center for Atmospheric Research (NCAR), also confirms the threat of a nuclear winter. While Aleksandrov and Stenchikov (1983) employ an annually averaged model with two vertical layers (up to 12 km) with a resolution of 12 degrees latitude by 15 degrees longitude, Covey et al. (1984) and Thompson et al. (1984) employ the NCAR model with its nine vertical layers (up to 30 km) and resolution of 4.5 degrees latitude by 7.5 degrees longitude. (The NCAR model also allows examination of the effects of a nuclear exchange for different seasons.) These writers reveal that, within ten days of a 6500 megaton nuclear exchange (the baseline scenario detailed in the 1985 National Academy of Sciences report), the average cooling of the Northern Hemisphere landmass beneath the smoke cloud for the summer case would be 15–20 degC (the comparable figure from the Soviet model is 25 degC). At this time, subfreezing temperatures would occur over substantial parts of North America and Europe (figure 7.4).

These results highlight how quickly the nuclear winter would come. Coastal regions, particularly in the western parts of the continents, would generally escape the intense surface cooling of continental interiors. During the first fortnight following an exchange the Northern Hemisphere cooling pattern might vary because smoke plumes and clouds would display heterogeneous density. Whenever dense patches of smoke drifted overhead and persisted for more than a few days, rapid freezing might occur. In effect, this implies almost random subfreezing temperatures, depending on initial weather conditions and the position of areas relative to extensive fires. For example, Covey et al. (1984) found that tempera-

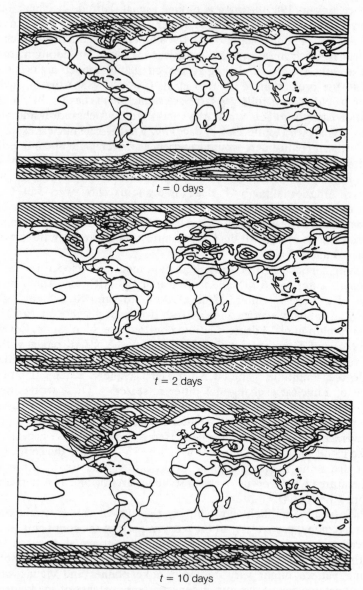

Figure 7.4 Surface temperature at three selected times: $t = 0$ is the time at which smoke is added to the atmosphere for the July simulation. Isotherms are at 10 degK intervals. Areas with temperatures less than 270 °K (−3 °C) are shaded. The warmest isotherm in the tropics is 300 °K (27 °C).

(*Source:* Covey et al., 1984)

tures could be below freezing in Western Europe eight days after a nuclear exchange but not ten days after.

Atmospheric circulation changes

Solar energy absorption by the upper layers of smoke and dust clouds will substantially warm the stratosphere and upper troposphere in the Northern Hemisphere; both one-dimensional and three-dimensional models point to temperature increases of up to 80 degC at these altitudes (figure 7.5). At the same time, with little solar energy reaching the surface, and with the escape of infrared radiation from the surface layers through the smoke clouds to space, ground temperatures would decrease greatly. Consequently the lapse rate of the Northern Hemisphere mid-latitudes would become stable. Convection would be suppressed, decreasing cloud formation and precipitation rates (MacCracken, 1983). Water clouds might even largely disappear in the middle troposphere because atmospheric heating decreases relative humidity. Even if clouds were present,

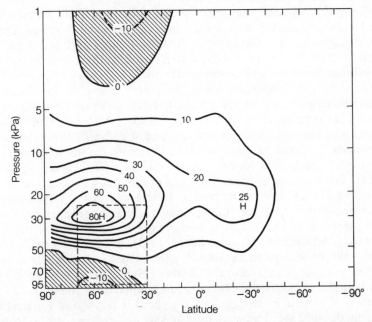

Figure 7.5 Zonally-averaged temperature changes (degC) averaged over days 10–20 after the injection of smoke into the atmosphere in the NCAR model simulation for July. The areas with negative numbers, indicating cooling, are shaded. The zone in which the smoke is injected is indicated by the dashed box.
(Source: Covey et al., 1984)

the increase in numbers of potential condensation nuclei would narrow the droplet size distribution, so suppressing the formation of rain droplets by coalescence (Crutzen and Birks, 1982; Crutzen, 1984). Whether changes in atmospheric ionisation would affect the process of precipitation formation has yet to be considered (Boeck, 1976; Kellogg, 1978). Fewer clouds and less precipitation would probably increase the residence time of particulates in the troposphere (typically one week to one month at present) by reducing the rainout and washout processes of particulate scavenging. Although precipitation rates would be less throughout the Northern Hemisphere, the oceans would continue to act as a moisture source for the marine boundary layer (Barton and Paltridge, 1984). With steep temperature gradients formed between oceanic and continental areas, strong monsoonal circulation might occur and coastal zones might be subject to severe storms with heavy snowfalls. Further consideration needs to be given to the extent of snowfalls during the first fortnight following a nuclear exchange, as snow may not only amplify surface cooling through positive feedback mechanisms but may also provide insulation. It could therefore increase survival potential for perennial plants and for animals with resting or hibernating phases (SANA, 1984).

The most significant change to the atmospheric circulation which may arise from the presence of massive smoke clouds in the Northern Hemisphere might be the disruption of interhemispheric airflows. Both the Soviet and the NCAR general circulation models indicate that the currently existing Southern and Northern Hemisphere Hadley cells would be replaced by one single-cell driven by rising motion in the Northern Hemisphere generated by the intense heating of the smoke layer (figure 7.6). This type of circulation would transport Northern Hemispheric smoke and ionising radiation upwards and southwards to the Southern Hemisphere, spreading these pollutants to regions beyond those in which the nuclear explosions occurred in less than a week (Thompson et al., 1984). The increased particulate loading of the atmosphere may cause the Southern Hemisphere to experience increased opacity, a reduction of solar energy reaching the surface, and marked temperature decreases. Temperatures in the Southern Hemisphere may fall by 3–4 degC on average (Aleksandrov and Stenchikov, 1983), by up to 8 degC (Turco et al., 1983b) or even more (Ehrlich et al., 1983) following a large-scale nuclear exchange confined to the Northern Hemisphere. The exposure of low latitudes of both hemispheres to low temperatures and reduced light levels is of particular concern, as many plants in tropical and subtropical regions do not have dormancy mechanisms that enable them to tolerate cold seasons, even at temperatures well above freezing. Ehrlich et al. (1983) conclude that, if cold temperatures or darkness or both were to become widespread, tropical forests could largely disappear.

The strength of the potential disruption of the interhemispheric circula-

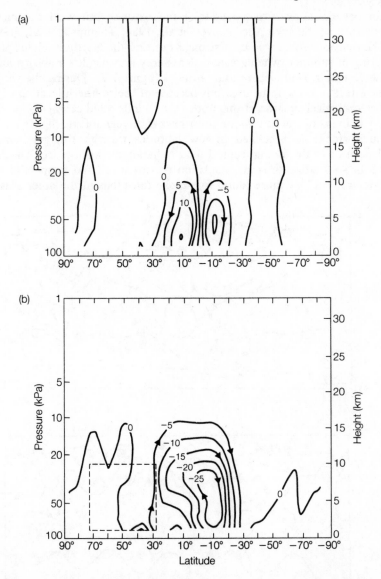

Figure 7.6   Zonally-averaged meridional airflow (units of 10^{10}kg s^{-1}) in the NCAR April simulation: (a) April control (days 16–20); (b) April perturbed (days 16–20). Arrows indicate the direction of meridional and vertical motion. The zone in which the smoke is injected is indicated by the dashed box.

(*Source:* Covey et al., 1984) Thompson (1984) reports that, when stratospheric dust is introduced into this simulation, the mid-tropospheric heating owing to insolation absorption by the smoke is decreased by a factor of 2 and that this in turn allows a Hadley circulation which is very similar to that of the control case.

tion patterns appears to depend upon the season within which the nuclear exchange would take place (Covey et al., 1984; Thompson et al., 1984). The dynamic effect would be strongest during the Northern Hemisphere spring or summer, when greater solar energy is available for absorption in the Northern Hemisphere mid-latitudes (figure 7.7). During the winter, the effect is likely to be less, but because of the southern location of the meteorological equator, strong upper-level winds could carry large patches or streamers of smoke into the subtropics relatively quickly (figure 7.7). If much smoke accumulated in low latitudes through this mechanism, absorption of the strong tropical solar radiation might produce dynamical feedbacks leading to large circulation perturbations and temperature reductions, such as those found for smoke injections in the other seasons

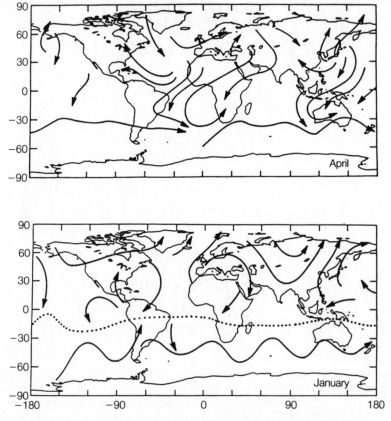

Figure 7.7 Airflow in the upper atmosphere (20 kPa, 200 mbar) for the NCAR large-scale nuclear exchange simulations for the spring and summer. The dotted line indicates the southern limit of southward winds in the winter simulation.
(*Source:* Covey et al., 1984)

(Thompson et al., 1984). A more confident prediction will have to await an improved interactive general circulation model, in which the particulates are moved by winds and affected by the convective activity, and precipitation rates are predicted by the model. Models need also to consider the strong coupling between the ocean and atmospheric circulation. One may expect significant alterations in ocean currents and upwellings such as El Niño (Rasmusson and Hall, 1983).

Until the next generation of general circulation models is available, additional insight into the atmospheric circulation changes that would follow a large-scale nuclear exchange may come from examining severe cold periods during the Quaternary. Atmospheric modelling of the general circulation at the peak of the Devensian (Wisconsin) glacial period approximately 18,000 years ago highlights that the cold continents – at that time covered by thick ice sheets – created extensive overlying anticyclones (Gates, 1976). For Europe this resulted in an increased incidence of easterly winds blowing outwards from the cold continental interiors. For regions such as the British Isles, this meant a reduction in the ameliorating influence of the westerlies which currently bring anomalous mildness to the region. This period also had climatic 'refuges', like those along parts of the west coast of North America (Johnson, 1977; Warner, Mathewes and Clague, 1982). However, the Devensian period lasted tens of thousands of years, and more appropriate climatic periods to examine may be short stadials such as the Loch Lomond (Younger Dryas) stadial approximately 10,500 years ago. The examination of periods of cooling following volcanic eruptions (Lamb, 1982) may also tell us more about atmospheric circulation changes, such as movements of the jet stream and increased storminess, which might follow the sudden cooling initiated by a large-scale nuclear exchange.

Increased tropospheric air pollution

Ionising radiation will be the pollutant of major concern in the aftermath of a nuclear war. However, in addition, widespread damage and destruction of industrial facilities, and the extensive fires in urban and rural areas, will generate enormous quantities of conventional pollutants and toxic chemicals, currently experienced only during accidents in the chemical industry (for example, dioxin at Seveso in Italy, methyl isocyanate gas at Bhopal).

Crutzen and Birks (1982) stressed the potential significance of the release by fires of oxides of nitrogen and hydrocarbons which could react in sunlight to form high concentrations of photochemical pollutants including ozone, PAN (peroxyacetyl nitrate) and ethane. Sunlight is required to initiate the necessary photochemical reactions, so photochemical pollution will become significant only when the particulate loading of the atmosphere decreases sufficiently to allow adequate sunlight to reach the lower atmosphere. Crutzen and Birks estimate that ozone concentrations in mid-latitudes of the Northern Hemisphere may reach 140–160 parts per billion by volume (ppbv), which is five times current background levels; ethane may reach 50–100 ppbv, and PAN may reach 1–10 ppbv. Such levels can seriously inhibit the growth and yield of certain plant species, as well as causing physiological effects in sensitive humans. Additional stress to terrestrial and oceanic ecosystems may come from increased acidity of precipitation (pH4 or even pH3) arising from the increased quantities of nitrates and sulphates in the atmosphere (Elsom, 1984).

Long-term recovery from the nuclear winter

The time taken for the global climate to return to contemporary norms will depend upon the rate of depletion of smoke and dust from the troposphere and stratosphere, the effect of altered surface albedo arising from fires and smoke, the potential for an enhanced infrared absorption effect owing to increased gaseous pollutants (water vapour, ozone, carbon dioxide), and the nature of atmospheric feedback mechanisms (Robock, 1984).

For many of the scenarios of nuclear war presented by Turco et al. (1983b), the subfreezing period in the Northern Hemisphere is estimated to last two to three months, and recovery to current temperature levels to take two to three years. Aleksandrov and Stenchikov (1983) suggest that a year after the nuclear conflict the nuclear winter may be followed by a period of pronounced warming by up to 35 degC over parts of the continents of the Northern Hemisphere. However, there are large uncertainties about climatic change in the years following a nuclear war because of uncertainties about the nature of the earth's surface and atmosphere following the nuclear winter. For example, nuclear-induced fires may have consumed a million or more square kilometres of urban area, forests and grasslands; low temperatures may have killed vegetation over large areas; soil disturbances may have accelerated surface erosion and led to dust storms, and massive quantities of sooty smoke will have been deposited on the snow and ice of polar regions (SIPRI, 1977; Turco et al., 1983b).

Surface albedo changes have the potential to cause regional and global changes in the climate through the triggering of positive feedback mechanisms (Catchpole, 1973; Otterman, 1974, 1977; Ramseier, 1974). This is why one cannot discount the possibility of the nuclear winter triggering a 'nuclear glacial'. Flohn (1974) has proposed an 'instantaneous glacierisation' model for explaining the formation of ice sheets during the Quaternary. According to this model, the key event is the survival of snow over a large area of the subarctic upland plateaus for a single summer; this then results in a series of feedback reactions leading to the establishment of permanent snowfields and, subsequently, ice sheet formation (Bray, 1976, 1977). One or a series of several closely spaced massive volcanic eruptions (1000 cubic kilometres or more of ejecta) have been proposed as a means of producing short-term cooling which may lead to the survival of subarctic snow over a single summer, so initiating positive feedback. Similarly, the dramatic cooling following a nuclear exchange may be a possible trigger for the instantaneous glacierisation mechanism. Further research is needed to assess the likelihood of a nuclear winter being followed by a nuclear glacial.

Conclusion, and the need for further research

Before 1982, few climatologists and meteorologists directed their attention to nuclear war as a trigger for major climatic change. Any potential climatological effects of a nuclear war were believed to be small and seemingly irrelevant, given the horrific consequences of the nuclear exchange itself. However, recent research has highlighted the error of this view. This research suggests that a large-scale nuclear exchange, or possibly even a 'limited' nuclear exchange, is likely to cause profound climatological changes in the Northern Hemisphere and even in the Southern Hemisphere. Extensive areas of the Northern Hemisphere continents would be subject to the sudden onset of subfreezing temperatures lasting for months, regardless of the season in which the nuclear exchange took place. Low temperatures and reduced sunlight would severely restrict productivity in natural and agricultural ecosystems for the first year after a nuclear war. Few survivors of the immediate effects of the war in the Northern Hemisphere could escape the hypothermia, famine and disease that would follow. If the Southern Hemisphere also experienced marked temperature reductions as a consequence of altered interhemispheric circulation patterns, then it is entirely possible that, globally, the greatest mechanism for death associated with a large-scale nuclear war could be starvation (Harwell, 1983).

The implications of a severe nuclear winter for survivors of the immediate effects of nuclear war demand increased attention by researchers from a wide range of fields. In this connection, the findings of Turco et al. (1983a, 1983b) and other atmospheric science research groups are being given widespread attention (Baum, 1983; Ehrlich et al., 1984; Greene, 1984; Grover, 1984; Rodhe, 1984; Sagan, 1983; Schneider and Londer, 1984; Turco et al., 1984). Already large groups of climatologists and atmospheric scientists have accepted the findings of the research which points to the serious likely climatological effects of a large-scale nuclear exchange (Council of the American Meteorological Society, 1983; National Academy of Sciences, 1985). Nevertheless, additional research using independent and improved models is essential so as to increase the confidence with which the intensity, duration and regional variation of the climatological effects of a nuclear war can be predicted (Thompson, 1984). Increased confidence in the predictions is vital for two reasons. First, predictions about the long-term global biological consequences of nuclear war depend upon the reliability of the predictions about climatological changes (Ehrlich et al., 1983). Second, the concept of the nuclear winter is potentially one of the most powerful arguments for nuclear disarmament (SANA, 1984). However, only confidently predicted climatological and biological consequences of nuclear war will convince a nation possessing nuclear weapons that the launching of a major nuclear attack, even against an unarmed opponent, will result in the aggressor itself experiencing punishment as severe as that imposed on its intended victim (Simon, 1984).

Unfortunately, one weakness in this argument is that it ignores the devastating consequences of a nuclear strike below the nuclear winter threshold (Plous, 1984). For example, nuclear strikes against missile silos and military airfields away from cities would not start urban conflagrations. Such fires are the most important factor in triggering the nuclear winter. Without them, the climatological disturbances following the nuclear strikes may be much less severe (Shepherd and Greene, 1984).

Nevertheless, realisation that a large-scale nuclear war would lead to environmental consequences affecting all nations on the earth may be the knowledge that generates sufficient worldwide pressure to eventually halt and reverse the nuclear arms race.

References

Aleksandrov, V.V. and Stenchikov, G.L. (1983), 'On the modelling of the climatic consequences of nuclear war', *The Proceedings on Applied Mathematics*. Moscow: Computing Centre of the USSR Academy of Sciences.

Alvarez, L.W., Alvarez, W., Asaro, F. and Michel, H.V. (1980), 'Extra-terrestrial cause for the Cretaceous–Tertiary extinctions', *Science*, 208, 1095–1108.

Alvarez, W., Kauffman, E.G., Surlyk, F., Alvarez, L.W., Asaro, F. and Michel, H.V. (1984), 'Impact theory of mass extinctions and the invertebrate fossil record', *Science*, 223, 1135–41.

Angell, J.K. and Korshover, J. (1973), 'Quasi-biennial and long-term fluctuations in total ozone', *Monthly Weather Review*, 101, 426–43.

Barton, I.J. and Paltridge, G.W. (1984), 'Twilight at noon overstated', *Ambio*, 13, 49–51.

Batten, E.S. (1966), 'The effects of nuclear war on the weather and climate', Memorandum RM-4989-TAB. Santa Monica, California: RAND Corporation.

Bauer, E. and Gilmore, F.R. (1975), 'Effect of atmospheric nuclear explosions on total ozone', *Review of Geophysics and Space Physics*, 13, 451–8.

Baum, R.M. (1983), 'Climate changes focus of research on effects of nuclear war', *Chemical and Engineering News*, 19 December, 16–17.

Boeck, W.L. (1976), 'Meteorological consequences of atmospheric Krypton-85', *Science*, 193, 195–8.

Bray, J.R. (1976), 'Volcanic triggering of glaciation', *Nature*, 260, 414–15.

Bray, J.R. (1977), 'Pleistocene volcanism and glacial initiation', *Science*, 197, 251–4.

Broido, A. (1960), 'Mass fires following nuclear attack', *Bulletin Atomic Scientists*, 16, 409–13.

Catchpole, A.J.W. (1973), 'The mystery of the glacial periods', *Weather*, 28, 314–21.

Chang, J.S., Duewer, W.H. and Weubbles, D.J. (1979), 'The atmospheric nuclear tests of the 1950s and 1960s: a possible test of ozone depletion theories', *Journal of Geophysical Research*, 84, 1755–65.

Council of the American Meteorological Society (1983), 'The atmospheric consequences of nuclear warfare: a statement', *Bulletin of the American Meteorological Society*, 64, 1302.

Covey, C., Schneider, S.H. and Thompson, S.L. (1984), 'Global atmospheric effects of massive smoke injections from a nuclear war: results from general circulation model simulations', *Nature*, 308, 21–5.

Crutzen, P.J. (1984), 'Darkness after a nuclear war', *Ambio*, 13, 52–4.

Crutzen, P.J. and Birks, J.W. (1982), 'The atmosphere after a nuclear war: twilight at noon', *Ambio*, 11, 114–25.

Ehrlich, P., Sagan, C., Kennedy, D. and Roberts, W.O. (1984), *'The Cold And The Dark: The World After Nuclear War*. London: Sidgwick and Jackson.

Ehrlich, P.R. and 19 others (1983), 'Long-term biological consequences of nuclear war', *Science*, 222, 1293–1300.

Elsom, D.M. (1984), 'Climatic change induced by a large-scale nuclear exchange', *Weather*, 39, 268–71.

Flohn, H. (1974), 'Background of a geophysical model of the initiation of the next glaciation', *Quaternary Research*, 4, 385–404.

Foley, H.M. and Ruderman, M.A. (1973), 'Stratospheric nitric oxide production from past nuclear explosions', *Journal of Geophysical Research*, 78, 4441–50.

Gates, W.L. (1976), 'Modelling the ice-age climate', *Science*, 191, 1138–44.

Glasstone, S. and Dolan, P.J. (1977), *The Effects of Nuclear Weapons* (3rd edn) Washington DC: US Department of Defense and Department of Energy.

Goldsmith, P., Tuck, A.F., Foot, J.S., Simmons, E.L. and Newson, R.L. (1973), 'Nitrogen oxides, nuclear weapon testing, Concorde and stratospheric ozone', *Nature*, 244, 545–51.

Greene, O. (1984), 'The nuclear winter', *Sanity*, June, 16–24.

Grover, H.D. (1984), 'The climatic and biological consequences of nuclear war', *Environment*, 26, 6–13, 34–8.

Harwell, M.A. (1983), 'The human and environmental consequences of nuclear war'. Paper presented at the Conference on the Long-term Biological Consequences of Nuclear War, Cambridge, Mass., April 1983.

Johnson, D.L. (1977), 'The late Quaternary climate of coastal California: evidence for an ice age refugium', *Quaternary Research*, 8, 154–79.

Johnston, H.S., Whitten, G. and Birks, J. (1973) 'Effect of nuclear explosions on stratospheric nitric oxide and ozone', *Journal of Geophysical Research*, 78, 6107–35.

Kellogg, W.W. (1978), 'Global influences of mankind on the climate', in J. Gribbin (ed.), *Climatic Change*. Cambridge: Cambridge University Press, pp. 205–27.

Lamb, H.H. (1982), *Climate, History and the Modern World*. London: Methuen.

Lewis, K.N. (1979), 'The prompt and delayed effects of nuclear war', *Scientific American*, 241, 35–47.

MacCracken, M.C. (1983), 'Nuclear war: preliminary estimates of the climatic effects of a nuclear exchange'. Paper presented at the 3rd International Conference on Nuclear War, Erice, Sicily, 19–23 August 1983 (Lawrence Livermore National Laboratory, 1983).

Maddox, J. (1984), 'Nuclear winter not yet established', *Nature*, 308, 11.

National Academy of Sciences (1975), *Long-term Worldwide Effects of Nuclear Weapon Detonations*. Washington DC: National Academy of Sciences.

National Academy of Sciences (1985), *The Effects on the Atmosphere of a Nuclear Exchange*.Washington DC: National Academy of Sciences.

Openshaw, S., Steadman, P. and Greene, O. (1983), *Doomsday. Britain After Nuclear Attack*. Oxford: Basil Blackwell.

Otterman, J. (1974), 'Baring high-albedo soils by overgrazing: a hypothesised desertification mechanism', *Science*, 186, 531–3.

Otterman, J. (1977), 'Athropogenic impact on the albedo of the Earth', *Climatic Change*, 1, 137–55.

Plous, S. (1984), 'Will deterrence survive a nuclear winter?' *Science*, 225, 268.

Pollack, J.B., Toon, O.B., Ackerman, T.P., McKay, C.P. and Turco, R.P. (1983), 'Environmental effects of an impact-generated dust cloud: implications for the Cretaceous–Tertiary extinctions', *Science*, 219, 287–9.

Rampino, M.R. and Self, S. (1982), 'Historic eruptions of Tambora (1815), Krakatau (1883), and Agung (1963), their stratospheric aerosols, and climatic impact', *Quaternary Research*, 18, 127–43.

Ramseier, R.O. (1974), 'How to melt the Arctic and warm the world', *Environment*, 16, 7–14.

Rasmusson, E.M. and Hall, J.M. (1983), 'El Niño – The great equatorial Pacific Ocean warming event of 1982–1983', *Weatherwise*, 36, 166–75.

Reinsel, G.C. (1981), 'Analysis of total ozone data for the detection of recent trends and the effects of nuclear testing during the 1960s', *Geophysical Research Letters*, 8, 1227–30.

Robock, A. (1984), 'Snow and ice feedbacks prolong effects of nuclear winter', *Nature*, 310, 667–70.

Rodhe, H. (1984), 'A nuclear winter', *Ambio*, 13, 43–4.

Sagan, C. (1983), 'Nuclear war and climatic catastrophe: some policy implications', *Foreign Affairs*, 62, 257–92.

SANA (Scientists Against Nuclear Arms) (1984), *Global Consequences of Nuclear War*, Report of the SANA Meeting on the Atmospheric and Long-term Biological Consequences of Nuclear War, Oxford, January 1984. Milton Keynes: SANA.

Schneider, S.H. and Londer, R.S. (1984), *The Coevolution Of Climate And Life*. San Francisco: Sierra Club Books, pp. 348–62.

Shepherd, J. and Greene, O. (1984), 'Nuclear winter: political, strategic implications', *Sanity*, June, 25–7.

Simon, H.A. (1984), 'Mutual deterrence or nuclear suicide', *Science*, 223, 775.

SIPRI (Stockholm International Peace Research Institute) (1977), *Weapons of Mass Destruction and the Environment*. London: Taylor and Francis.

Teller, E. (1983), 'Deadly myths about nuclear arms', *Readers Digest*, 122, 21–6.

Thompson, S.L. (1984), 'An evolving nuclear winter', *Climatic Change*, 6, 105–7.

Thompson, S.L., Aleksandrov, V.V., Stenchikov, G.L., Schneider, S.H., Covey, C. and Chervin, R.M. (1984), 'Global climatic consequences of nuclear war: simulations with three-dimensional models', *Ambio*, 13, 236–43.

Toon, O.B. and Pollack, J.B. (1980), 'Atmospheric aerosols and climate', *American Scientist*, 68, 268–78.

Turco, R.P., Toon, O.B., Ackerman, T.P., Pollack, J.B. and Sagan, C. (1983a), 'Long-term atmospheric and climatic consequences of a nuclear exchange'. Paper presented at the Conference on Long-term Global Atmospheric and Climatic Consequences of Nuclear War, Cambridge, Mass., April 1983.

Turco, R.P., Toon, O.B., Ackerman, T.P., Pollack, J.B. and Sagan, C. (1983b), 'Nuclear winter: global consequences of multiple nuclear explosions', *Science*, 222, 1283–92.

Turco, R.P., Toon, O.B., Ackerman, T.P., Pollack, J.B. and Sagan, C. (1984), 'The climatic threat of nuclear war', *Scientific American*, 251, 23–33.

Turco, R.P., Toon, O.B., Park, C., Whitten, R.C., Pollack, J.B. and Noerdlinger, P. (1981), 'The Tunguska meteor fall of 1908: effects on stratospheric ozone', *Science*, 214, 19–23.

Warner, R.G., Mathewes, R.W. and Clague, J.J. (1982), 'Ice-free conditions on the Queen Charlotte Islands, British Columbia, at the height of late Wisconsin glaciation', *Science*, 218, 675–7.

Westing, A.H. (1982), 'Environmental consequences of nuclear warfare', *Environmental Conservation*, 9, 269–72.

Whitten, R.C., Borucki, W.J. and Turco, R.P. (1975), 'Possible ozone depletions following nuclear explosions', *Nature*, 257, 38–9.

CHAPTER 8

The Geography of Civil Defence

Donald J. Zeigler

An irreconcilable conflict has threatened the cumbersome peace-keeping machinery that has somehow managed to stave off nuclear war for the first half-century of the atomic era. Tension between the two superpowers has been mounting for years and has escalated to crisis proportions in the past few weeks. Suddenly US satellites detect the beginning of a massive evacuation of Soviet cities, the first concrete sign that a nuclear war is to begin, a sign that will be interpreted by the US military that a Soviet first strike is to follow.

How ironic it is to envisage a scenario which projects the *protection* of civilians as the first *offensive* act of the Third World War. Yet, this scenario is the one most often painted by those who decry the impotency of US civil defence and call for elaborate plans to evacuate US cities in the event of impending holocaust. How would the USA respond to satellite intelligence that indicated the commencement of a Soviet evacuation? Without plans for wartime civilian protection, civil defence advocates offer the prospect of a Soviet ultimatum, with the US population held hostage and the Soviet population well protected. But *with* evacuation plans, the President of the USA would order crisis relocation to begin, and because the US population is inherently mobile, so the theory goes, it would take the nation less time to empty its cities than it would take the USSR. Since it would be just as senseless for the Soviets to drop their missiles on empty US cities as it would be for them to risk a counterstrike before their own cities were empty, they would be thwarted in their offensive acts. Even if they did launch their nuclear arsenal, the US population would survive and recovery would soon begin.

Preparation for place annihilation

The primary stimulus for US civil defence planning since the early 1970s has been Soviet civil defence planning: part of a broader trend that Wieseltier (1983, p. 39) calls the 'Sovietisation of American strategy'. If the USSR is prepared for what Kenneth Hewitt (1983) calls 'place annihilation', then the USA must be, too. The USA fears that the USSR could empty its cities, aim its missiles and demand surrender, knowing that if the USA refused its demands US cities would be annihilated along with their inhabitants. Hewitt calls a nation's cities 'the definitive human places' and promises that place annihilation will be one of the dominant themes of the next world war just as it was during the First and Second World Wars.

War has been taken off the battlefield; casualties are as likely to be civilian as military, and no target today is geographically out of range. The time–space convergence that has restructured global geopolitics has also restructured the likely complexion of global war. Civilian vulnerability increased with the airplane and again with the intercontinental ballistic missile. Today, we all might as well think of ourselves as living on the battlefield of the Third World War. US civilians now stand as much chance of being hit by the ultimate bullet as a Civil War soldier did at Gettysburg.

Proponents of civil defence planning believe that civilians must be prepared to survive an attack even if the physical shells which they inhabit cannot. Two methods constitute the basis of almost all population protection plans: sheltering, and evacuation. Evacuation, sometimes referred to as 'dispersal' or 'relocation', requires people to move out of 'risk areas', the likely targets of attack, and into 'host areas', those designated to receive evacuees. Evacuation is a geographical solution to the problem of protecting oneself from a severe place-specific hazard. In response to a wartime threat, it may take three forms: tactical evacuations are ordered when an attack is imminent; strategic evacuations are ordered in advance of an attack which is thought likely; and post-attack evacuations are implemented to rescue the survivors. The first two are designed to protect people by removing them from the danger zone, but only the second might be employed to change the strategic balance of power by demonstrating the futility of bombing population centres. As the time between missile launch and missile strike has diminished to minutes, tactical evacuation has become an impractical defensive strategy. Evacuation planning in the nuclear era has come to mean planning for strategic evacuation.

As an alternative to evacuation, people may be ordered to retreat to hardened steel blast shelters under or near the places where they live and work. The advantage of sheltering in the risk zone is that it can be quickly implemented and is easily reversible should an expected attack not occur. The obvious disadvantage is that it does not remove people from the places most likely to be annihilated by a direct hit. If the attack were to materialise, those caught in blast shelters run the risk of being buried alive or incinerated underground. Moreover, after the blast survivors would emerge into an environment of total devastation which would have to be

Table 8.1   Sheltering versus evacuation

Advantages	Disadvantages
Sheltering in place	
1 Could be implemented within hours	1 People remain in areas most likely to be bombed
2 Inexpensive to implement during a crisis	2 Seemingly incompatible with behavioural inclinations to flee
3 More likely to be ordered because of time and cost advantages	3 Expensive to plan for because of need to construct shelters
4 Easy to reverse should an attack fail to materialise	4 Comparatively incompatible with the concept of 'all hazards' planning
5 Workforce remains close to critical industries which need to remain in operation	5 Evacuation may need to take place after an attack anyway, under more difficult conditions
Evacuation to host areas	
1 People are removed from areas most likely to be bombed	1 Three to seven days would be required to evacuate large cities
2 Compatible with natural behavioural inclination to flee	2 Expensive to implement during a crisis
3 Inexpensive to plan for when compared with cost of building individual blast shelters	3 Less likely to be ordered because of time and cost disadvantages
4 Compatible with the concept of 'all hazards' planning	4 Not easily reversible should an attack fail to materialise
	5 Workforce far removed from critical industries
	6 An attack during evacuation would increase number of casualties
	7 Doubtful that host areas could provide for basic needs of evacuees

abandoned anyway. Another disadvantage of sheltering lies in the tens of billions of dollars required to construct blast shelters in the cities, a high price when compared with the cost of developing a paper plan for evacuation, and designating host-area fallout shelters in basements and building interiors. Several of the advantages and disadvantages of sheltering and evacuation are spelled out in table 8.1. The emphasis in the USA is now on evacuation, but in the early 1960s sheltering was perceived to be the better strategy for civilian protection. Indeed, there is no consensus on how to prepare for thermonuclear annihilation since risk analysis for nuclear war has no direct precedent.

Although currently the primary basis for civilian protection in both the USA and the USSR, evacuation is intended to be applied selectively. The elite of politics, business and industry, plus the so-called 'essential' workers and decision-makers, would be treated differently from what seems to be considered the expendable population. A portion of the chosen few would be whisked away to specially prepared, blast-resistant command posts far underground, while others would remain in the cities to staff industries critical to the war effort and human survival.

Civil defence planning in the USSR

Leon Gouré (1983), the leading US authority on Soviet evacuation planning, calls Soviet civil defence plans 'well developed' and 'quite comprehensive'. Gouré paints a picture of a tightly controlled evacuation in which essential Soviet workers will be 'dispersed' to locations from which they can commute to work in the cities, while the non-essential elements of the population will be 'evacuated' to host areas. All evacuees will be organised by place of employment or residence. They will assemble and register at evacuation assembly points, whereupon they will be loaded into mass transit vehicles or formed into marching columns of 2000–3000 people. Gouré concludes that most of the urban population of the USSR could be evacuated in two to three days. The host areas for each city are planned to be within the boundaries of the *oblast* where the city is located, with the 'dispersed' population being resettled as close as 30 miles to the city and the 'evacuated' population posted farther away. Evacuees will be received at evacuation reception points and will be housed with local residents and in public housing. In case accommodation is insufficient, evacuees will be expected to live in dugouts and cabins built by civil defence personnel, local citizens and evacuees.

In addition to relocation planning, the USSR also has an active blast shelter programme in urban areas, with priority given to sheltering the political, economic and scientific elite as well as essential workers and the civil defence staff (Gouré, 1982, p. 91). One estimate cited by Gouré indicates that blast shelters alone could accommodate 10–20 per cent of the urban population, and the Soviets intend eventually to have enough space to shelter the entire population. The main advantage to the Soviets of being able to shelter the population in place is that this can be accomplished within hours rather than days. Douglas (1983, p. 673) has reported that since 1970 regulations have required new and renovated buildings to include a shelter, and industrial plants to be built in duplicate so that if one is destroyed the other can continue to operate.

Civil defence planning in the USA

With the passage of the Federal Civil Defense Act in 1950, the USA committed itself to protecting the civilian population during a nuclear attack and handling the civilian aspects of the emergency and recovery periods. A bureaucratic framework, the Federal Civil Defense Administration (FCDA), was established to carry out this charge. Today, the FCDA has evolved into the Federal Emergency Management Agency (FEMA), a 1978 creation designed to consolidate the federal government's myriad emergency management activities.

In the early 1950s civilian protection plans revolved around tactical evacuation, but by 1954 the hydrogen bomb was operational and tactical evacuation became anachronistic. The Kennedy administration turned firmly to sheltering as a defence against nuclear attack, but was unable to gain congressional approval for a sustained, full-scale national sheltering programme. When the Shelter Incentive Bill was buried in the Senate in 1964, civil defence entered a period of limbo until 1978, when President Carter breathed new life into a moribund programme. The rebirth of civil defence saw a reorientation towards evacuation, a direction that had begun to take form in the mid-1970s under the name of 'crisis relocation planning'. This new policy emphasised 'dual use', that is, the development of emergency plans applicable to both nuclear attack and other disasters. In 1981 the trend towards amalgamated planning culminated in amendments to the Federal Civil Defense Act which was broadened to encompass all natural and technological disasters. Today, all FEMA emergency plans must be justified by 'dual use' and all single-purpose emergency plans must be integrated into 'full-spectrum' plans. Hurricanes, floods and nuclear attack should ultimately be handled by implementing the same

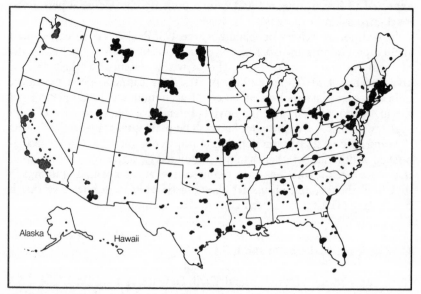

Figure 8.1 Evacuation zones in the USA: areas to be evacuated 'during extreme nuclear crisis'.
(*Source:* Federal Emergency Management Agency (FEMA), 1982)

basic plan. Since 1983 crisis relocation planning for nuclear emergencies has been folded into a broader programme known as the Integrated Emergency Management System, a federal–state–local partnership. By the end of the 1980s 'comprehensive emergency management plans' (formerly known as 'crisis relocation plans') should exist for all 400 high-risk areas portrayed in figure 8.1. These targets comprise military, economic and civilian sites which are subject to a 50 per cent or greater probability of receiving blast over-pressures of 2 pounds per square inch, assuming a circular error probability of no more than 0.5 nautical mile. They include military installations and support facilities, basic industries and organisations, and population concentrations of 50,000 or more. Ground rather than air bursts, however, would generate fallout plumes downwind from each of the blast sites. These would cover much of the host areas, requiring fallout shelter protection for the millions of Americans that would find themselves refugees in small rural towns.

A geographical critique of civil defence planning

'Every government study of civil defence published . . . has indicated that civil defence measures can mean the difference in millions of lives saved in a nuclear attack', concluded Blanchard (1979, p. 465) in his detailed study of US civil defence between 1945 and 1975. The chief responsibility of the federal government is to provide for the common defence of the US citizens, and the Federal Civil Defense Act orders it to protect the civilian population and assure the continuity of government during a crisis. The US public expects to be protected, but its support of civil defence measures has been ambivalent. Some people have not been supportive at all. Opposition to crisis relocation planning mounted as it evolved during the 1970s because some thought it would make war more likely and could not be operationalised to cope with the reality of a nuclear war. Some of the arguments against civil defence grow out of more general opposition to the nuclear arms race; others are based on logistical and behavioural considerations. The following questions certainly do not exhaust the gamut of criticisms against civil defence planning; they do, however, address some of the major geographical issues which cast doubt on its overall efficacy.

Flash flood equals nuclear war

For the present the US government seems intent on answering the question, 'How are nuclear disasters similar to other disasters?' and on avoiding the question, 'How are they different?' FEMA policy is based on the premise (indeed, the promise) that planning for one disaster is equivalent to planning for all disasters. What seems to be lacking in federal plans is a healthy measure of scepticism that normal disaster plans will not work in the event of a nuclear war. Perry (1982), for instance, compared nuclear attack with several other disasters and concluded that there was as much variation among the three natural hazards which he studied as there was between the natural hazards and nuclear attack. For Perry to have arrived at such a counterintuitive conclusion may mean that he had chosen to examine the wrong dimensions of variation. Only if emergency planning is viewed as a *logistical* phenomenon rather than as a challenge of behavioural geography may all disasters be considered in the same category. Human perceptions of nuclear hazards differ in the extreme from other hazards (Slovic, Fischhoff and Lichtenstein, 1979; 1980), and for that reason their associated behaviours differ as well. The US population is free-willed, mobile and not fond of being ordered to take action by those in authority. As will be discussed later, there are several behavioural tendencies that may make planning for a nuclear attack different from planning for flash floods.

Going on a camping trip

'You should take those items you would take on a camping trip for a minimum of two weeks', advises a model emergency operations plan developed by FEMA (1980). 'Leave your pets at home, however, in the basement with two weeks of food and water.' Opponents of nuclear attack planning object to the message communicated by such instructions. Is not leaving your home during the nuclear attack more serious than leaving your home on a vacation? Families are even advised to take books, games and toys. That a crisis evacuation could last longer than two weeks seems not worth disseminating to the general public. Nor does it seem worth mentioning that there may not be a home to return to after the attack.

Just as Churcher and Lievan (1983, p. 122) have found in their study of UK civil defence planners' internal documents, these instructions present 'an image of nuclear war as short and survivable, with well-organized authorities in control and a relatively rapid return to normality after the attack'. Here again, the contrast between nuclear and non-nuclear disasters comes into sharp focus. We cannot think about nuclear holocaust in the same terms as natural disasters. As Baum, Fleming and Davidson (1983) have argued, nuclear and many other technological disasters are not 'over and done with' as are natural disasters. If, as Hewitt (1983, p. 279) suggests, 'one can forsee an agonisingly slow, inconsequential, but ecologically devastating warring continuing for years or decades', crisis relocation planning seems poorly adapted.

Human behaviour: the evacuation shadow phenomenon

The catastrophic potential of nuclear attack, the dread with which people view ionising radiation, and the delayed, transgenerational characteristics of the nuclear hazard make any disaster of nuclear origin qualitatively different from other disasters. Because nuclear hazard perceptions differ from those of natural hazards, behavioural responses will differ as well. Plans built on assumptions about human behaviour during floods and hurricanes may be unworkable during nuclear disasters. Also unworkable may be plans that presume to control human behaviour rather than take advantage of the natural protective inclinations of the population. One plan developed for the evacuation of New York City, for instance, includes instructions that all cars should be transporting three or more people; those with any fewer will be required to stop so that passenger loads can be consolidated and extra vehicles abandoned. Is such a directive workable or in the best interest of the evacuation process? How many emergency workers would it take to count the number of passengers in outbound cars, let alone select car loads for amalgamation?

Americans today are mobile and free to act upon their perceptions. If the 1979 disaster at Pennsylvania's Three Mile Island (TMI) nuclear generating station is even a rough indication of how people perceive and respond to nuclear threats, then we can expect a significant gap between how officials expect people to react and how they actually will react. At TMI only pregnant women and preschool children within five miles of the plant (about 3000 individuals) were advised to evacuate their homes. But what should have been a limited evacuation turned into one of mammoth proportions, with over 144,000 people leaving the area within 15 miles of the plant and thousands more from as far as 25 miles away from the threatening reactor (Flynn, 1979; Zeigler, Brunn and Johnson, 1981). More recently we found that, in the event of a hypothetical emergency, residents' intentions to evacuate the area around New York's Shoreham nuclear power station would produce a similar experience to that of TMI (Johnson and Zeigler, 1983; Zeigler and Johnson, 1984). According to our social survey there, an evacuation advisory directed at everyone within ten miles of the Shoreham plant (about 4 per cent of Long Island's total population) would prompt half of all Long Island households to evacuate; only 19 per cent indicated that they intended to follow directions in the event of a general emergency severe enough to warrant a ten-mile evacuation advisory.

My colleagues and I have termed this high level of spontantous evacuation the 'evacuation shadow phenomenon' – the tendency of people to evacuate from a wider area than was officially designated (Zeigler, Brunn and Johnson, 1981). The extensive evacuation shadow which developed around TMI was perhaps the most significant behavioural response of the local population. If the threat of a radiological accident at a nuclear power plant is enough to cause such a geographically widespread 'over-response' to official advisories, what could we expect in the face of the ultimate nuclear hazard, thermonuclear war? Is it not reasonable to expect extensive evacuation shadows to materialise around all high-risk areas portrayed in figure 8.1? In all likelihood, the evacuation will not be limited to the areas which have been officially advised to evacuate. Although FEMA's director has recently cited spontaneous movement as a strong argument for developing evacuation plans and capabilities, current planning does not seem to have accepted the geographical realities of spontaneous evacuation in response to nuclear disasters. It may assume spontaneous evacuation from within the high-risk zone, but it does not seem to occur to planners that there will also be significant numbers leaving from the periphery.

Twenty miles or two hundred?

It is not likely that evacuees from high-risk zones in the USA will conform to expectations when it comes to selecting places to stay while away from home. The purpose of evacuating is to protect yourself and your family as completely as possible from the effects of nuclear weapons. Since geographical distance is perceived to be the best protection, evacuees will try to maximise that distance. Unlike evacuations from other disasters, there will probably be little pereived benefit in staying close to home and much in retreating to the lowest-risk part of the host areas. The distance which evacuees put between themselves and the threatening reactor at Three Mile Island betrays the fear with which people view nuclear hazards. That was the longest evacuation ever recorded (Flynn, 1979; Zeigler, Brunn and Johnson, 1981): over half of the evacuees fled over 100 miles from their residences, a response very different from that in other nature- and technology-induced evacuations. Few of those who evacuate are likely to be satisfied with destinations on the margins of the high-risk zones, margins which will themselves be characterised by high rates of spontaneous evacuation. Indeed, at Three Mile Island the vast majority of evacuees originated from beyond the official evacuation zone. Yet crisis relocation plans for nuclear attack do not consider such natural human inclinations.

In the Norfolk–Portsmouth–Virginia Beach metropolitan area of southeastern Virginia, for instance, each city has been assigned to a specific host community beyond the risk zone. If the crisis relocation plan were to be implemented, Norfolk residents would be routed to a small town 150 miles away, while those of neighbouring Portsmouth would be routed to portions of Suffolk, only 20 miles away. Can the people of Portsmouth be expected to feel secure when they are only marginally beyond the high-risk zone? Can the people of Suffolk be expected to remain in place while the metropolitan population pours through their community, bound for safer destinations farther west? If not, they too may be expected to head west, creating unexpectedly crowded conditions in villages and small towns there. Under other circumstances, evacuees might be expected to take refuge with family and friends rather than in public shelters, but in a nuclear war not everyone who wanted to evacuate would be able to find private accommodation in rural areas.

Evacuees from impending nuclear attack originate from both the high-risk zones and the territories beyond. They will not be satisfied with locations only 20 miles from where the bombs are supposed to land. After all, bombs do not always arrive on target; and fallout spreads from the point of impact covering vast areas in unpredictable geographical patterns shaped by the winds. On the other hand, some populations may refuse to move at all, a process resulting possibly from the 'psychic numbing' described by Janis (1962); or many could be so overwhelmed with the enormity of the disaster that they could closely conform with emergency directives.

Role conflict

Evacuation plans assume that there will be no conflicting loyalties among emergency workers. But these workers might well have a conflict and resolve it by choosing to be with their families in host communities beyond the high-risk zone, rather than at their assigned posts in target areas. This role conflict is likely to be an even more serious problem during nuclear emergencies than during other technological and natural disasters. Disaster research suggests that families make every effort to assemble before taking any action during a disaster and also tend to evacuate as a unit. This may conflict with responsibilities to help to manage or direct the disaster response. Role conflict may result in the non-response or delayed response of key emergency management people.

Prototype emergency response plans assume that key workers, needed to keep strategic industries operating, will be satisfied to remain behind or be relocated in the closest host areas, from where they can commute. They also assume that other personnel will automatically stay behind to direct traffic, drive buses and ambulances and help remove institutionalised populations from the high-risk zone. These people, however, may end up resolving their role conflict in favour of their families, who may be loath to let them remain in or return to target areas. At TMI, role conflict created severe problems for physicians, nurses and technicians in area hospitals (Smith and Fisher, 1981; Maxwell, 1982) and for nuclear power plant personnel (Kasl, Chisholm and Eskenazi, 1981). In New York, the

Nuclear Regulatory Commission threatened to shut down the Indian Point plants because bus drivers had testified that they would be reluctant to enter a radiation zone (Zuckerman, 1984, p. 110). Research near the Shoreham nuclear power station has also indicated a serious potential for role conflict among volunteer firemen and bus drivers, and around the Diablo Canyon reactor in California schoolteachers were found to be subject to role conflict pressures (Zeigler, Johnson and Brunn, 1983).

Ordering an evacuation

We assume that the President of the United States will be perspicacious enough to know when an attack is coming, presumably a week ahead of time, and when to issue an evacuation order. This assumption is another key component of the idealised scenario painted by the proponents of civil defence planning. In reality, we should expect that a diversity of information and opinion – factual and fanciful, responsible and irresponsible – will make it very difficult for anyone to know when to order an evacuation. Once again, we seem to be thinking of evacuation from a nuclear attack as being an analog of the tactical evacuations of the Second World War. What will complicate the decision on when to evacuate will be the absolute necessity to decide a week ahead of time, in response not to a specific incident such as a missile launch but to a set of circumstances that point, however ambiguously, to impending attack.

Because so many factors favour an early evacuation and so many factors weigh against, there is unlikely to be consensus on when to begin crisis relocation. Already, one major study (Gastil, 1969) seems to be permeated by a concern that encouraging evacuation prematurely would threaten the war effort by reducing our 'production capabilities'. And an early evacuation runs a greater risk of being unneeded. Moreover, the earlier the evacuation commences before the attack, the longer will evacuees have to be supported in host areas, increasing both the cost of the evacuation and the risk of running out of supplies before the attack even begins.

On the other hand, if the order comes too late there may be no time even to begin an evacuation, or else the blast may occur while the relocation effort is in progress. If political officials wait until the signs of attack are abundantly clear because they fear 'crying wolf', it may be too late for crisis relocation to do much good.

The government risks losing credibility in such circumstances and would undoubtedly be accused of having known that an attack was imminent but not advising protective action. To order an evacuation of two-thirds of the US population will not be an easy decision; yet, to know the optimal time to send people scattering is one of the most critical components of a successful strategic evacuation.

Urban interdependence replaced by rural self-reliance

In our highly interdependent urban society, long-distance lifelines supply us with an abundance of necessities and amenities. We take these interconnections for granted and know very little about the man-made food chains and resource networks that span the globe to bring us the best of earth's bounty. We thus tend to underestimate the life-threatening problems that are bound to arise when these flows of food, water, energy and medicine are interrupted. Even the flow of information is likely to be interrupted by the electromagnetic pulse of the hydrogen bomb, which would destroy the microchips of telecommunications, computer and surveillance systems. National and international interdependence have largely replaced local and regional self-reliance. Yet in the event of a nuclear war, rural host areas (themselves dependent on nearby cities) would have to become as self-sufficient as possible – perhaps only for a few weeks, but possibly for years. Since cities, all of them high-risk bombing targets, occupy the strategic foci of the transport network, their annihilation would also disrupt long-distance transportation. It is doubtful, first, that urban populations would know how to exploit the local resource base and, second, that the local resource base could be coaxed into producing enough for city-sized masses, particularly in the absence of capital and technology.

By virtue of its host-city designation, Greenfield, Massachusetts, with a population of 18,000, would swell to 176,000 during a nuclear crisis. Platt (1984), in a critique of the crisis relocation plan, estimated that 26,000 truckloads of earth would be needed for fallout protection, along with 22,500 55-gallon drums of water for two weeks in shelters and enough food and medicine to supply city-size numbers of people in country-size places. Food would ostensibly come through 'ordinary commercial channels' (Billheimer, 1976), albeit under extraordinary circumstances, and all evacuees would be expected to bring two weeks' worth of food with them. In terms of medical needs, Panofsky (1966) correctly observed almost two decades ago that civil defence is geared towards the 'well population'. During a nuclear war, the demand for drugs and medical expertise would increase exponentially, while the supply would be close to nil. Sickness and death would affect nearly everybody, either directly or indirectly, as exposure, malnutrition and radiation poisoning took their toll. Nuclear war planners fail to understand the geographically complx human ecosystems which supply us with even the basic necessities of life. Although they will lack the physical infrastructures and the extensive tributary regions that provide city populations with their biological needs, rural host areas will have to function as cities during a crisis. Planning for life in host areas is no task to be permeated with glib assumptions about the availability of food, water and medical supplies – but to acknowledge this fact undermines the cause of civil defence and emphasises the maleficence of nuclear war rather than its survivability.

Does population dispersal fuel the arms race?

Crisis relocation planning is designed to defend the population in the event of war, but critics maintain that it is an offensive weapon in defensive clothing. As Gayler (1982) has put it, 'Our civil defence program will generate requirements for even more nuclear warheads, just as Russian civil defence generates requirements for more of ours.' In essence, a densely settled population requires fewer warheads to exterminate them than a population that is spread out over rural areas. Every time one side improves its civil defence plan, it forces the other side to devise a host of new malevolent retaliations. As the population is dispersed, for instance, we become more intent on developing the potential to retarget nuclear warheads to new population clusters. Just as the development of elaborate Soviet civil defence plans precipitated a US effort to beef up its civil defence efforts, so US planning will encourage a response on the part of the USSR to reduce the USA's ability to withstand attack.

Proponents believe that civil defence is instituted only as a safeguard and has no impact on the risks of a nuclear war. Opponents contend that civil defence plans actually increase the risks of nuclear war. If a nation believes that 80 per cent or more of its population will survive, it will perceive the consequences to be less disastrous and thus will be more likely to launch a nuclear attack. As Platt (1984) put it, the more that civil defence planning 'succeeds in diminishing public fears of nuclear war, the less security it provides since it enhances willingness to risk catastrophe'. Thus the mentality of a military arms race seeps into the fabric of civilian society. Now we can add new civilian defence plans to the list of new offensive weapons, new early warning systems, new basing systems and new intelligence-gathering networks, all of which have moved civilisation along the path to armed destruction.

Conclusions

We are caught in a nuclear arms race that seems to make civil defence planning a necessity. Perhaps the majority of US citizens do favour civil defence, but currents of opposition are strong and questions about its efficacy are being raised with increasing frequency. The questions arising from the public, however, are different from the questions that civil defence planners seem prepared to answer. The contrast seems to be best characterised by Panofsky (1966, p. 17), who has pointed out that 'the easy technical questions have been "over-analysed" while the hard questions have been "under-analysed'". Indeed, because of the unprecedented nature of nuclear war, some of the hard questions, many of which are geographical in scope, seem to have no answers. For this reason Mitchell (1984) has argued that we have overemphasised emergency management (what we do before, during and after an emergency) and neglected hazard mitigation (what we do to reduce our susceptibility to the hazard).

If 'integrated emergency management' is pursued, however, we must understand that the presumption of similarity between natural and technological disasters may undermine any plans for population protection during a nuclear war. If we can use our knowledge of nuclear power plant accidents as a basis for suggesting likely patterns of human response to another – indeed, the ultimate – nuclear hazard, then people are likely to react quite differently from the obedient automatons conjured up by crisis relocation planners who have not grasped the significance of the evacuation shadow phenomenon, long-distance spontaneous relocations and role conflict among emergency personnel. Nor have they used geography's ecological approach to analyse the problems of supporting city populations in rural shells. Questions about the duration of evacuation, the timing of an evacuation order and the overall efficacy of population protection are treated only in idealised scenarios of what might happen in a nuclear war. Why? Perhaps because, for a civil defence plan to work as a strategic weapon, not just a protective strategy, both sides must fully believe in its effectiveness. To civil defence planners, believing that the plans will work and convincing the enemy of this may be more important than assuring that they can be operationalised to save not only lives, but human society.

References

Baum, A., Fleming, R. and Davidson, L.M. (1983), 'Natural disaster and technological catastrophe', *Environment and Behaviour*, 15, 333–54.

Billheimer, J.W. (1976), 'Food for evacuees: meeting the distribution problem', *Foresight*, 3, 8–13.

Blanchard, B.W. (1979), *American Civil Defense 1945–1975*. PhD dissertation, University of Virginia.

Churcher, J. and Lieven, E.V.M. (1983), 'Images of nuclear war and the public in British civil defence planning documents', *Journal of Social Issues*, 39, 117–32.

Douglas, J.D. Jr (1983), 'Strategic planning and nuclear insecurity', *Orbis*, 27, 667–94.

FEMA (Federal Emergency Management Agency) (1980), *Blue Print for Emergency Response*. Washington, DC: FEMA.

FEMA (1982), *High Risk Areas for Civil Nuclear Defence Planning Purposes*. Washington, DC: FEMA.

Flynn, C.B. (1979), *Three Mile Island Telephone Survey*. Washington, DC: US Nuclear Regulatory Commission.

Gastil, R.D. (1969), *Scenario for Post-Attack Social Organization: Final Report*. Croton-on-Hudson, NY: Hudson Institute.

Gayler, N. (1982), *Statement before the Arms Control Subcommittee of the Foreign Relations Committee of the US Senate*. Washington, DC: US Government Printing Office.

Gouré, L. (1982), 'Soviet views on, and some characteristics of, USSR civil defense', *Hearings, US Senate*. Washington, DC: US Government Printing Office.

Gouré, L. (1983), *The Soviet Crisis Relocation Program*. McLean, Va.: Science Applications.

Hewitt, K. (1983), 'Place annihilation: area bombing and the fate of urban places', *Annals of the Association of American Geographers*, 73, 257–84.

Janis, I.L. (1962), 'Psychological effects of warnings', in G. W. Baker and D. W. Chapman (eds), *Man and Society in Disaster*. New York: Basic Books.

Johnson, J.H. Jr and Zeigler, D.J. (1983), 'Distinguishing human reponses to radiological emergencies', *Economic Geography*, 59, 386–402.

Kasl, D., Chisholm, R.F. and Eskenazi, B. (1981), 'The impact of the accident at Three Mile Island on the behaviour and well-being of nuclear workers', *American Journal of Public Health*, 71, 474–95.

Maxwell, C. (1982), 'Hospital organizational response to the nuclear accident at Three Mile Island', *American Journal of Public Health*, 72, 275–79.

Mitchell, James K. (1984), 'Nuclear war and hazards research'. Paper presented at the annual meeting of the Association of American Geographers, Washington, DC.

Panofsky, W.K.H. (1966), 'Civil defense as insurance and as military strategy', in E. Eyring (ed.), *Civil Defense*. Washington, DC: American Association for the Advancement of Science.

Perry, R.W. (1982), *The Social Psychology of Civil Defense*. Lexington, Mass.: Lexington Books.

Platt, R.H. (1984), 'The planner and nuclear crisis relocation', *Journal of the American Planning Association*, 50, 259–60.

Slovic, P., Fischhoff, B. and Lichtenstein, S. (1979), 'Rating the risks', *Environment*, 21, 14–20, 36–9.

Slovic, P., Fischhoff, B. and Lichtenstein, S. (1980), 'Facts and fears: understanding perceived risk', in R. C. Schwing and W. A. Albers Jr (eds), *Societal Risk Assessment*. New York: Plenum Press, pp. 181–214.

Smith, J.S. and Fisher, J.H. (1981), 'Three Mile Island: the silent disaster', *Journal of the American Medical Association*, 245, 1656–9.

Wieseltier, L. (1983), *Nuclear War, Nuclear Peace*. New York: Holt, Rinehart, and Winston.

Zeigler, D.J., Brunn, S.D. and Johnson, J.H. Jr (1981), 'Evacuation from a nuclear technological disaster', *Geographical Review*, 71, 1–16.

Zeigler, D.J. and Johnson, J.H. Jr (1984), 'Evacuation behavior in response to nuclear power plant accidents', *Professional Geographer*, 36, 207–15.

Zeigler, D.J., Johnson, J.H. Jr and Brunn, S.D. (1983), *Technological Hazards*. Washington, DC: Association of American Geographers.

Zuckerman, E. (1984), *The Day After World War III*. New York: Viking Press.

PART III

The Geography of Peace

CHAPTER 9

Nuclear Weapon Free Zones

Frank Barnaby

In plain language, a totally nuclear weapon free zone is an area from which nuclear weapons are excluded. The area covered may be part of a country, a whole country or a number of countries in a region. Nuclear weapons would never be allowed in a nuclear weapon free zone under any circumstances; for example, a nuclear weapon power would not be allowed to land military aircraft carrying nuclear weapons in any country which is part of a nuclear weapon free zone.

A legal definition of a nuclear weapon free zone is given in a United Nations Resolution of 11 December 1975. It is a zone

> recognised as such by the UN General Assembly, which any group of states, in the free exercise of their sovereignty, has established by virtue of a treaty or convention whereby: (a) the statute of total absence of nuclear weapons to which the zone shall be subject, including the procedure for the delimitation of the zone, is defined; and (b) an international system of verification and control is established to guarantee compliance with the obligations derived from that statute.

It would be normal for countries joining a nuclear weapon free zone to ratify a treaty establishing the zone. In a typical treaty the parties would commit themselves to use any nuclear material and facilities under their jurisdiction exclusively for peaceful purposes. They would agree not to produce, or to acquire in any way, or to test, nuclear weapons and to prohibit the storage, receipt, installation or deployment of any other country's nuclear weapons.

For the purposes of a treaty, nuclear weapons could be defined as follows (as in the Treaty of Tlatelolco):

> A nuclear weapon is any device which is capable of releasing nuclear energy in an uncontrolled manner and which has a group of characteristics that are appropriate for use for warlike purposes. An instrument that may be used for the transport or propulsion of the

device is not included in this definition if it is separable from the device and not an indivisible part thereof.

A nuclear weapon free zone agreement could be verified by the International Atomic Energy Agency (IAEA). In this case, each party to the treaty would negotiate an agreement with the IAEA whereby the Agency's safeguards would be applied to its peaceful nuclear activities. Or a Supervisory Commission could be set up by the parties to carry out inspections in their territories to verify compliance with the obligations in the treaty.

It should be noted that the Treaty on the Non-Proliferation of Nuclear Weapons (NPT) commits the non-nuclear-weapon parties to the Treaty

not to receive the transfer from any transferor whatsoever of nuclear weapons or other nuclear explosive devices or of control over such weapons or explosive devices directly, or indirectly; not to manufacture or otherwise acquire nuclear weapons or other nuclear explosive devices; and not to seek or receive any assistance in the manufacture of nuclear weapons or other nuclear explosive devices.

Thus, if a region contains a group of countries that have ratified the NPT it automatically is a nuclear weapon free zone – provided that these countries also refuse to allow existing nuclear weapon states to deploy nuclear weapons on their territory. However, the NPT does allow such deployment if the weapons remain under the control of the nuclear weapon state that owns them.

One of the problems in establishing nuclear weapon free zones is to decide what to do about peaceful nuclear explosions. Some Third World countries want to retain the right to manufacture their own nuclear explosives for peaceful purposes. The snag is that technically there is essentially no difference between peaceful and military nuclear explosives.

The problem should have been solved by the NPT. This treaty contains a legal obligation to make available to parties the 'potential benefits from any peaceful applications of nuclear explosions' at a cost to be kept 'as low as possible' and to 'exclude any charge for research and development'. The NPT envisaged an international body to supervise any peaceful nuclear explosion in non-nuclear-weapon states. But the international arrangements for the supply and supervision of peaceful nuclear explosives have not yet been set up.

The Treaty for the Prohibition of Nuclear Weapons in Latin America, or Treaty of Tlatelolco (the Latin American Treaty), solves the peaceful nuclear explosion problem by allowing the parties to carry them out under the observation and supervision of the IAEA. In practice, however, no party to the Latin American Treaty has been in a position to produce and use a nuclear explosion for peaceful purposes – or in fact has desired to make a peaceful nuclear explosion. Attitudes to peaceful nuclear explosions, and the wish to retain the option of using them, constitute the main ostensible reason why a number of important Third World countries have kept out of the NPT and, in the case of Latin America, why they prefer the Latin American Treaty to the NPT.

Existing nuclear weapon free zones

Nuclear weapon free zones have been established in a number of uninhabited regions. The Antarctic Treaty, signed in 1959, declares the Antarctic an area to be used exclusively for peaceful purposes. Any nuclear explosion is banned in the area.

The 1967 Outer Space Treaty Prohibits placing in orbit around the earth any objects carrying nuclear weapons or any other kinds of weapons of mass destruction, the installation of such weapons on celestial bodies, or their stationing in outer space in any other manner.

The 1971 Seabed Treaty prohibits emplanting or emplacing on the seabed and the ocean floor, or in their subsoil, nuclear weapons or any other types of weapons of mass destruction as well as structures, launching installations or any other facilities specifically designed for storing, testing or using such weapons (this generally applies beyond a 12-mile shore zone). The SALT II Treaty, signed in 1979 by the USA and the USSR but not yet ratified by the US Senate, prohibits the two superpowers from developing, testing or deploying fixed ballistic or cruise missile launchers in or on the seabed, the ocean floor or the beds of inland waters. SALT II also bans mobile launchers for such missiles which move only in contact with the ocean floor, the seabed or the beds of internal waters or inland waters.

These three nuclear weapon free zones were relatively easy to negotiate because the military have little interest in the activities which are banned, and because the environments concerned are uninhabited. The Antarctic Treaty is interesting, however, because it established for the first time a control system based on national verification. Each party has the right to carry out inspections in the Antarctic by observers chosen from its nationals. The inspectors have complete freedom of access to any area at any time, including access to installations and all ships and aircraft at points of disembarking or embarking cargoes or people on the continent.

The only inhabited region of the earth to be declared a nuclear weapon-free zone is Latin America. The 1967 Treaty for the Prohibition of Nuclear Weapons in Latin America (Treaty of Tlatelolco) prohibits the testing, use, manufacture, production or acquisition by any means, as well as the receipt, storage, installation, deployment and any form of possession of any nuclear weapons, by Latin American countries. The parties should conclude agreements with IAEA for the application of safeguards to their nuclear activities.

The Tlatelolco Treaty established a system of international control under a permanent supervisory body, the Agency for the Prohibition of Nuclear Weapons in Latin America. The control system deals with suspected violations of the Treaty; the measures to be taken in case of violation are spelt out. As in the Antarctic Treaty, the parties to the Tlatelolco Treaty accept on-site inspection. In this case the verification is international and administered by the IAEA; in the Antarctic Treaty verification is on a national basis. The Tlatelolco Treaty is also unusual for an arms control measure because it is a permanent treaty.

The Tlatelolco Treaty contains two protocols. Some countries – specifically the UK, the USA, France and the Netherlands – outside the region are legally responsible for territories lying within the limits of the geographical zone defined in the Treaty. These four countries undertake in Protocol I, to cooperate in keeping nuclear weapons out of the zone. Under Protocol II the nuclear weapon states agree to respect the denuclearisation of Latin America as defined in the Treaty, and they agree not to threaten to use nuclear weapons against the parties to the Treaty. (If the British had nuclear weapons on the ships of the naval task force sent to the Falklands during that war, it can be argued that they broke the spirit if not the law of the Latin American Treaty because the UK has ratified Protocol II.)

The Tlatelolco Treaty is in force for 22 Latin American states. Argentina, Brazil and Chile have signed it but it is not yet in force for them; Cuba, Guyana, Saint Lucia and Saint Vincent are outside the system. Protocol I is in force for the Netherlands, the UK and the USA; Protocol II is in force for China, France, the UK, the USA and the USSR. France has signed but not ratified Protocol I.

The Latin American nuclear weapon free zone was established because of a common political will for it in the region. It was seen as a way to improve the security of the states there, and it contains 'negative security' guarantees from the nuclear weapon states – that they will not use, or threaten to use, nuclear weapons against the parties to the Treaty. Much of the credit for obtaining the Treaty goes to one man, the Mexican diplomat and ex-Foreign Minister Garcia Robles, who was awarded the Nobel peace price for his efforts.

Proposed nuclear weapon free zones

Although only one inhabited region – Latin America – has been established as a nuclear weapon free zone, many other areas have been proposed (Delcoigne, 1982; Lodgaard and Thee, 1984). Perhaps the most famous proposal was that made in 1957 by Adam Rapacki, the then Foreign Minister of Poland. At the UN General Assembly, Poland offered to prohibit the production and stockpiling of nuclear weapons on its territory if both East and West Germany would do the same. Czechoslovakia, East Germany and the USSR supported the Rapacki plan. It might have succeeded but for the opposition of West German Chancellor, Konrad Adenauer.

Proposals for a nuclear weapon free zone in central Europe seem to have been abandoned, at least by governments. Central Europe is, of course, the region in which it is most urgent to establish a nuclear weapon free zone (Blechman and More, 1983). It is here that the military alliances stand face to face. About 10,000 nuclear warheads have been assigned to the region by NATO and the Warsaw Treaty Organisation.

A nuclear war in Europe would almost certainly escalate to a strategic nuclear war between the superpowers. A nuclear world war would destroy the Northern Hemisphere and severely damage the Southern Hemisphere. Since a nuclear weapon free zone would reduce the danger of nuclear war in Europe by removing battlefield nuclear weapons, it would considerably increase world security. The modernisation of battlefield nuclear weapons in Europe would lead to the deployment of tactical nuclear weapons seen to be useful for fighting a nuclear war; and the deployment of significant numbers of nuclear war fighting weapons in Europe would lead to the perception that a nuclear war in Europe is 'fightable and winnable', a perception that would increase the probability of nuclear war.

Western objections to proposals for a nuclear weapon free zone in central Europe revolve around questions of verification, the dependence of NATO on the first and early use of nuclear weapons in any major war in Europe, and perceived differences in the geopolitics of the USA and the USSR.

There have been recent attempts to revive interest in making at least part of central Europe free of nuclear weapons. For example, the Report of the Independent Commission on Disarmament and Security Issues, under the chairmanship of Olaf Palme (now the Prime Minister of Sweden), recommends a nuclear-free zone, or strip, 300 kilometres wide centred on the East–West German border. No nuclear weapons would be allowed in the zone (see figure 9.1). It would contain parts of West Germany, East Germany and Czechoslovakia. But, unlike the Rapacki plan, it would leave some of all three countries available for the deployment of nuclear weapons with ranges greater than 150 kilometres. It was felt by the Independent Commission that this difference might make the 300 kilometre nuclear weapon free zone more acceptable to the West than the Rapacki plan was. The idea was eventually to extend the zone to the northern and southern flanks of the alliances.

Although the USSR has endorsed this proposal, NATO countries are

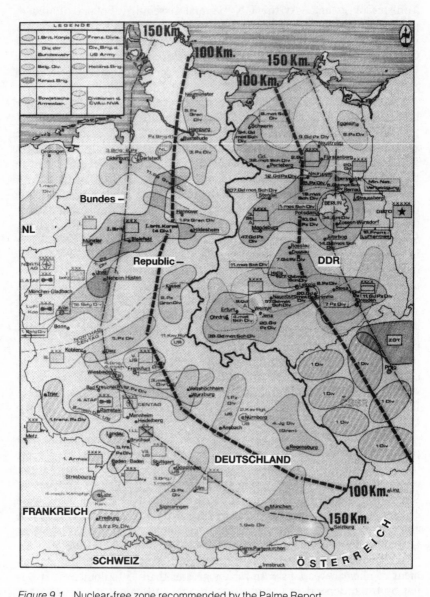

Figure 9.1   Nuclear-free zone recommended by the Palme Report.
(*Source:* Berg and Lodgaard, 1983)

not enthusiastic about it even though there is increasing opposition within NATO circles to battlefield nuclear weapons. These are usually regarded, however, as weapons with ranges greater than 30 or so kilometres, and so a 300 kilometre zone in NATO may be seen as too wide.

The Palme Commission thought that the successful negotiation of a 300 kilometre nuclear weapon free zone should be accompanied by measures to restrain conventional offensive weapons and chemical weapons in the zone. It was, in other words, seen as leading to a disengagement zone in central Europe. Specifically, the implementation of such a denuclearised zone could be linked with an agreement, at the mutual and balanced forces reduction negotiations in Vienna, to limit conventional forces in central Europe.

One proposal which seems to be acquiring a new lease of life is that for a Balkans nuclear weapon free zone. This has some support from the present governments of Bulgaria, Greece, Yugoslavia and Romania. The idea is that all Balkan states should become members of the zone; except for Albania, all are already parties to the NPT. Given the importance of the region to both alliances, though, it is unlikely that the establishment of a Balkans nuclear weapon free zone will be an easy process because of the opposition of some countries (like Turkey) in the Balkans.

Nor will it be easy to establish a nuclear weapon free zone in the Nordic region, another proposal under discussion. President Kekkonen of Finland proposed a Nordic zone in 1963, to include Denmark, Sweden, Norway, Finland and possibly Iceland. In 1981 the USSR indicated its willingness to discuss its nuclear weapons targeted on the Nordic region. The USA, however, argues that a Nordic nuclear weapon free zone would be destabilising and would make arms control negotiations more difficult. Nevertheless, all Nordic countries are *de facto* nuclear weapon free; although Norway and Denmark are members of NATO, they will not have nuclear weapons deployed on their territory.

The UN General Assembly has devoted particular attention to, and passed resolutions about, nuclear weapon free zones in Africa, the Middle East, South Asia, the Pacific and the Indian Ocean. The problem in Africa is South Africa, which according to many has, or soon will have, nuclear weapons. Moreover, many other African states are not parties to the NPT. In South Asia, differences between India and Pakistan are a major difficulty, with India arguing that South Asia cannot be separated from Asia and the Indian Ocean.

A major obstacle to the establishment of a nuclear weapon free zone in the Middle East is the probable development of nuclear weapons by Israel. The attack by Israel in 1981 on an Iraqi nuclear installation also adversely affected the already dim prospects for a nuclear weapon free zone in the region.

The main impetus for proposals for a nuclear weapon free zone in the

South Pacific comes from the continuing French nuclear weapon tests in the region. The Australian Labor Party has, since the early 1960s, advocated such a zone. Its recent re-election, and that of the New Zealand Labour Party, has stimulated speculation about renewed attempts to negotiate a zone. The small island countries in the region, led by Fiji, are pushing the concept; they complain that they receive scant support from the major powers in the region.

The importance of establishing nuclear weapon free zones in oceans

Perhaps the most important regions for the establishment of nuclear weapon free zones – apart from central Europe – are the oceans, at least in so far as world security is concerned. The territory of states can be covered by the NPT if they wish to renounce land-based nuclear weapons. (It is true, of course, that the NPT does not prevent a party from allowing a nuclear weapon state to deploy nuclear weapons on its territory provided that the nuclear weapons remain under the ownership and control of the nuclear weapon state. So in this sense a nuclear weapon free zone is superior, for the participants would usually not be allowed to have any nuclear weapons on their territory, no matter who owned them.)

The importance of the oceans in this context is that they are being used by the major powers to deploy large numbers of nuclear weapons, and for anti-submarine warfare activities. The danger for world security of this situation provides the impetus for proposals that the Indian Ocean should be declared a 'zone of peace'. Such zones date back to 1964, when Sri Lanka suggested the concept to the UN. Since then it has been realised in numerous resolutions adopted by the UN General Assembly. Basically, the concept is that the great powers should halt the further escalation and expansion of their military presence in the Indian Ocean, and eliminate from the Indian Ocean all bases, military installations and facilities, and the deployment of nuclear weapons.

The importance of the oceans to the superpowers can be appreciated by considering, for example, their use of them for operating fleets of strategic nuclear submarines which carry ballistic missiles with nuclear warheads. This use is becoming more crucial since both the USA and the USSR have improved the accuracy of their nuclear delivery systems and the yield-to-weight ratios of their nuclear warheads to such an extent that each country's land-based missiles can destroy the other's land-based missiles, and so each side is vulnerable to a surprise attack from the other. Strategic nuclear submarines are, however, still relatively invulnerable to a sudden attack. Neither side can detect and destroy instantaneously all of the other's strategic nuclear submarines at sea at any one time. But both sides are working on anti-submarine warfare (ASW) techniques for doing this.

If these efforts succeed, they may lead one side to believe that it can gain a large advantage in making a sudden first-strike nuclear attack on the other side. Such a perception would considerably increase the risk of a nuclear world war.

Strategic nuclear submarines

As of September 1983, the USSR was operating 62 strategic nuclear submarines and the USA was operating 34 (data in this section from SIPRI, 1984). The missiles carried by these submarines are targeted on cities and provide an element of assured destruction in the superpower nuclear policies. A single US strategic nuclear submarine, for example, carries about 160 warheads, enough to destroy every Soviet city with a population of more than about 200,000 people. US cities are targeted by Soviet strategic nuclear submarines to the same extent that Soviet cities are by US submarines. Just four strategic nuclear submarines on appropriate stations in the oceans could destroy most of the major cities in the Northern Hemisphere.

In 1980 the USSR launched a very big strategic nuclear submarine, the Typhoon. The Typhoon is 160 metres long and displaces, when submerged, 25,000 tons. It carries 20 submarine-launched ballistic missiles (SLBMs). Each Typhoon will carry the newest Soviet SLBM, the SS-N-20. The missile is more accurate than other Soviet SLBMs and carries between six and nine multiple independently targetable re-entry vehicles (MIRVs) over a range of about 8300 kilometres.

In September 1983, the USSR had about 7700 independently targetable warheads deployed in its strategic nuclear forces, with a total delivery capability of approximately 6000 megatons. Of the Soviet warheads, about 23 per cent are on SLBMs, 73 per cent are on intercontinental ballistic missiles (ICBMs) and about 4 per cent on long-range bombers. Of the Soviet megatonnage, 12 per cent is carried on SLBMs and 83 per cent on ICBMs.

The USA now operates two types of SLBM, the Poseidon and the Trident-1. Each Poseidon missile carries, on average, 10 warheads (the maximum number is 14); each Trident-1 carries, on average, 8 (the maximum number is probably 10, although some sources say 14). The maximum range of the Poseidon SLBM is 4600 kilometres; that of the Trident-1 is 7400 kilometres (IISS, 1984).

The US Navy, as of September 1983, could deliver 568 SLBMs, carrying a total of about 5150 warheads with a total delivery capability of about 360 megatons. Of these warheads, about 3100 are ready for immediate launch. Of the US nuclear warheads, 53 per cent are carried on SLBMs, 22 per cent on ICBMs and 25 per cent on strategic bombers. Of the total

US megatonnage, 9 per cent is carried on SLBMs, 33 per cent on ICBMs and 58 per cent on bombers.

Modern strategic nuclear submarines are huge. The Trident (Ohio-class) submarine, for example, is twice as big as its predecessor, the Poseidon (Lafayette-class); the former is a 170 metre long boat, displacing 18,700 tons. The Soviet Typhoon is even bigger than the Trident submarine.

Trident and Typhoon submarines may be deployed under the Arctic icepack, well hidden but still in range of their targets. The Trident submarine, for example, will have a patrol period of 70 days. The period is limited by the stamina of the 164-man crew rather than by the endurance of the submarine; theoretically, the latter could remain submerged for the lifetime of the reactor fuel elements, a few years.

It should be possible for the US Navy to keep about two-thirds of the Trident fleet at sea at any one time, whereas only about a half of the Poseidon submarines are at sea at any one time. These fractions are much higher than those which the Soviets achieve. Only about one in eight of the Soviet strategic nuclear submarines are at sea at any one time – that means a total of about eight submarines. This is because of a shortage of trained crews and the high cost of maintaining and operating the submarines.

Another disadvantage of the Soviet submarine fleet is geographical. The submarines have to pass through relatively narrow channels to get out from their bases to the Atlantic and Pacific Oceans. On the Atlantic side, for example, they have to pass through the channel north of Scotland to Iceland and up to the ice. This channel and the one through which the submarines have to pass to get out into the Pacific are monitored by the West, so that it is known when a Soviet submarine goes into the oceans. US strategic nuclear submarines, on the other hand, have total access to both the Atlantic and Pacific Oceans.

Anti-submarine warfare (ASW)

As described above, a crucial component in the USSR–US nuclear arms race is the efforts being made on both sides to develop effective ASW techniques. Strategic ASW aims to limit severely the damage which the other side can do in a retaliatory attack with its submarine-launched ballistic missiles, by being able to detect and swiftly destroy all the enemy's strategic nuclear submarines at sea at the time. Success here would, of course, enhance perceptions of a nuclear first-strike capability. Of all naval developments, there is little doubt that those in strategic ASW are potentially the greatest threat to world security, in that they may significantly contribute to increasing the probability of a nuclear world war.

There is unusual secrecy about ASW developments. For example, the US Navy is working with blue–green lasers to detect submarines, possibly from satellites, but little is known about the progress of this work. From time to time statements are made, for example by US naval spokesmen, implying an existing capability to detect Soviet submarines, at least when they are close to the US coast. But we know few details about current strategic ASW capabilities. We can assume, though, that even in the absence of a technological breakthrough – which cannot, of course, be discounted – steady progress will be made in limiting the damage that can be done by enemy strategic nuclear submarines.

In ASW, detection is the critical element. Once detected, an enemy submarine can be destroyed relatively easily. Detection methods are being improved by increasing the sensitivity of sensors, improving the integration between various sensing systems and improving the computerised processing of data from all the sensors.

All types of ASW sensors are being further developed: electronic ones based on infrared, radar, lasers and optics; acoustic ones, including active and passive sonar; and magnetic ones, in which the disturbance to the earth's magnetic field caused by the presence of the submarine is measured. Airborne, space-borne, ocean–surface, and seabottom sensors are being increasingly integrated into detection systems which are thereby made more effective. ASW aircraft, surface ships and hunter–killer submarines are also being made more complementary to each other. Each system has its own characteristics, and their integration considerably improves the effectiveness of ASW activity as a whole.

ASW sanctuaries

Strategic ASW developments are extremely destabilising. To preserve the invulnerability of the sea-based nuclear deterrent – and thereby reduce the risk of a nuclear world war – by hindering ASW operations, it has been suggested that certain areas of the oceans should be declared ASW sanctuaries, so that strategic nuclear submarines can operate in them without fear of detection. Purver (1981), for example, has suggested that this could be achieved by a Polar Basin Treaty. He would first limit the treaty to the surface and seabed areas of the Polar Basin, which would prohibit such ASW systems as bottom-mounted or moored surveillance systems, moored mines and surface warships. This would seriously hamper ASW activities, and should be supported by the USSR, which deploys strategic nuclear submarines in the area. The West would, however, still retain control over the exit channels so that it could monitor the passage of Soviet submarines into the Atlantic.

Conclusions

As those that follow the proceedings at the United Nations and the Conference on Disarmament in Geneva will appreciate, great efforts have been made to negotiate nuclear weapon free zones. Progress has been slow. The many UN General Assembly resolutions have produced only one treaty covering an inhabited region: the Tlatelolco Treaty.

The main reason for this lack of progress is the absence of a firm political will to create nuclear weapon free zones. It is clear that a number of countries want to retain the option to produce nuclear weapons at some future date. Some countries in military alliances believe that their alliance policies would suffer if they did not allow the deployment of nuclear weapons on their territory. A first-use-of-nuclear-weapons policy is, of course, not compatible with membership of a nuclear weapon free zone. Unfortunately, there seem to be very few regions which do not contain countries that have objections to making the region nuclear weapon free. The effort to create nuclear weapon free zones must however go on, because such zones could be a crucial element in nuclear disarmament.

In the meantime, particular attention needs to be given to providing sanctuaries for strategic nuclear submarines to maintain their invulnerability, until far-reaching nuclear disarmament is achieved, in the face of continued progress in ASW techniques. A partial zone of peace in, for example, the Arctic would achieve this by banning military activities on the seabed and surface. Although a very primitive concept, this is probably the best we can hope for in the context of nuclear weapon free zones in the short term. The irony is that the purpose of the establishment of such a zone would be to enhance the survivability of a nuclear weapons system. The fact that such a thing can be regarded as very desirable is an indication of the parlous state of the nuclear arms race.

References

Berg, P. and Lodgaard, S. (1983), 'Disengagement zones: a step towards meaningful defence?' *Journal of Peace Research*, 20(1), 5–15.
Blechman, B. and Moore, M.R. (1983), 'A nuclear weapon-free zone in Europe', *Scientific American*, 248, 29–35.
Delcoigne, G. (1982), 'An overview of nuclear-weapon-free zones', *International Atomic Energy Bulletin*, 24, 50–5.
IISS (International Institute of Strategic Studies) (1984), *The Military Balance 1983–4*. London: IISS.
Lodgaard, S. and Thee, M. (eds) (1984), *Nuclear Disengagement in Europe*. London: Taylor and Francis.

Purver, R.G. (1981), *Arms Control in the North*, National Security Series no. 5, Queen's University, Kingston. Ontario: Centre for International Relations.

SIPRI (Stockholm International Peace Research Institute) (1984), *World Armaments and Disarmament*, SIPRI Yearbook. London: Taylor and Francis.

CHAPTER 10

The Geography of Peace Movements

Stanley D. Brunn

Peace movements, associations and organisations are an important part of the social and political fabric of an increasingly large number of local communities and countries in Europe and North America. Their activities are significant because they address timely local, national and global issues of disarmament, human rights, nuclear war, nuclear proliferation and pollution, draft resistance, ecological balance and the idea of a nuclear freeze. Some chapters and groups are involved directly in local and state politics, while others choose to influence opinion by working through and with other community organisations and associations. The activities of peace groups include conferences, workshops, political lobbying, letter-writing campaigns, speakers' bureaus, exchange programmes, awards and research into contemporary issues. The membership of peace movements and activities ranges from a few people in local study and action groups to major national and international organisations with memberships approaching 50,000 and networks of branches and regional offices.

In this chapter I shall examine the diversity, extent, purposes and activities of peace-related groups, the locations of their headquarters, the number of their branches or chapters and the scale of their networks. I will concentrate mainly on movements within the USA, though the appendix giving the current state of peace research also refers to European movements and those further afield.

Major peace organisations

Very many peace associations and organisations exist in North America (see Akey, 1984), Europe, the USSR, Japan, Australia, New Zealand and some countries in the developing world. Their orientation, objectives and goals may differ. While some may be religious in focus, others are concerned with nuclear war and disarmament, and still others about human rights violations. Many centres, fellowships and associations were established during the Vietnam War.

Some of the earliest peace groups were affiliated with religious communities, for example the Friends Peace Committee (est. 1892), International Fellowship of Reconciliation (1919), Jewish Peace Fellowship (1941) and Presbyterian Peace Fellowships (1943); or they were concerned about pacifism and the counselling of conscientious objectors, for example the Women's International League for Peace and Freedom (1915), War Resisters International (1921) and War Resisters League (1923).

The membership size of the groups ranges from over 50,000 (e.g. Coalition for Peace through Strength, War Resisters International, International Fellowship of Reconciliation, World Peace through Law and Women's International League for Peace and Freedom) to between 10,000 and 30,000 members (e.g. the National Peace Academy Campaign (federally funded), Clergy and Laity Concerned, Another Mother for Peace, Fellowship of Reconciliation, International Association of Educators for World Peace, World Association of Judges, US Peace Council, National Council for a World Peace Tax Fund and War Resisters League) to under 1000 members, of which there is a large number.

The location of the headquarters of these associations is important, in enabling them not only to associate with other groups, but also to contact the print and television media, lobbyists, government and non-government agencies and officials. The largest concentrations in the USA are in the Boston, New York City, Philadelphia and Washington DC areas; a smaller number is in southern California, while there is a scatter throughout the rest of the country. Outside the USA, Toronto, Geneva, London and Tokyo are notable centres for peace groups.

Activities

There is a wide and varied range of peace group activities. The Center for Nonviolent Alternatives is interested in developing renewable energy. The War Resistance League is concerned about class struggle, disarmament, feminism, nuclear power, prisons and training in non-violence. The World Association of Judges includes 15,000 members in almost all countries; it 'seeks to promote world peace through the expansion of the role of law in the world community and by advancing and improving the administration of justice of all peoples'. Most of the religious fellowships counsel conscientious objectors. Several groups are concerned about tax reform, tax resistance and escalating arms spending; included among these (in the USA) are the Center for Law and Pacifism, the Center for Nonviolent Alternatives, the National Council for a World Peace Tax Fund and the Conscience and Military Tax Campaign. Human rights are a major concern of Amnesty International, Humanitas International Human rights Committee, the National Coalition of American Nuns, the International Association for the Defense of Artists, the Center for International Policy and the Sakharov International Committee. The Latin American Human Rights Association, with headquarters in Quito, Ecuador, and offices in Washington DC, sponsors seminars, takes international delegates to countries where human rights are allegedly being violated, and supports families of prisoners and missing persons. The Irish National Caucus, headquartered in Washington DC, is an educational organisation concerned about protecting human rights in Northern Ireland; its interests include the desire for a United Ireland. The Bertrand Russell Peace Foundation aids political prisoners. The Episcopal Peace Fellowship provides support to prisoners and is concerned about capital punishment. Among those sponsoring international exchange programmes are the Christian Movement for Peace, Friends of the Peaceful Alternatives, International Peace Research Association and Peace Corps Partnership Program; Promoting Enduring Peace also has summer peace camps. The Peace Development Fund provides small grants to community groups to promote peace study and coordinate peace activities.

Some associations and groups have a distinct regional focus to their activities. Those with interests in promoting peace in Third World countries include the Center for New National Security, the International Peace Research Institute and the National Council of Peace Corps Volunteers. The US Peace Council and Committee to Bridge the Gap are concerned about Arab–Israeli peace. Other peace groups with a Middle East focus include Women for Peace in the Middle East (est. 1982), Search for Justice and Equality in Palestine (1971), Americans for Justice in the Middle East (1967), Americans for Safe Israel (1971), Middle East Peace Project (1969) and Catholic Near East Welfare Association (1976). Interns for Peace (1976) has a training programme to foster cross-cultural relations for those wishing to live in rural Jewish and Arab communities in Israel. Ecological and environmental issues are important to the Coalition for International Cooperation and Peace, the International Student Peace Network and the World Council on Religion and Peace.

Peace, disarmament and nuclear war are also a concern of professionals in the sciences, arts and engineering. Since 1980 a number of groups have been formed – some with large memberships – including Physicians for Social Responsibility (formed in 1961; 18,000 members), Educators for Social Responsibility, Business Executives for National Security and Lawyers Alliance for Nuclear Arms Control. Among those with smaller memberships are Social Scientists Against Nuclear War, Nurses Alliance for the Prevention of Nuclear War, Artists for Nuclear Disarmament and Social Workers for Nuclear Disarmament. Psychologists for Social Responsibility have 6 regional, 20 state and 30 local chapters. High Technology Professionals for Peace has 200 members, publishes *Technology and Responsibility* (quarterly), holds an annual meeting, sponsors a lecture series, has a speakers' bureau and works with the clergy and Defense Department on moral and ethical issues including the draft and nuclear war. The efforts of this group are discussed by Halpern (1984).

Whereas some groups emerged out of concerns about the Vietnam war, other organisations have become defunct since that time, including the Business Executive Movement for Vietnam, Americans for Peace, the Peace Brigade, and Citizens Concerned for Peace and Freedom in Vietnam. Other groups have lost membership, for example Another Mother for Peace, which had 100,000 members during the 1960s. Some of the newest groups have organised to protest against draft registration such as the New Party (est. 1978), the Committee Against Registration and the Draft (1979), the National Resistance Committee (1980) and Draft Action (1981).

Publications

Many of the successes which peace associations and organisations enjoy are reaped by informing their memberships of events, views, opinions and activities via quarterly, bimonthly or monthly newsletters and journals. The print media is one of the more important vehicles through which voluntary associations can inform and educate their own memberships and others in society about disarmament, nuclear freeze options, draft registration, human rights, regional conflicts and conscience-raising issues. Many publications come from religious groups and have a strong moral orientation, for example *Shalom*, *Sojourners*, *FCLN Newsletter* and *CALC Report*; others address law issues (*World Jurist*), nonviolence (*WIN Magazine*) and disarmament (*Cooperation for Disarmament*). Still others are designed to keep abreast of legislative activities (*Legislative Alert*), to advise pacifists (*Newsletter*, by War Resisters International) and to inform women of issues important to them (*Peace and Freedom*, by Women's International League for Peace and Freedom). Readers learn about peace issues and legislation, taxation, military spending, human rights violations and ecology. Newsletters may contain feature articles, information about progress on legislation, the names of politicians to write to supporting or opposing a particular issue, forthcoming activities and recent publications.

Study groups

The peace network is further strengthened by study groups or chapters at local, state and regional levels. The local groups may have a dozen, 50 or in excess of 100 members who are also part of state and regional groups. Extensive networks at the local levels are very important in enabling movements to maintain contact with their members and to fulfil their objectives, whether that means influencing public opinion, supporting or opposing particular pieces of legislation or mobilising public demonstrations in concert with other groups.

In the USA the largest number of study groups is concerned with disarmament, nuclear issues and human rights. Campaign for Nuclear Disarmament, Committee to Stop Chemical Atrocities, Amnesty International and Ground Zero all have 200 or more local study groups; Women's International League for Peace and Freedom, Conscience and Military Tax Campaign and World Peacemakers have 100 or more. Some of those with a small number of local groups are nevertheless very important in raising the public awareness of issues, for example the Environmental Coalition on Nuclear Power, SANE: a Citizen's Organisation for a Safe World, and United Campuses to Prevent Nuclear War.

Peace research

Another important element of peace movements is the scholarly research that is conducted on peace and peace-related issues. In North America there are a number of centres and institutes that are devoted to research on peace, disarmament, war and conflict resolution. Most of these are associated with a university and are in or near one of the major urban centres mentioned above. Whereas most institutes and centres have three or fewer research professionals, the Institute for War and Peace Studies associated with Columbia University has 15 professionals and the World Peace through Law Center has 10. Most of these peace research centres were established during the Vietnam war years of the 1960s and 1970s.

The World Peace through Law Center investigates topics of major interest to the legal profession, including international law, world peace through law, a world law code, an international court system, foreign investment disputes, treaties and agreements, and disarmament. The Peace Research Institute carries out research on the prediction of wars, United Nations voting patterns and the roots of violence. The Institute for War and Peace Studies conducts research on peace and security, US foreign policy, strategic studies, arms control and theoretical and empirical investigations in international comparative politics. The National Action/Research on the Military Industrial Complex, a project of the American Friends Service Committee, undertakes research on military intervention, global resources, companies with military contracts, apartheid, US budget priorities and nuclear weaponry. The Inter-University Seminar on Armed Forces carries out interdisciplinary research on military institutions, civil–military relations, peacekeeping and conflict resolution. The Peace Studies Program at Cornell University conducts research on moderation and avoidance of war, on the social, political and economic consequences of progress towards peace and on arms control. The Center for International Catholic Studies investigates international peace and conflict from the vantage point of international politics and Catholic theology and the moral dimensions of nuclear war.

In addition to these centres, there is a larger number that are wholly or partially devoted to disarmament issues. While some are associated with colleges and universities, others are independent of public support. The centres with the largest numbers of research professionals are associated with Yale University (Institute for Social and Policy Studies), Princeton University (Center for Energy and Environmental Studies) and Harvard University (Center for Science and International Affairs). The political and social scientists, military scientists and historians in these centres are engaged in other work besides disarmament, arms control, arms trade and transfers, nuclear proliferation, international security, military balance and political changes in the less developed countries (LDCs). The Churches' Center for Theology and Public Policy examines disarmament, health care, minority rights and the world political economy. The Foreign Policy Research Institute addresses a variety of issues including arms control, power projections, strategic nuclear weapons and political risks. The Center for Defense Information offers internship programmes, monitors US military programmes and politics and provides references to Congress. The World Policy Institute studies the politics of food distribution, protecting human rights, the eventual elimination of nuclear and conventional weapons and the development of an equitable and ecologically sustainable world economy. The Center for Energy and Environmental Studies investigates energy and environmental problems, nuclear policy alternatives, arms control and hazardous waste management. The International Peace Academy conducts research on ocean disputes, disarmament skills, negotiations and conflict.

Some nongovernmental organisations (NGOs) are also concerned with disarmament. These include the American League for Exports and Sales Assistance, which promotes multilateral restraint in the areas of foreign military sales and provides information on export controls and preservation of US jobs. The Coalition of a New Foreign and Military Policy, which is a federation of religious, peace, labour, public interest, professional and education groups concerned about US relations with the Third World, studies federal spending priorities, human rights and the de-escalation of the arms race. The International Peace Research Association, the Non-Governmental Organizations Committee on Disarmament, the American Peace Academy and the Arms Control Association are additional NGOs.

The research centres are important not only for the serious study of peace and peace-related issues, but also for the publications generated by their staff, which appear in major scholarly journals. The impact of research by these institutes and centres, the testimony of the research staff in legislative hearings and their availability to peace organisations and associations for seminars, conferences and workshops cannot be underestimated (see, for example, Martin's (1982) work on the extent of population losses following a nuclear exchange).

The peace network

The peace movement network includes scholars, editors, publishers, organisers, local chapter leaders and the staff of national organisations who influence their own constituencies and other like-minded associations. Examples of the impact of networks and networking were apparent during the Vietnam war among a wide variety of religious, draft-resisting and human rights groups.

Today, religious, disarmament, military tax refusal, ecology-oriented and nuclear energy protest groups all call for a halt to the arms race and support for a nuclear freeze. Associations of educators, judges, women, clergy and university campuses also play an important role in informing and influencing public opinion, pushing for specific legislation, organising petition drives, public marches and demonstrations, holding conferences and planning workshops, and providing information for churches, schools and local study groups. When international problems emerge that bring into question issues of human rights violation, the spiralling arms purchases by Third World countries and their production by North American and European countries, the threat of local or regional nuclear war, civil wars or the plight of refugees, the peace network can be seen to operate at international, national, state and local scales. Some current issues of concern to peace associations and movements include regional war in Central America; the lack of any serious talk between the major superpowers to reduce the likelihood of nuclear war; the space wars game; arms reduction; the proliferation of nuclear weapons by Third World governments and terrorist groups; the protracted conflict in the Middle East, including the Iraq–Iran war; human rights violations in South Africa, Chile, El Salvador and Afghanistan; the placement of cruise and Pershing missiles in West Germany, Netherlands and the UK; halting the continued underground testing of nuclear weapons; and the human and environmental consequences of a nuclear war. Letter-writing and telegram campaigns, local and state petition drives and peace-related fund raising events are among the efforts that unite peace groups in their drive to influence public opinion, legislation and elected politicians.

Examples of networks and networking are the Fellowship of Reconciliation, and the Peace Fellowships associated with the Baptists, Buddhists,

Catholics, Disciples, Lutherans, Methodists and Presbyterians. Local chapters or committees are a part of larger national associations. The Jobs for Peace National Network (est. 1981) with headquarters in San Francisco promotes the transfer of dollars from military programmes to domestic needs; the network publishes reports, pamphlets and information packets, and holds an annual convention. The Nuclear Network (1981) in Washington DC serves 45 groups and aims 'to support and coordinate the efforts of anti-nuclear war groups; to empower people and show them they can make a difference in preventing nuclear war'. The International Peace Research Association (1964), with headquarters in Tokyo, includes 368 individual memberships, 57 research institutes and 75 scientific organisations. World Union, headquartered in Pondicherry, India, has 2000 members in 25 countries. The International Students Peace Network and World Pen Pals (40,000 young people aged 12–20 in 150 countries) also promote global understanding. The Committee Against Registration and the Draft (1979) has 12 regional and 66 local groups. The Coalition for Peace through Strength includes 125 national organisations with 300,000 individual members and 217 members of Congress. It also produces television documentaries and holds press conferences. The International Peace Bureau, which is concerned about chemical and biological weapons, among other issues, is affiliated with local groups that total 30 million individuals. The Campaign against Nuclear War provides a toll-free telephone number to members to inform them of current legislation and activities. Human Rights Internet maintains an international communications network or organisations monitoring human rights. Speakers' bureaus are provided by the Center for Nonviolent Alternatives, the Friends Peace Committee, Members of Congress for Peace through Law, and World Peacemakers. The Disarmament Educational Fund is willing to send speakers to address groups on Central America. Peace Links–Women Against Nuclear War promotes an International Peace Day on 10 October. An innovative project named the Ground Zero Pairing Project aims to link communities in the USA and USSR to promote a better understanding of each other's country and the dangers they both face from nuclear war. Workshops and seminars are organised by the Center for Law and Pacifism, the Institute for Peace and Justice and the International Students Peace Network. Some groups provide materials for education in the schools, which is another important part of networking – they include the Christian Movement for Peace, the International Association of Educators for World Peace and the National Action/Research on the Military Industrial Complex. The Fellowship of Reconciliation has a Children's Creative Response to Conflict programme. The Center for Law and Pacifism, the Center for Peace Studies and the Friends Coordinating Committee on Peace are clearing-houses on peace materials. World Peacemakers also provides information to peace groups across the nation.

One of the major successes among peace movements that is evident in peace networking has been in the support for nuclear freeze referenda at local and state levels and in Congress (Peirce and Anderson, 1982; Pressman, 1984). At the end of 1983 statewide referenda had led to approval of a freeze in California (52 per cent), Massachusetts (74 per cent), Michigan (57 per cent), Montana (57 per cent), New Jersey (66 per cent), North Dakota (58 per cent), Oregon (62 per cent), Rhode Island (59 per cent) and Wisconsin (75 per cent). Only in Arizona (41 per cent) did a statewide referendum fail. Cities and counties throughout the USA have voted on the freeze issue, and they have won in 51 locations and lost in only 3. Among the major cities and largest urban counties supporting the freeze are Denver, New Haven, Washington DC, Dade County (Miami), Cook County (Chicago), Suffolk County (Long Island) and Philadelphia.

With coordinated successes in nuclear freeze resolutions at local and state levels, supporters took their resolution to Congress. In 1982 the freeze failed to win passage by only two votes. In May 1983 the resolution, after numerous attempts to weaken the language, passed by 278 to 149. The issue received bipartisan support, from 218 Democrats and 60 Republicans. Delegations from California, Massachusetts, Michigan, New Jersey, North Carolina, Pennsylvania, Washington and Wisconsin were unanimous or nearly so in support of the measure. This was seen as a first step towards a reduction in the arms race.

Some communities have also considered establishing themselves as nuclear free zones (Colfax, 1984). Others have voiced strong opposition to trains carrying missiles, weapons and hazardous materials through their area (Van Biema, 1984). Cambridge, Massachusetts, debated on whether to ban research on nuclear weapons; the referendum failed (Gladstone, 1984; *Technology Review*, 1984). Several communities have voted to halt the building of nuclear power facilities, the dumping of nuclear wastes in their vicinities and the resumption of the damaged nuclear power unit at Three Mile Island (TMI). Among states voting on such facilities, opposition to nuclear plant operations increased following the TMI accident in March 1979.

Summary

The peace movements are an important part of the total social and political mosaic of any country. They play a significant role not only in what they do – that is in bringing peace and conflict resolution issues to the attention of the public and the government – but also in how they accomplish their goals. Small local study groups that are tied into state organisations and represented at national annual meetings are just as important in keeping the peace issue before the public as are newsletter and journal readers, research conferences, speakers' bureaus, available education materials and libraries. The large and small organisations are important in influencing their own members and other peace groups and also in informing and influencing individuals not associated with them and organisations, associations and groups for which peace studies and peace issues are not of paramount concern. While the national headquarters for the associations may be in London, New York, Washington or Toronto, the information disseminated by newsletters, magazines, educational materials, speakers and inter-library loans reach even the smallest and most isolated parts of any country. The national and international communications networks of telephone, television and newspaper help to coalesce public opinion on peace-related issues and to unite like-minded individuals and groups who may be separated by geographical or social distances. Peace is one of the issues that transcends regional and sectional boundaries. The peace movement is therefore a tightly integrated network connecting legislators, lawyers, scholars, students, clerics, educationalists, engineers, business and industry leaders, the unemployed (and employed), husbands and wives, the youth and the aged in First, Second and Third World countries.

Appendix: Current Research on Peace Movements

Recent research on peace movements can be considered in six categories. First are those studies by social scientists, economists, social critics and popular religious writers who discuss the peace movements in a broad context. Dixon (1982) questions the Reagan policy of a huge arms buildup and discusses the peace movement's relationship to cuts in public services and to workers' movements. The role of the peace movements in nuclear deterrence and anti-nuclear crusades (Silber, 1982; Sweet, 1983; Tanter, 1983; and Van Voorst, 1983) can also fit into this category. Wittner (1984) has a good historical discussion of the US peace movement. A second group of studies is concerned with disarmament issues, not only in a general context (Albert and Dellinger, 1983; Chomsky, 1983) but in Europe in particular (Kaldor and Smith, 1982; Gordon, 1983). Studies on the freeze include those by Cockburn and Ridgeway (1983), Cole and Taylor (1983) and Drinen (1983).

Most studies are in the third category, of scholarly and journalistic accounts of peace movements in various countries. More studies have been done on European movements than elsewhere (*World Press Review*, 1981; Zupan, 1982). Movements in West Germany have been discussed by Armus (1983), Boutwell (1983), Merkl (1982), Musladen (1984), O'Connell (1981), Sanford (1983), Van Bredow (1982) and Wörner (1982). Groups in France are described by Touraine (1983) and Van Bredow (1982), in Northern Ireland by Lumsden (1978), in the UK by George and Marcus (1984) and *Nation* (1984), in the Netherlands by Faezel (1984), in Finland by Pakaslahti (1983) and in Turkey by Margaronis (1984). Eastern European peace movements, while small, are important; those in Hungary are described by Koszegi and Szent-Ivanyi (1982) and in East Germany by Loeser (1984) and Musladen (1984). Peace groups in the USSR are described by Brand (1982), Kalven (1982), Zagladin (1983) and Crozier (1984). Outside Europe, peace groups are important in Israel (Goss-Meyer and Forest, 1982; Peled, 1981; Schenker, 1984; Swartz, 1983), in Japan (Boulding, 1984; *Japan Quarterly*, 1984), in Canada (Muntan, 1984) and in Australia (Redner and Redner, 1983; York, 1983/4).

A fifth category examines the direct influences of peace movements and antiwar activities in foreign policies. Gladkow and Kortunov (1982) discuss these activities in light of US and USSR relations. Nelkin and Pollak (1980) examine them in France. How these groups in Europe influence US policy is the subject of *US News and World Report* for 1981 and Smith (1984); and the means by which US groups influence Middle East policies are discussed by Smith (1983). Soviet attempts to manipulate European peace movements are described by Joshua (1981) and Wettig (1984).

The sixth and final category discusses peace movements in a philosophical and ideological context and considers their influences among other groups. Scott (1983/4) presents a Marxist approach to peace studies; recent antiwar movements are described in *Wilson Quarterly* (1983) and *World Marxist Review* (1981). Green movements (Capra and Spretnak, 1984) are seen to share many common goals with peace movements; West Germany's Green Party activities are examined by Papadakis (1984).

A very useful data source on peace movements in the USA has recently been prepared by the Institute for Defense and Disarmament Studies. The *American Peace Directory, 1984* (Fine and Steven, 1984) contains lists of: national peace groups, peace-oriented educators' groups, peace-oriented educational programmes, local peace groups and local chapters of national peace groups. This data source of names and addresses is valuable in identifying the variety and extent of networks and linkages that exist within and across the USA. It is the single most useful source on peace movements currently available in the USA.

Lists of some 80 peace organisations, mostly in the USA, of some 50 regular publications of peace associations and groups, of US peace and peace-related organisations with study groups and of centres conducting research on peace and disarmament are all available from the author.

References

Akey, S. (ed.) (1984), *Encyclopedia of Associations, 1985*. Vol. I, *National Organizations of the USA*. Detroit.

Albert, M. and Dellinger, D. (1983), *Beyond Survival: New Directions for the Disarmament Movement*. Boston: South End Press.

Armus, Ronald D. (1983), 'Is there a peace movement in the GDR?' *Orbis*, 27, 301–41.

Associations' Publications in Print (1981). New York: R. R. Bowker.

Boulding, E. (1984), *Peace Movements Over Two Decades in Japan and China*. Hanover, NH: Dartmouth College.

Boutwell, J. (1983), 'Politics and the peace movement in West Germany', *International Security*, 7, 72–92.

Brand, D. (1982), 'Russian doves: Soviet peace groups have official sanction to denounce America', *Wall Street Journal*, 21 June, p. 1.

Capra, F. and Spretnak, C. (1984), *Green Politics: The Global Promise*. New York: E. P. Dutton.

Chomsky, N. (1983), 'The present danger: what directions for the disarmament movement?' *Worldview*, 26 February, pp. 8–11.

Cockburn, A. and Ridgeway, J. (1983), 'The freeze movement versus Ronald Reagan', *New Left Review*, January/February, pp. 5–21.

Cole, P.M. and Taylor, W.J. (eds) (1983), *The Nuclear Freeze Debate: Arms Control Issues for the 1970s*. Boulder, Colorado: Westview Press.

Colfax, J.D. (1984), 'Peace in one county?' *Progressive*, 48, 18–19.

Crozier, B. (1984), 'Peace and repression', *National Review*, 36, 26.

Dixon, M. (1982), *The Role of the Peace Movement in a Period of World Economic Crisis*. San Francisco: Institute for the Study of Labor and Economic Crisis.

Drinen, R.F. (1983), *Beyond the Nuclear Freeze*. New York: Seabury Press.

Faezel, M. (1984), 'Dutch renew debate on missile basing', *Aviation Week and Space Technology*, 120, 79–80.

Fine, M. and Steven, P.M. (eds) (1984), *American Peace Directory, 1984*. Cambridge, Mass.: Ballinger.

George, B. and Marcus, J. (1984), 'Unilateralism's second wave: the 1983 general election and after', *Political Quarterly*, 55, 60–71.

Gladkow, P. and Kortunov, A. (1982), 'The antiwar movement in the USA', *International Affairs* (Moscow), November, pp. 34–42.

Gladstone, D. (1984), 'Cambridge nixes ban on nuclear weapons activity', *Physics Today*, 37, 77.

Gordon, S. (1983), 'From the other shore: movements for nuclear disarmament in Eastern Europe', *Working Papers for a New Society*, 10, 32–40.

Goss-Meyr, H. and Forest, J. (1982), 'Violence and reconciliation: notes on the peace movement in Israel', *Transnational Perspectives*, 8, 15–18.

Halpern, J. (1984), 'Working with technology for peace', *Bulletin of Atomic Scientists*, 40, 61–2.

Japan Quarterly (1984), 'The Japanese disarmament movement on the upsurge', *Japan Quarterly*, 29, 287–90.

Joshua, W. (1981), 'Soviet manipulation of the European peace movement'. *Strategic Review*, 11, 9–18.

Kaldor, M. and Smith, D. (eds) (1982), *Disarming Europe*. London: Merlin Press.

Kalven, J. (1982), 'Arms control advocates protest harrassment of Soviet peace groups', *Bulletin of Atomic Scientists*, 38, 62–3.

Koszegi, F. and Szent-Ivanyi, I. (1982), 'A struggle around an idea: the peace movement in Hungary', *New Society*, 62, 115–17, 120.

Loeser, F. (1984), 'On East Germany's peace movement', *New Leader*, 67, 12–14.

Lumsden, M. (1978), 'Peace by peace? Socio-economic structures and the role of the peace people in Northern Ireland', *Current Research on Peace and Violence*, 1, 41–52.

Margaronis, M. (1984), 'The crackdown goes on', *Nation*, 238, 480.

Martin, B. (1982), 'Critique of nuclear extinction', *Journal of Peace Research*, 19, 287–300.

Merkl, P. (1982), 'Pacifism in West Germany', *SAIS Review*, [School of Advanced International Studies] Summer, pp. 81–91.

Muntan, D. (1984), 'The Canadian winter of nuclear discontent', *Current History*, 83, 202–5.

Musladen, J.M. (1984), 'Anti-politics and successor generations: the role of youth in the West and East German peace movements', *Journal of Political and Military Sociology*, 12, 171–90.

Nation (1984), 'The end of END?' *Nation*, 238, 339–40.

Nelkin, D. and Pollak, M. (1980), 'Antinuclear movement in France', *Technology Review*, 82, 36–7.

O'Connell, G. (1981), 'West Germany's peace movements: a troubled tradition', *America*, 145, 174–8.

Pakaslahti, S. (1983), 'Rejecting false impartiality', *World Marxist Review*, 26, 59–62.

Papadakis, E. (1984), *The Green Movement in West Germany*. London: Croom Helm.

Peirce, N.R. and Anderson, W.R. (1982), 'Nuclear freeze proponents mobilize on local referenda, House elections', *National Journal*, 14, 1602–5.

Peled, M. (1981), 'PLO and the Israeli peace camp', *New Outlook*, February/March, pp. 23–7.

Pressman, S. (1984), 'Nuclear freeze groups focus on candidates', *Congressional Quarterly Weekly Report*, 42, 1021–4.

Redner, H. and Redner, J. (1983), *Anatomy of the World: The Impact of the Atom on Australia and the World*. London: Collins.

Sanford, J. (1983), *The Sword and the Ploughshare: Autonomous Peace Initiatives in West Germany*. London: Merlin Press.

Schenker, H. (1984), 'The Israeli peace movement: a symbol of hope', *Israel Horizons*, 32, 25–7.

Scott, P.D. (1983/4), 'Peace, power, and revolution: peace studies, Marxism, and the academy', *Alternatives*, 9, 351–72.

Silber, J.R. (1982), 'Apocalypses then and now: the peace movement and the antinuclear crusade', *Public Opinion*, 5, 42–6.

Smith, D. (1983), 'US peace movements and the Middle East', *Freedomways*, 23, 70–80.

Smith, R.J. (1984), 'Missile deployments shake European politics', *Science*, 223, 665–7.

Swartz, J. (1983), 'Israel's peace crusaders', *Macleans*, 96, 6.

Sweet, W. (1983), 'Christian peace movement', *Editorial Research Reports*, 13 May, pp. 355–72.

Tanter, R. (1983), 'Breaking the nuclear faith: an introduction to the US Catholic bishops' letter on war and peace', *Alternatives*, 9, 99–110.

Technology Review (1984), 'Nuclear research mounts a defense', *Technology Review*, 87, 72–3.

Touraine, A. (1983), *Anti-nuclear Protest: The Opposition to Nuclear Energy in France*. Cambridge: Cambridge University Press.

Van Biema, D.H. (1984), 'Radical Catholic Jim Douglas fights a grass-roots war against a full train of nuclear weapons', *People Weekly*, 21, 50–2.

Van Bredow, W. (1982), *The Peace Movements in France and in the Federal Republic of Germany: Objective and Subjective Dimensions in a Comparison.* Marburge: Institut Politik-wissenschaft.

Van Voorst, L.B. (1983), 'The churches and nuclear deterrence', *Foreign Affairs*, 61, 827–52.

Wettig, G. (1984), 'The Western peace movement in Moscow's longer view', *Strategic Review*, 12, 44–54.

Wilson Quarterly (1983), 'Antiwar movement, the new left and public opinion', *Wilson Quarterly*, 7, 106–7.

Wittner, L.S. (1984), *Rebels Against War: the American Peace Movement, 1933–1983.* Philadelphia: Temple University Press.

World Marxist Review (1981), 'Antiwar movements and organisation', *World Marxist Review*, 24 December, 66–8.

World Press Review, (1981), 'Europe's peace marchers: the movement shaking US–European relations', *World Press Review*, 28, 24–6.

Wörner, M. (1982), 'The "peace movement" and NATO: an alternative view from Bonn', *Strategic Review*, 10, 15–21.

York, B. (1983/4), 'The Australian anti-Vietnam movement, 1965–1971', *Melbourne Journal of Politics*, 15, 24–41.

Zagladin, V. (1983), 'Communists and the antiwar struggle', *Current Digest of the Soviet Press*, 35, 9–10.

Zupan, B. (1982), 'The mass peace movement in Europe', *Review of International Affairs*, 3, 26–8.

CHAPTER 11

Geography of Peace and War: a Soviet View

Innokentiy P. Gerasimov

Nowadays people the world over are aware of the great significance of *global* socioeconomic problems, whose early scientific solution is vital for the destiny of mankind. One such problem is the poverty and undernourishment of a considerable part of the world's population arising from certain social reasons and also from the inability of many developing countries to produce a sufficient amount of necessary foodstuffs. Another grave problem is the increasing pollution and deterioration of the urban environment, especially in the most technologically developed countries. This results from the fact that the intensive industrialisation and urbanisation of these countries has not been accompanied by the necessary concern for a conservation of the natural environment. Other global problems include disproportionate regional development, the degradation of large areas of land and an increasing deficit of the natural resources necessary for further industrial production, the last owing to an excessively intensive and irrational use of such resources and the lowering of their natural potential for renewal. There are also problems of anthropogenic desertification and impoverishment, and the disappearance of nature's gene pool owing to the destruction and extinction of many species of plants and animals.

Global problems and geographical science

It is most important for all sciences, including geography, to attempt to solve these problems. The geographers' contribution is indispensable, primarily because a purely general, or universal, approach to such problems, without regard for geographical differences and peculiarities in the nature, economy and population of different countries and regions, is quite inadequate. Geographers will be able to contribute to the problem-solving in three ways. First, the geographical sciences have two major branches – natural–historic and socioeconomic (social) – which deeply interpenetrate and enrich each other. This provides for particularly effective and substantial analyses of and prognoses for the complex and diverse situations that characterise global problems. Second, geography can reveal general (global) laws concerning the interaction of society and nature and can provide for their application in specific areas of the continents (and the world oceans). And third, the transition of geography from a descriptive to a constructive–prognostic science, and its formation of a constructive paradigm, make its possible contribution to the study and solution of global problems especially effective.

Turning to the global problems themselves, the significance of different problems is, of course, variable, but there is one that is unquestionably the most crucial: the preservation of world peace, specifically by preventing a global nuclear conflict. All other global problems are relatively unimportant by comparison, as any efforts to solve them will be brought to nothing by a nuclear war. We (Soviet geographers) believe that we have proved that even a so-called 'limited' nuclear war would not only destroy mankind, but also make human environments quite unfit for the life of the entire earth's biota, including man himself.

We feel that geographers the world over should provide not only a scientific analysis of the consequences of a nuclear war, but also global and regional scientific forecasts aimed at the preservation, and the all-round improvement of, the material and cultural life and the activities of future generations. In other words, the geographical aspects of the problems of peace and war should comprise a special branch of modern geography called 'political geography', and Lenin's teachings about peaceful coexistence between countries with different social structures should be made the basis of it.

Ecological consequences of a nuclear war

Political geography should, first of all, analyse the ecological aspects of the problems of war, particularly the consequences of nuclear war which nowadays threatens the world. At present, in both Soviet and foreign scientific literature there is a growing interest in this problem, and the first results of research (naturally prognostic in its nature) are accumulating. Alongside the special studies of different official services, whose work is usually kept secret, there is an intensification of research undertaken on the initiative of different social and scientific organisations.

The basis of such research is the scientific analysis of various consequences of a nuclear conflict. The following major forms of such consequences are distinguished.

1   *Primary (direct) effects of nuclear explosions*   These are expressed in a

huge discharge of freed energy in three main ways:

(a)   *a mechanical impact wave* of an unprecedented force, sweeping away in its course all buildings, trees, transmission lines and other obstacles, and so causing extensive damage to population settlements, industrial centres, forests, etc.;

(b)   a tremendous *heat emanation* (hundreds and thousands of degrees), which is capable of burning a human body completely and leaving only its shadow on a spared part of a stone wall (I have seen this myself when I visited Hiroshima);

(c)   *a destructive effect on the ozone screen in the atmosphere*, as a result of the formation of nitric oxide, which plays the role of a catalyst in the chain reaction whereby atmospheric nitrogen is reduced. The weakening of this screen, even if it is not completely destroyed, will intensify ultraviolet radiation and be ruinous to all forms of life.

2   *The main radioactivity effect*   This would produce gamma-rays, with catastrophic doses greatly surpassing the current level of radioactive isotopes in the environment (especially of lasting strontium-90 and caesium-137), reaching lethal doses for living organisms.

3   *Secondary (indirect) consequences of nuclear explosions*   These include an increased radioactive pollution of all the earth's spheres (atmosphere, hydrosphere, pedosphere, biosphere, etc.) and a general, catastrophically high, dust input into the atmosphere (troposphere and stratosphere). There are also aerosol particles and various gases emitted during explosions, which are generated in huge quantities when forests, oil and gas installations, urban settlements, industrial centres, etc., catch fire. An excessive dust content in the atmosphere will cause a sharp change in the whole radiation balance of the earth, and particularly a considerable reduction in the amount direct solar radiation to the earth's surface. This will result in cooling, a disturbance of atmospheric circulation, an increase of hurricane winds and many other climatic consequences of a catastrophic character (see below). In addition, there will be false seismic shaking caused by underground explosions, catastrophic movements of the ground on slopes (avalanches, landslides, etc.), and (as shown by research undertaken after the explosions of nuclear bombs in Hiroshima and Nagasaki) a growth of oncological diseases and negative genetic phenomena in all the living organisms that survive the explosions.

When making scientific forecasts of the catastrophic consequences of a nuclear conflict, it is important to evaluate, in addition to the above effects, the cumulative (integrated) consequences, which differ for surface, atmospheric and underground nuclear explosions and also between explosions on the continents and over oceans, and between blasts of differing force and concentration. In other words, a nuclear war may not be just one terrible event, but a whole chain of such events, beginning with an explosion of nuclear weapons during a relatively short time – hours or days – and then continuing for a very long time in the form of repercussions from these explosions. The limits of this last period are quite diffuse and conditional, but they range from dozens to hundreds of years and more.

The geographical element in peace studies

It is clear that in this sphere of scientific investigation there is a great number of variables requiring a very broad range of corresponding studies. Such studies are now being conducted in all developed countries; but the progress made, judging by the literature, is somewhat irregular. Nevertheless, the geographical aspect in the current research is quite prominent. To illustrate this, let us consider the two main trends in modern research.

Ecological impact of nuclear war

The first concerns prognostic studies devoted to an analysis of the impact of a nuclear war on the earth's atmosphere and, via this, on the climatic conditions in which mankind exists. In this sphere of research one should mention the work of a number of Soviet scientists (M. I. Budyko, G. S. Golitsyn, Yu. A. Izrael, A. M. Obukhov, V. V. Aleksandrov, G. L. Stenchikov and others). The following conclusions may be drawn from their studies.

1   As a result of nuclear explosions, the earth's atmosphere will be infected by radioactive pollutants in the form of a cloud which will stretch over many hundreds and thousands of kilometres, including practically the whole territory of Europe and the USA, with the dose of gamma-rays at over 400–1000 rems.

2   The formation from atmospheric nitrogen during nuclear explosions of nitric oxides in the troposphere, and their transport to the stratosphere, will bring about photochemical smog. Also, 40–60 per cent of ozone in the ozone screen of the stratosphere in the Northern Hemisphere will be destroyed. This will lead to a sharp increase of the ultraviolet irradiation of the earth's surface, which is extremely harmful (if not lethal) to all the living organisms;

3   A very serious consequence of nuclear explosions and the fires caused by them will be the discharge of dust and ash to the atmosphere. Surface explosions will raise dust (a mushroom-like cloud of dust up to the height from 10–15 to 30–40 km), part of which will evaporate. The weight of the dust will range from 100,000 to 600,000 tons for each megaton of explosion force; i.e., if the power of a nuclear explosion is 500 megatons,

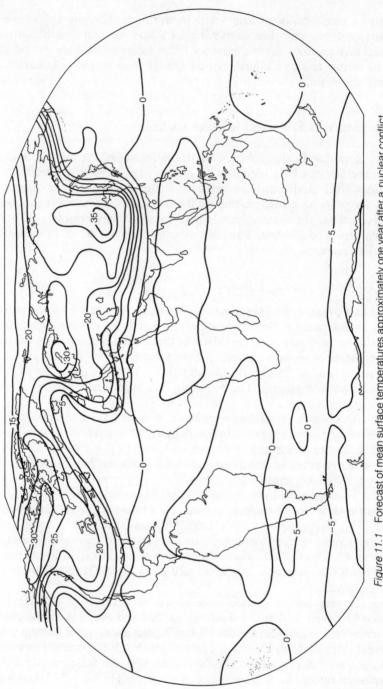

Figure 11.1   Forecast of mean surface temperatures approximately one year after a nuclear conflict.

the dust and ash will reach 1 billion or more tons. Most of this dust will precipitate, but a considerable amount will turn into an aerosol fraction, which will get into the stratosphere. The ash and the dust will quickly envelop the Northern Hemisphere, if not the whole earth. The heating of the dust and ash by the sun will increase winds and accelerate the spreading of dust. As a result, the transparency of the atmosphere to solar radiation penetration will drop to 1 per cent of the usual amount; i.e., the greater part of the earth will be in darkness. This will lead to a sharp cooling of the near-surface layer of air, while changes in atmosphere stratification will bring about an almost complete lack of atmospheric precipitation. This will cause, along with a sharp cooling, the dessication (desertification) of the earth's surface.

Figure 7.3 (p.134) shows a forecast of the mean temperatures on the surface of the continents and the ocean approximately six weeks after a nuclear conflict. As seen from this, the Northern Hemisphere will have the lowest temperatures: in North America and Eurasia temperatures will range from -20 °C or -25 °C or -40 °C or -50 °C.

However, several months after the last fall out of dust, the general cooling of the troposphere will be replaced by its heating by 20–30 degC (see figure 11.1). This will lead to a catastrophic thawing of snow and glaciers and to many other consequences; for instance, even the highest mountains will be heated, resulting in powerful mudflows. The unevenness of temperature rise in the Northern and Southern Hemispheres will form an integrated system of transequatorial atmospheric circulation and will destroy the trade wind systems, while irregular temperature changes over the land and the ocean will generate global hurricanes.

The climatic conditions on earth, at least during the first four to six months after an exchange, will create a physio-geographical situation which has been called a long 'nuclear winter'. This winter will gradually turn into a hot and extremely dry 'summer'. These climatic changes alone will be enough for an immediate and complete destruction of agricultural production throughout the world and for a shattering blow to the whole biota of the earth, including man.

Measurement of losses arising from nuclear war

The second type of prognostic studies in a number of papers by Soviet scientists (for instance, A. A. Bayev, N. M. Bochkov, E. I. Chazov, L. A. Ilyina, M. G. Shandel, N. N. Trapeznikov and others), as well as by scientists from other countries, presents certain concepts and estimates directly concerning those losses which mankind will suffer as a result of a nuclear war. In certain measure these forecasts are based on data obtained during the study of the consequences of the explosion of the US nuclear bombs in Japan in 1945 and of chemical weapons used by the US for 'ecocide' in the Vietnam war. According to these estimates, in the case of a megaton nuclear attack on a city with 1 million population, 200,000–310,000 people will be dead and 350,000–380,000 will suffer different degrees of damage by the end of the first day. If the nuclear conflict is global and nuclear weapons of greater force are used, losses will naturally be much greater. For instance, according to some foreign authors, in the Northern Hemisphere 750 million of our 1290 million people will be killed, while 340 million will suffer from radiation injuries (*Ambio*, 1982).

A further question concerns the fate of those lucky enough to survive the nuclear conflict. Soviet medical scientists and biologists give the following answer to this question:

> People who will be wounded or who will suffer radiation injuries will have practically no chance of surviving, because of the grave consequences of the explosions, sometimes overlapping; because of disorganisation in the medical services; and because of the inability of those who remain alive to work hard enough to counter the destructive consequences of a nuclear attack. (Bayev and Bochkov, 1983)

The general conclusion which can be drawn from the above studies is quite definite. The direct impact of very high doses of heat and radiation caused by nuclear explosions on the human organism and on other living creatures is lethal. It is so strong in biological and geographical respects that it makes us question the possibility of the continued existence of man as a biological species at all, after a nuclear conflict.

As for the secondary consequences of a nuclear war, even those who manage to survive (in dugouts or in some very remote places) will undoubtedly suffer an increased number of malignant tumours, as well as very unpleasant genetic disturbances which will manifest themselves over several generations. All this will bring terrible sufferings to mankind. And that, Soviet scientists believe, is why it would be naive to count on some sort of renovation of the human genus or even on a new coil of evolution. Man will enter the post-nuclear era with practically the same biological features which existed before it, but these features will be mutilated by inherited defects and by somatic and psychiatric diseases. In addition, the environment to which he will have to adapt will be more unfavourable than in any known prehistoric epoch (Bayev and Bochkov, 1983).

However, there remains the general question concerning the situation on earth after all these immediate and catastrophic changes in the environment become weaker and disappear; although some aspects of this question have been considered, to date it has been inadequately investigated. So it is still not clear whether nuclear war would turn the earth into an eternally lifeless and infertile cosmic body, or whether, somewhere on the planet, life would survive or appear anew, and again repeat the long path of evolution which has taken, as is known, many millions of years.

The major task of political geography

It appears to us that the above studies developed by experts in different branches of science, are of great political–geographical importance. And these studies do not cover all aspects of this now most urgent problem; within the framework of modern political geography, many other important issues should be considered – in particular, the need to prevent the very threat of nuclear war. One issue is the problem of the 'nuclear-free zones' spontaneously suggested by progressive people who are fighting for peace. These should be the subject of comprehensive scientific political–geographical investigations.

Great attention and thorough investigation should be accorded the numerous statements by some politicians calling for a cessation of the reckless waste of material resources and intellectual efforts in the production of armaments, and for the diversion of these huge resources into fighting the numerous natural disasters which jeopardise modern humanity – above all, the disasters of hunger, which affect a considerable proportion of the world's population, desertification and devastation of human environments and many others.

It is well known that Soviet statesmen have persistently stressed the close interrelation of the problems of disarmament and socioeconomic development of the world. Over two decades ago, in 1962, the USSR brought to the attention of the Seventeenth Session of the UN General Assembly the 'Declaration on Diversion to Peaceful Needs of the Means and Resources Freed due to Disarmament'. There were also other well-known political initiatives from our country.

Thus, the general range of problems studied by modern Soviet political geography, which gives a priority to the major task of preventing the threat of possible nuclear war, should nevertheless be very broad. It should cover comprehensively the problems of both peace and war, including among the latter the whole range of problems of maintaining peace throughout the world, and of fostering the prosperity of all humanity.

Anti-war declaration of geographers

Taking all this into account, a most important declaration was adopted recently at the session of the National Committee of Soviet Geographers, attended by representatives of some National Committees of Geographers from other socialist countries. This session was devoted to a discussion of the preparation for the Twenty-fifth International Geographical Congress to be held in Paris in autumn 1984. It unanimously approved the proposal, by the National Committee of Soviet Geographers, that the Congress should adopt a special anti-war declaration. This calls for geographers throughout the world to strengthen in any way possible their struggle against the threat of nuclear war, and to make their scientific contributions to this struggle. I conclude this paper with the draft text of this declaration.

APPEAL

to geographers of the world to organise a large-scale public movement

GEOGRAPHERS FOR PEACE, AGAINST THE ARMS RACE AND THE NUCLEAR WAR THREAT

We, geographers of socialist countries, address participants of the 25th International Geographical Congress, geographers of the world. The alarming international situation, the acceleration of the arms race, the location of US medium-range missiles in Western Europe, the increased threat of nuclear war and of the militarisation of space all make it necessary for geographers to act.

We have to disclose the truly global after-effects of a nuclear catastrophe, including those of 'limited' nuclear conflicts, in order to show that in modern war there will be no victors and no vanquished, that the population of neutral countries will also be doomed to perish – even of those situated many thousands of kilometres from battlefields – and that radioactive contamination and other kinds of degradation of environment will jeopardise the very existence of life on earth.

In the struggle for peace it is important to indicate clearly the sources of the threatening catastrophe. Geographers can oppose imperialistic propaganda by telling the truth about the actual lives and peaceful aspirations of people of different countries. At the same time, experts in the field of economic and social geography can help in exposing the actual initiators of arms race – bosses of the military–industrial complex, who pursue superprofits and governmental orders, and with these aims are ready to keep our planet on the brink of war.

We are deeply convinced that it is necessary to put an end to the wasting of productive forces and of natural resources on the arms race, that the use of the contemporary scientific and technological potential of humanity for peaceful co-existence – and not for military conflicts – would open new prospects for satisfaction of material and spiritual needs of people and for a better quality of life, especially in the developing countries. Overall disarmament would improve the international climate, would contribute to scientific and economic collaboration in solving the problems which concern all honest people: those of fighting hunger and maladies, of supplying food products, energy and raw materials, of conserving the environment, of using marine resources and space research for peaceful purposes. Geographers of the world and the International Geographical Union should make their contribution to the scientific solution of these problems.

We call for geographers of all countries to join the movement, 'Geographers for Peace, Against the Arms Race and the Nuclear War Threat', to use their professional knowledge and potential for strengthening peace among the nations.

References

Aleksandrov, E. A. and Sedunov, Yu. S. (1979), *Chelovek i stratosfernyi ozon* (Man and stratosphere ozone). Leningrad: Gidrometeoizdat.

Aleksandrov, V.V. and Stenchikov, G.L. (1983), *Modelirovaniye klimaticheskikh posledstviy atomnoi voiny* (Modelling of climatic consequences of a nuclear war). Moscow: Moskovskiy vychislitel'nyi tsentr.

Ambio (1982), Special issue on 'The Aftermath of Nuclear War', *Ambio*, 11, 2–3.

Bayev, A.A. and Bochkov, N.I. (1983), 'Yadernaya voina postavit pod somneniye sushchestvovaniye cheloveka kak biologicheskogo vida' (A nuclear war will make the existence of man as a biological species doubtful), *Priroda*, 10.

Budyko, M.I. (1979), *Global'naya ekologiya* (Global ecology). Moscow: Izd-vo 'Mysl'.

Golitsyn, G.S. (1983), 'Vystupleniye na Vsesoyuznoi konferentsii uchenykh za izbavleniye chelovechestva ot ugrozy atomnoi voiny, za razoruzheniye i mir' (An address at the All-Union Conference of Scientists for Saving Mankind from the Threat of a Nuclear War, for Disarmament and Peace), *Vestnik AN SSSR*, 9.

Izrael, Yu.A. (1983), 'Ekologicheskiye posledstviya vozmozhnoi yadernoi voiny' (Ecological consequences of possible nuclear war), *Meteorologiya i gidrologiya*, 10.

Izrael, Yu.A. and Petrov, V.N. (1970), 'Rasprostraneniye radioktivnykh produktov podzemnykh yadernykh vzryvov na bol'shiye rasstoyaniya' (Spreading of radioactive products resulting from underground nuclear explosions at great distances), in *Atomnye vzryvyev mirnykh tselyakh*. Moscow: Atomizdat.

Izrael, Yu.A., Petrov, V.N. and Severov, D.A. (1983), 'O vliyanii atmosfernykh yadernykh vzryvov na soderzhaniye ozona v stratosfere' (The influence of nuclear explosions in the atmosphere on the content of ozone in the stratosphere), *Meteorologiya i gidrologiya*, 9.

Obukhov, A.M. and Golitsyn, G.S. (1983), 'Vozmozhuye atmosfernye posledstviya yadernogo konflikta' (Possible atmospheric consequences of a nuclear conflict), *Zemlya i vselennaya*, 6.

Trapeznikov, N.N., Chazov, E.I., Ilyina, L.A. and Gus'kova, A.K. (1982), *Opasnost'yadernoi voiny. Tochka zreniya sovetskikh uchenykh-medikov* (The threat of a nuclear war. The point of view of Soviet physicians-scientists). Moscow: APN.

CHAPTER 12

Peace Education and the Geography Curriculum

Alan Jenkins

> Peace education attempts to sharpen awareness about the existence of con-
> flict between people, and within and between nations. It investigates the
> causes of conflict and violence embodied within the perceptions, values and
> attitudes of individuals, as well as within the social, political and economic
> structures of society, and encourages the search for alternatives, including
> non-violent solutions and the development of skills necessary for their
> implementation.
>
> (Nottinghamshire County Council Education Committee, 1982)

Introduction

Many readers will have seen the film *The Atomic Café*. Using extracts from
newsreels and public information films by US government agencies, it
shows how the US public has been systematically misinformed about the
threats of nuclear warfare. Among its most grotesque scenes are extracts
from a civil defence film shown to US schoolchildren in the 1950s. With
the help of an animated cartoon character, 'Bert the Turtle', it instructs
the children (and presumably the teachers) in a recommended civil defence procedure, the 'atomic head clutch position'. Should a bomb fall
while they are at home or at school, they are to adopt a position with their
'backs to the windows, faces buried beneath their knees, hands clasped on
the back of their necks, ears covered with their arms and eyes closed'
(Carey, 1982, p. 116). At the time, the National Educational Association
and other professional teaching organisations and educational authorities
gave strong support to this utterly useless procedure.

It is easy to pour scorn on this and similar responses by government and
teaching organisations to the threat of nuclear war; however, it is far from
easy to suggest how we, as teachers, should respond. In this chapter I set
out my reflections on how teachers of geography might construct a curriculum that tries to grapple realistically but constructively with the threat
of nuclear warfare. I start by considering the role that geography courses

can play and how their content should be organised. However, while recognising the importance of course content, the central theme of this chapter is that teachers of peace studies have to give particular attention to teaching methods and to what educationalists have called the 'hidden curriculum' – that is, the latent messages of the classroom and the institution (Snyder, 1971). In addition, they must confront difficult questions about the degree to which their courses can be 'objective', and whether peace education can give students any sense of security in the face of the nuclear threat.

The role and content of geography courses

I suspect that many of the geographers who want to teach about peace and war will be politically on the left. They will thus be well aware that much of the recent Marxist or structuralist criticisms of academic geography attack it for its emphasis on spatial pattern and its lack of attention to social processes. This analysis criticises the geography curriculum in higher education and in schools for being partial, unreal and irrelevant to people's lives (Johnston, 1977). It has argued for a more problem-centred and multi-disciplinary or interdisciplinary curriculum.

An explicit educational message of peace studies is that a fundamental understanding of the issues which they examine should lead one into many disciplines. I would argue that interdisciplinary-style courses that are fundamentally geographical can play an important educational role in creating a peace curriculum.

These interdisciplinary links are not hard to establish, for geography embraces both the physical and the social world, and a knowledge of both is essential in order to understand not only the nature of the nuclear threats we face but also what should be done about them. Similarly, understanding and action require both scientific 'objectivity' and the expression and discussion of feelings and emotion. Again, geography courses can address peace issues using both approaches. They can incorporate discussions and activities which hinge on the kind of scientific analysis that Openshaw and Steadman show in this volume; equally, they could use a phenomenological perspective to help students appreciate what 'place annihilation', caused by (nuclear) bombing means (Hewitt, 1983). The film *The Day After* can be examined for the scientific accuracy of its account of the spatial and environmental consequences of a nuclear blast but students could also consider its landscape iconography. Thus, the opening scenes are classic arcadian images of the American 'West', showing Kansas grain fields and a man on a horse herding cattle to the music of Virgil Thompson (Boyd-Bowman, 1984). There are few disciplines that use such widely differing approaches to study such a diversity of subjects, and peace studies needs the wide knowledge of subject content and epistemological variety which geography fosters.

In addition, conventional and discrete courses on political and economic geography, climatology or biogeography can very easily incorporate 'nuclear' themes. This is very important, because as trained geographers we must recognise that we have a professional contribution to make in emphasising the significance of spatial or environmental aspects of the arms race. And it is my experience that, while students (certainly in higher education) can appreciate why their geography courses should be broadened into other disciplines and should be problem-centred, they also find security in seeing the link back into 'pure' geography.

Indeed, a fundamental failure in many 'pure' geography courses is not so much their preoccupation with spatial pattern at the expense of process, but rather their failure to use their concerns for, and knowledge of, such patterns to confront the central economic, social and ecological issues of our times. Indeed, at a time when geographers are rediscovering the importance of their key concepts of place, region and environment, it is salutary to note how many people working in peace education emphasise the importance of these concepts in building their curricula. For example, one of the leaders in this field argues that it is very important for students 'to have a realistic map of the world' (Galtung, 1976, p. 91). He sets out four fundamental values to explain what he means by peace: viz., not only the absence of violence, but also the presence of economic welfare, social justice and ecological balance. He then draws up a 'conflict map of the world' that indicates the threat to peace in these four dimensions (Galtung, 1975, 1976).

The importance of teaching methods

Thus geographers, through their knowledge of the content and methods of the discipline, have much to offer peace education either in specialist geography courses or in a different framework. However, questions of content are perhaps less significant than those of the processes that occur in and out of the classroom. As academics who spend much of our time teaching, we geographers none the less often ignore this, tending to put tremendous emphasis on content and to be less concerned with teaching methods and how students learn. This is bad teaching in any context: it is indefensible when, as we have to do in peace education, we must enable students individually and collectively to bring greater control and security to their lives.

Let me give some substance to this argument by a simple example. A typical classroom in higher education has a person standing at the front telling many more people what to write down and learn. In a curriculum that is seeking to bring a 'peace' perspective to our students, it is not just that the conventional lecture is poor teaching (Gibbs and Jenkins, 1984): more fundamental in this context, it can be hierarchical, authoritarian and patriarchal. For the form of the lecture tends to assert that one person has knowledge which is to be passed down to others. It does not emphasise that we all have skills and knowledge which we can give to others. Moreover, the person likely to have the overt power in the classroom is a male teacher. For any teacher who is at all convinced that there is a connection between Western concepts of masculinity and aggressive behaviour (Spretnak, 1983), care should be taken in using a form of teaching that can be patriarchal.

This is not to state that one should never lecture, but it is to assert that questions of teaching method are central in constructing a peace curriculum (Hicks, 1982). If you as a teacher of geography are willing to consider this argument, then you can draw on a developing body of teaching expertise that has been created in various disciplines, particularly political, global, developmental, world, multi-cultural, disarmament and peace education. You will find that most of the fundamental thinking has come from those working in schools. We have to be open to their experience and adapt it to our needs (see in particular Richardson, 1976, and Richardson, Flood and Fisher, 1979).

From authoritarian teaching to teaching for cooperation

We must therefore be warned. We cannot fall into the trap of teaching in an authoritarian manner a set of skills and knowledge that is meant to liberate. In peace education one has got to create a classroom which is in some way a microcosm of the society one is trying to create, where force is absent and/or democratically controlled, where first the opposing value systems of class participants are understood and then a *modus vivendi* is sought, and where each person is enabled to contribute.

Here the teacher's role is crucial, both in creating a structure that will enable cooperation, and in carefully limiting his or her own role. The teacher should try to ensure that subject matter expertise does not lead to an authoritarian role in the classroom. One should be *an* authority; but seldom, if ever, should one act *in* authority (Peters, 1966). Therefore the dominant methods in geographical peace education should have individuals and groups cooperating to achieve mutually agreed aims, and should not only draw on expert knowledge (including the teacher's) but should also allow all class members to feel that they are actively contributing to the course. Some appropriate methods would be individual student research, carefully organised group discussions (Bridges, 1979), debates, role-playing games and simulations. In addition to specific methods, the teacher (and the students) must pay particular attention to their attitudes towards each other, and here questions of voice and body language are central. One has to try to create a classroom in which all opinions are critically tested against the evidence and yet where feelings and emotions can be made open. Teaching this way is difficult, not least because it can involve lengthy class discussions on how the course should be taught, on how (if at all) it should be assessed, or on larger issues such as 'what's the point of this course, it won't stop the bomb falling'. This pulls one far away from overt content which some students can find bewildering and frustrating. Some, at least, may well want to get on with the 'subject matter'; other students may want to forget the 'original' subject matter and get to grips with these important issues.

The hidden curriculum

Getting the appropriate balance between content and method is difficult but essential. Those who initially reject the emphasis I place on method should consider carefully the work of a number of educationalists (in particular Snyder, 1971) who have developed the concept of the 'hidden curriculum'. The hidden curriculum is not that which is expressly taught (rank size rule, number of cruise missiles to be placed in the UK) but the implicit messages of the institution and the classroom. In some peace education courses the hidden curriculum becomes the central subject matter of the course. As the HMI (Her Majesty's Inspector of Schools) who is responsible for peace education stated, 'Frequently education for peace is concerned in the first place, and sometimes almost exclusively so, with the ruthless re-examination of how the school organises itself and teaches its pupils' (Slater, 1984, p. 23). Many geography courses could profit from such an examination.

Problems of objectivity

Whether they like it or not, geographical peace educators are likely to have to face up to the question of whether their courses should or should not be objective. For as questions of peace and war have come to the centre of political debate, so the growing number of teachers who develop courses on them have found themselves the source of political controversy. In the UK, Conservative Party spokesmen have attacked the growth of peace education. Rhodes Boyson, when Under-Secretary for Education, referred in the House of Commons to the growth of 'appeasement studies' (cited in Rathenow and Smoker, 1984, p. 184) and accused peace educators of bias and indoctrination. Sir Keith Joseph, the Secretary of State for Education and Science, has argued that in an oversubscribed curriculum issues to do with 'one-sided and two-sided disarmament . . . will come up naturally in the curriculum . . . [and thus] there seems no need to make special space for studies labelled peace' (Joseph, 1984, p. 5). He encouraged parents with any complaints about how their children were taught these issues to take them up with the school, the local education authority and his own department. Right-wing organisations have argued that 'peace studies is not a respectable subject for a first degree, and is even less respectable – indeed downright disrespectable – as part of the school curriculum . . . [for] children have yet to acquire the historical knowledge, articulate expression, and grasp of argument that might enable them to discuss them profitably, (Cox and Scruton, 1984, p. 2). Meanwhile the right-wing sections of the UK press recount the horrors of the indoctrination of our children by 'left-wing' teachers. Clearly, this context will affect the political climate within one's own institution (and classroom) when one tries to introduce or teach a course on peace studies.

Most of the overt objection is over the question of balance. The frequent charge is that peace studies teachers are politically motivated and will thus give an unbalanced viewpoint and fail to be objective. Sir Keith Joseph has argued that, when a teacher discusses peace issues,

> His or her presentation needs to be as objective as it can be made, in the sense that he or she ensures that what is offered as a fact is indeed true; that the selection of facts gives a picture which is neither unbalanced or superficial; that facts and opinions are clearly separated; and that the pupils are encouraged to weigh evidence and argument so as to arrive at rational judgements. (Joseph, 1984, p. 5)

When one looks at curricula that people such as Joseph endorse, it is easy to pick holes in their professed arguments in favour of 'objectivity'. Thus, Joseph himself has argued that school history should emphasise *British* history, and that school physics courses, in studying nuclear fission and fusion, should not go into the social implications of nuclear power. Meanwhile the Foreign Office, the Ministry of Defence and NATO provide schools and colleges with literature and films that give exceedingly one-sided and simplistic versions of events and issues in the Cold War. Indeed, geographers interested in propaganda cartography can usefully analyse *The Peace Game*. The NATO-supporting British Atlantic Committee, in a proposed syllabus for peace and conflict studies, states: 'In order to be able to understand deterrence and to discuss policies based on deterrence we need to establish why states maintain armed forces in the first place. Such forces are defence forces: *they exist to maintain the interests of the state which maintains them*' (British Atlantic Committee, 1983, p. 6; my emphasis). It is easy to show that such statements are highly value-laden and 'unbalanced'. But the teacher will ignore them at his peril. I have heard versions of them stated as the soundest academic truth in recent meetings within my own institution to validate existing and proposed 'peace' courses.

Though many of the protestations over bias are intellectually naive, simply to point this out does not satisfactorily answer what is a genuine problem. For, as I have said, it seems to be the case that most teachers interested in peace studies will be politically on the left, and will also be members of nuclear freeze groups or the Campaign for Nuclear Disarmament (CND) or some other 'peace' organisation. Will they not, indeed, give a very one-sided, partial and even bigoted viewpoint? And is it anyway educationally desirable that such studies should be exclusively taught by people broadly of the same viewpoint (whatever it is)?

Ideally, peace studies should be taught by a range of people of differing political persuasions. I say this not from some absurd notion that there are two equally valid sides to every question, but from a recognition that different individuals and groups see peace-related issues differently, and that as educators one of our aims must be to get students to analyse and understand these various positions. We should therefore invite colleagues of different political persuasions into our classes to set out their own analyses – but these invitations may well be declined. (And I have considerable sympathy for people who do not wish to be the token spokesman for the 'other side'.) However, we should ensure that the reading and films we select offer alternative viewpoints (see Suddaby, 1983), and that all viewpoints are critically analysed.

To an extent, one can use one's involvement in peace campaigning as a valuable educational strategy. My own course opens with students discussing among themselves their views on nuclear warfare, and the extent to which teachers should be 'objective' and emotionally detached from the issues they teach. Many of them strongly assert that teachers should be objective. I then openly declare my membership of CND and confess that my views are biased. This strategy of hiding nothing fundamental from students evokes respect and thought, but it can also evoke concern – partly over questions of whether grading will (consciously or unconsciously) be on the basis of political beliefs. We then discuss papers by highly committed geographers such as Bunge (1973) and contrast them with ostensibly more objective analyses, such as that of Openshaw and Steadman (1982) to explore the merits and disadvantages of scientific method, objectivity and value freedom. That is one possible strategy. Another may be simply not to teach about issues in which we are closely involved. And, in certain cases, if we are merely teaching to provide some emotional catharsis for ourselves we might be better teaching the rank-size rule or methods of soil taxonomy.

But the issues of peace and war are so important to students' lives that educational institutions must somehow provide a means to understand them (Elam, 1983). I do not accept Collier's view that, in the 'training of students in the analysis of values and perceptions . . . it is necessary for the teacher to select topics of study which will elicit the felt engagement of the students, yet be at a sufficient emotional distance to allow of appropriate detachment in the analysis' (Collier, 1984, p. 31). Following this principle, he commends a course at Harvard entitled 'Moral Dilemmas in a Repressive Society: Nazi Germany'. While such a course may have potential value, it suffers from having no immediate relevance to students' lives. The very immediacy of the nuclear threat demands that we analyse it in the classroom.

But how does the teacher conduct him or herself in the classroom when discussing contentious social issues? I would caution against haranguing students from a particular ideological position. Those who profess concern about potential 'bias' seem to view students as empty vessels into which prejudice may be poured; but they should think back to their own school and college days and remember those teachers who were immediately written off by their students for trying to peddle a particular line.

This can be less of a difficulty if we return to the distinction between a teacher being *an* authority and being *in* authority. As Peters (1966, pp. 260–1) states, 'the . . . danger is that of those who are authorities becoming authoritarian . . . [when] in the sphere of knowledge no-one can be regarded as more than a provisional authority.' But this argument itself can come up against hard moral and philosophical objections – that we expect everyone to ascribe to certain moral positions, and that perhaps the teacher is there to propagate them. Thus, Walford argues that geography teachers must oppose racism and sexism, but that they should strive 'for impartiality in *most* of the contentious issues that we handle' (Walford, 1984, p. 196; my emphasis).

Educational theorists and practitioners have sought to guide the teacher on how to teach controversial issues, e.g. Bridges (1982), Stradling (1984), Stradling, Noctor and Baines (1984). In analysing their arguments, one is drawn back to the importance of a careful choice of teaching methods and, relatedly, of ensuring that the 'hidden curriculum' accords with the expressed liberal ethos of the institution and the classroom. Thus Stradling, after extensive research on the classroom practice of teaching controversial issues, concludes:

> More and more teachers in those areas of the curriculum where controversial issues are likely to be taught are becoming less directive in their teaching. They divide tutor groups and classes into discussion groups in which the proceedings are controlled by the pupils themselves; they rely on a good deal of experimental learning including role play and simulations but also direct involvement with a community; and they emphasise enquiry based learning through projects, community profiles, analysis of the output of the media and

so forth. In other words, *their expertise lies more in their ability to choose and utilise the most appropriate learning capacities than in their capacity for imparting received knowledge.* (Stradling, 1984, p. 128; my emphasis)

The desired effects of geographical peace studies

The emphasis I give to method does not deny the importance of a careful choice of subject matter in building a geographical peace curriculum. Indeed, in one major respect the choice of subject matter presents a major dilemma for the teacher. For by discussing issues such as the environmental consequences of nuclear warfare or the casualties to be expected in the UK from a 200 megaton Soviet attack, is there not a danger of so terrifying one's students (and oneself) that one's course is in no sense liberating? We do not want to adopt a similar stance to those who taught pupils unquestioningly to adopt the 'atomic head clutch position', but if, by 'teaching about war and peace . . . [we] merely leave a class full of frightened children without skills or perceptions with which they can come to terms with their fears, then schools will have done young people a great disservice' (Slater, 1984, p. 27). We must not doubt that to confront these issues is usually uncomfortable, and at times overwhelming in the sense of powerlessness which it can bring; yet we have to face them within ourselves and our students, partly because of the need for our fears to find expression.

If they are properly constructed, peace studies courses may well enable students to take much greater control over their lives and, in certain small ways, help them to work for peace. One reason for this is that students become highly involved in such courses; the issues matter, and if taught with the methods outlined above students can obtain much knowledge and develop skills of analysis and evaluation. In an oblique attack on those who criticise peace education, Slater points out:

If you are going to encourage young people to understand complicated controversial issues, and to develop demanding intellectual tools to enable them to critically evaluate evidence concerned with these issues, we have to make unusually high demands on literacy and numeracy. Political education, education for peace . . . is not distracting schools from doing their basic job. It can reinforce it and increase its demands (Slater, 1984, p. 24).

To impart this sense that one can do something is largely a question of teaching methods that develop students' knowledge and confidence in their own abilities and their ability to cooperate. But it is also a matter of the content of peace studies courses. We should ensure that, besides indicating what is to be feared, we also include examples of what can be done to avert the threat of nuclear war. Some of the work in this volume indicates the sorts of positive themes that could be incorporated into geography courses: thus, Barnaby's chapter suggests that the geographical device of disengagement or nuclear-free zones could help us to move towards peace; Isard and Anderton indicate that we could substitute our economic dependence on war expenditure by alternative regional economic strategies. Class projects can be devised to get students to construct a non-nuclear defence for our countries. Filip (1984) shows, through a study of East and West Germany, how one can examine the geography curriculum to see if it legitimates state boundaries and desires for 'national' expansion, or inculcates loyalty to political blocs. Students could critically examine their own curriculum in this light while teachers should develop alternative programmes of geographical education which establish a more global perspective (Hicks and Townley, 1982).

However, for some teachers (and students) this would not be enough. They would want their courses and institutions to be much more clearly linked to action towards peace, through campaigning and broader educational projects in the local community. How far can one go in this direction as an educator? How far can one ask students to take part in action? What might they ask of their teacher? We should openly discuss these dilemmas and admit our uncertainties. As academics this is our responsibility, and it may also help to open up a dialogue between ourselves and those who initially disagree with us.

What can peace education achieve?

I conclude with this fundamental question as to whether peace education in schools and colleges can make any contribution towards peace. I have no doubt that it can motivate students to learn, but can it really help them to work towards peace? I am not certain. One is all too aware that developments in peace education are very limited in our educational institutions, and more critically that recent UK and US attempts to use education for engineering social equality and freedom from racism and sexism have shown how limited the autonomy of the educational system is and how schools and colleges mirror society at large. Any prospect for change through the educational system must be linked to much wider action by communities and governments. Part of me agrees that 'teaching efforts alone are more or less useless' (Nicklas and Ostermann, 1979, p. 377; Curle, Freire and Galtung, 1976). Another part of me wants to argue with Humphrey (1981, p. 493) that, although 'we behave as though we have been hexed by the bomb – put under a spell, we nevertheless have the power to change things, and should remember Dylan Thomas's words to his ageing father:

Do not go gentle into that good night.
Rage, rage against the dying of the light.

Yet though it feels good to write that quotation – though it does give me some strength – my doubts return. What do *you* think? How, if at all, do *you* (intend to) teach these issues?

References

Boyd-Bowman, S. (1984), 'Film representations of nuclear warfare: *The Day After*', *Screen*, 25, 71–97.

Bridges, D. (1979), *Education, Democracy and Discussion*. Windsor: National Foundation for Educational Research.

Bridges, D. (1982), 'So truth be in the field . . .? Approaches to controversy in world studies teaching', in D. Hicks, and D. Townley, *Teaching World Studies: An Introduction to Global Perspectives in the Curriculum*. London: Longman, pp. 37–54.

British Atlantic Committee (1983), *Peace and Conflict Studies: A Syllabus in Peace Studies*. London: British Atlantic Committee.

Bunge, W. (1973), 'The geography of human survival', *Annals of the Association of American Geographers*, 63, 275–95.

Burns, R. and Aspeslaugh, R. (1984), 'Objectivity, values and opinions in the transmission of knowledge for peace', *Bulletin of Peace Proposals*, 15, 139–48.

Carey, M.J. (1982), 'The schools and civil defence: the fifties revisited', *Teachers College Record*, 84, 115–27.

Collier, K.G. (1984), 'Higher education as preparation for the handling of controversial issues', *Studies in Higher Education*, 9, 27–35.

Cox, C. and Scruton, R. (1984), *Peace Studies: A Critical Survey*. London: Institute for European Defence and Strategic Studies.

Curle, A., Freire, P. and Galtung, J. (1976), 'What can education contribute towards peace and social justice?' in M. Haavelsrud (ed.), *Education for Peace*. Guildford, Surrey: Science and Technology Press, pp. 64–97.

Elam, S.M. (1983), 'Educators and the nuclear threat', *Phi Delta Kappan*, April, 533–8.

Filip, K. (1984), 'Political geography around the world, III: Facing the political map of Germany', *Political Geography Quarterly*, 3, 251–8.

Galtung, J. (1975), 'Educating to understand the problems of peace', *Futures*, February, 52–7.

Galtung, J. (1976), 'Peace education: problems and conflicts', in M. Haavelsrud (ed.), *Education for Peace*. Guildford, Surrey: Science and Technology Press, pp. 80–7.

Gibbs, G. and Jenkins, A. (1984), 'Break up your lectures, or Christaller sliced up', *Journal of Geography in Higher Education*, 8, 27–40.

Hewitt, K. (1983), 'Place annihilation: area bombing and the fate of urban places', *Annals of the Association of American Geographers*, 73, 257–84.

Hicks, D. (1982), *Education for Peace: What does it Mean? Some Thoughts for the 1980s.* Lancaster: Centre for Peace Studies.

Hicks, D. and Townley, D. (eds) (1982), *Teaching World Studies: An Introduction to Global Perspectives in the Curriculum.* London: Longman.

Humphrey, N. (1981), 'Four minutes to midnight', the Bronowski Memorial Lecture, *The Listener*, 29 October, 493–9.

Johnston, R.J. (1977), 'On geography and the organisation of education', *Journal of Geography in Higher Education*, 1, 5–12.

Joseph, K. (1984), Speech to the National Council of Women, in *Educating People for Peace*. London: National Council for Women of Great Britain.

Nicklas, H. and Ostermann, A. (1979), 'The psychology of deterrence and the chances of education for peace', *Bulletin of Peace Proposals*, 10, 368–73.

Nottinghamshire County Council Education Committee (1982), *Report to the Education Committee of the Working Party on the Development of a Curriculum for Peace Education.* Nottingham: Nottingham County Council Education Committee.

Openshaw, S. and Steadman, P. (1982), 'On the geography of a worst case nuclear attack on the population of Britain', *Political Geography Quarterly*, 1, 263–78.

Peters, R.S. (1966), *Ethics and Education.* London: Allen and Unwin.

Rathenow, H.F. and Smoker, D. (1984), 'Peace education in Britain: some results of a survey', *Bulletin of Peace Proposals*, 15, 171–84.

Richardson, R. (1976), *Learning for Change in World Society: Reflections, Activities, Resources.* London: World Studies Project (2nd edn, 1979).

Richardson, R., Flood, M. and Fisher, S. (1979), *Debate and Decision: Schools in a World of Change.* London: One World Trust.

Slater, J. (1984), Speech to the National Council of Women, in *Educating People for Peace*. London: National Council of Women of Great Britain.

Snyder, B.R. (1971), *The Hidden Curriculum.* New York: Alfred Knopf.

Spretnak, C. (1983), 'Naming the cultural forces that push us towards war', *Journal of Humanistic Psychology*, 23, 104–14.

Stradling, R. (1984), 'The teaching of controversial issues: an evaluation', *Educational Review*, 36, 121–9.

Stradling, R., Noctor, M. and Baines, B. (1984), *Teaching Controversial Issues.* London: Edward Arnold.

Suddaby, A. (1983), *The Nuclear War Game.* London: Longman.

Walford, R. (1984), 'Geography and the future', *Geography*, 69, 193–208.

Notes on Contributors

CHARLES ANDERTON is a graduate student at Cornell University having received an MA in economics in 1984. His current interest is in arms race modelling.

FRANK BARNABY is the Director of the World Disarmament Campaign (UK) and the Co-Director of 'Just Defence'. He is visiting Professor of Peace Studies at the Free University of Amsterdam, and in 1985 was holder of the Harold Stassen Chair in World Peace at the University of Minnesota, Minneapolis.

STANLEY BRUNN is Professor and Chair at the Department of Geography, University of Kentucky. His interests include the political and social geography of the USA and he is author of *Geography and Politics in America* (1974) and co-author of *Technological Hazards* (1984). His current research projects include US voting behaviour, propaganda maps and votes on nuclear power issues.

ALAN BURNETT is a Principal Lecturer at Portsmouth Polytechnic. His current research interests include urban political participation and public services, the impact of residential facilities on dependent groups, propaganda mapping and the residential structure of socialist societies. He is co-editor of *Political Studies from Spatial Perspectives* (1981).

DEREK ELSOM is a Principal Lecturer in Geography at Oxford Polytechnic. His research interests include air pollution meteorology and applied climatology. He is author of *Atmospheric Pollution: Causes, Effects and Control Policies* (forthcoming).

INNOKENTIY P. GERASIMOV is Director of the Institute of Geography of the USSR Academy of Sciences and a full member of the Academy of Sciences of the USSR (Academician). His research interests include environmental problems and the protection of nature. He is author of over 2000 papers.

WALTER ISARD is Professor of Economics at Cornell University and has been active in peace research for many years. His current interests are in arms race modelling and conflict theory. He is author of many books and papers including *General Theory: Social, Political, Economic and Regional* (1969) and *Conflict Analysis and Practical Conflict Management Procedures* (1982).

TONY IVES is currently practising as a professional geographer and planner in the Oxford area. He has a special interest in Third World social geography and is a member of the UK Campaign against the Arms Trade and of the Oxford Project for Peace Studies.

ALAN JENKINS is a Senior Lecturer in Geography at Oxford Polytechnic. His interests include the application of educational research to the teaching of geography in higher education. He is co-founder and co-editor of the *Journal of Geography in Higher Education*, and is researching the representations of China in western documentary films.

STANLEY OPENSHAW is a Lecturer in the Department of Geography, Newcastle University. His research interests include the application of computer modelling and spatial analysis to nuclear war and nuclear power. He is co-author of *Doomsday: Britain After Nuclear Attack* (1983).

PATRICK O'SULLIVAN is Professor and Chair at the Department of Geography, Florida State University. His research interests include geopolitics, military geography and regional identity. He is author/editor of *Geographical Economics* (1981) and *The Geography of Warfare* (1983).

DAVID PEPPER is a Principal Lecturer in Geography at Oxford Polytechnic. He has developed courses on peace studies, and also specialises in environmentalism. He is author of *The Roots of Modern Environmentalism* (1984), and is a member of the Oxford Project for Peace Studies.

PHILIP STEADMAN is Lecturer in the Faculty of Technology and Director of the Centre for Configurational Studies at the Open University. His research interests include the computer modelling of nuclear attack scenarios. He is co-author of *Doomsday: Britain After Nuclear Attack* (1983). He is currently serving on a Royal Institute of British Architects enquiry into the effects of nuclear attack on the built environment.

HERMAN VAN DER WUSTEN is a Professor in Geography at the University of Amsterdam. His research interests include the distribution of educational facilities, support patterns of political movements and spatial patterns of violence.

DONALD ZEIGLER is Assistant Professor and Director of the Geography Program at Old Dominion University, Virginia. His current research interests include social and behavioural responses to technological hazards. He is co-author of *Technological Hazards* (1984).

Index

218 Index